PLYMOUTH ARGYLE

THANKS FOR THE MEMORY

Season 1958-59 Revisited

Steve Rhodes

Copyright © 2009 by Steve Rhodes

Published in Great Britain by
Stevrho Publishing
Unit 4b Frobisher Industrial Centre
Budds Lane
Romsey
Hampshire
SO51 0EZ
01794 511442

e-mail stevrho@btinternet.com

Printed by
Short Run Press Limited
25 Bittern Road
Sowton Industrial Estate
Exeter
Devon
EX2 7LW
01392 211909

e-mail estimates@shortrunpress.co.uk

ISBN 978-0-9562482-0-6

Cover :
The cover design is a replica of the front page of the
Club Handbook from 1959-60.
It was produced to coincide with the start of the new season and
contained full details of the previous season's results.
Published by the Plymouth Argyle Supporters' Club, the Chairman
and the Manager also contributed. It featured an article each year
by 'Man In The Crowd,' penned by WS (Bill) Tonkin.
The picture was taken on 29 April 1959 and shows Len Casey lead-
ing the team out for the final match of the season.
With promotion assured, Bradford City formed the customary
Guard of Honour.
Courtesy Greens On Screen/Plymouth Argyle FC

Contents

Final Table

Football League Division Three

1958-59

Team	Played	W	D	L	F	A	Pts
PLYMOUTH ARGYLE	46	23	16	7	89	59	62
Hull City	46	26	9	11	90	55	61
Brentford	46	21	15	10	76	49	57
Norwich City	46	22	13	11	89	62	57
Colchester United	46	21	10	15	71	67	52
Reading	46	21	8	17	78	63	50
Tranmere Rovers	46	21	8	17	82	67	50
Southend United	46	21	8	17	85	80	50
Halifax Town	46	21	8	17	80	77	50
Bury	46	17	14	15	69	58	48
Bradford City	46	18	11	17	84	76	47
Bournemouth & BA	46	17	12	17	69	69	46
Queens Park Rangers	46	19	8	19	74	77	46
Southampton	46	17	11	18	88	80	45
Swindon Town	46	16	13	17	59	57	45
Chesterfield	46	17	10	19	67	64	44
Newport County	46	17	9	20	69	68	43
Wrexham	46	14	14	18	63	77	42
Accrington Stanley	46	15	12	19	71	87	42
Mansfield Town	46	14	13	19	73	98	41
Stockport County	46	13	10	23	65	78	36
Doncaster Rovers	46	14	5	27	50	90	33
Notts County	46	8	13	25	55	96	29
Rochdale	46	8	12	26	37	79	28

Leading scorers:
Towers (Brentford) 32, Bradbury (Hull City) 30, McCole (Bradford City) 28, Rowley (Tranmere Rovers) & Smith (Hull City) 26

Author's Note

Thanks For The Memory was written to celebrate the 50th anniversary of Plymouth Argyle's 1958-59 Third Division title winning campaign. But to tell the full story of the people who came together to effect that season's triumph, the 1958-59 campaign became just a catalyst. Research showed that many of the players had rubbed shoulders with the true greats of the game, while the manager Jack Rowley turned out to be one of the greatest goal scoring forwards British football had ever seen.   As a 10 year old autograph hunter, armed with my book and pen, I spent every waking hour at Home Park. These men were my first heroes, a pleasant group of people who brought me, and thousands of others, great pleasure. They came into my life for a few years and then were gone again. I neither knew where they came from nor where they went afterwards. I never forgot them and always wondered what had become of their lives.

In January 2008 I went into an Estate Agent's office in Romsey. The lady who dealt with my enquiry noticed the Argyle badge on my fleece, telling me that her Dad had played for Argyle. She was Harry Penk's daughter, one of my original green and black heroes. Within days Harry and his wife Barbara came around for lunch and *Thanks For The Memory* was up and running. Since then it has consumed every hour of my leisure time. The meeting with Harry and Barbara led me to most of the other players from that era. I have met or spoken to all of the surviving players. I spent many enjoyable hours chatting to them about their lives before, during and after their time at Plymouth Argyle.

I was also fortunate enough to trace Chairman Ron Blindell's delightful wife Kay and Manager Jack Rowley's charming daughter Susan. Blindell and Rowley were each giants in their respective arenas. Blindell was the Sir Alan Sugar of his day, a self-made man who became a millionaire. Despite the passage of time, Jack Rowley remains one of the best players ever to grace Old Trafford. Only Bobby Charlton and Denis Law have scored more goals for the club and no one has yet matched his total of hat-tricks for United. As a youngster it was the players who mattered most to me. I now see that this was my loss and I am glad to have had the opportunity to study and document the contributions of others. Through George and Moira Baker I traced Trainer George Taylor's daughter Margaret Callan, giving me the chance to record his magnificent contribution to football in general and Argyle in particular.

There are so many people to thank. I hope that the list of acknowledgements at the back of the book contains everyone who helped. To those I have forgotten please accept my sincere apologies. Special thanks must go to my partner Rose for her patience, as every evening and weekend was consumed by this project. Also Trev Scallan and Steve Dean at *Greens on Screen* for their help and encouragement and to Colin Parsons for allowing me free and constant access to his fantastic collection of Argyle memorabilia. Gordon Sparks at BBC Radio Devon, Chris Errington at the *Plymouth Evening Herald* and John Collings at the *Sunday Independent* also warrant a mention for their support and interest, as do the historians at Charlton, Everton, Hull, Mansfield, Swindon, Wolves and Alfreton FC. Latterly, academic football writer Joyce Woolridge volunteered to read the manuscript and offered much needed direction and advice.

I have but one regret. It is that my late mother did not survive to see the lifelong effect her early encouragement had on me. After my father died in 1955 she and my sister Lorna started and then nourished my interest in football in general, and Argyle in particular. Without their love and encouragement I would never have been able to say —*T hanks For The Memory.*

Steve Rhodes
Romsey

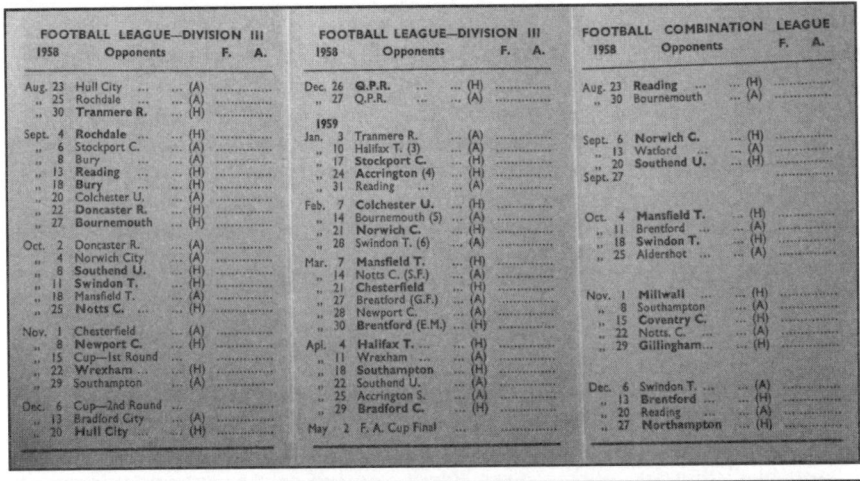

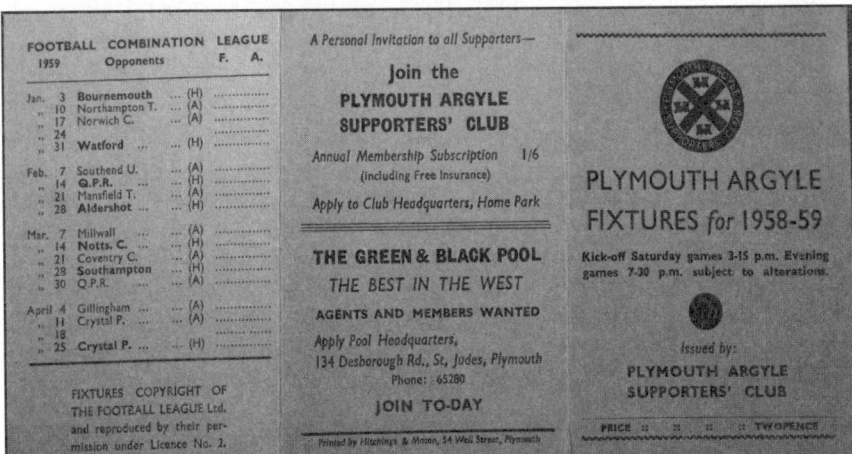

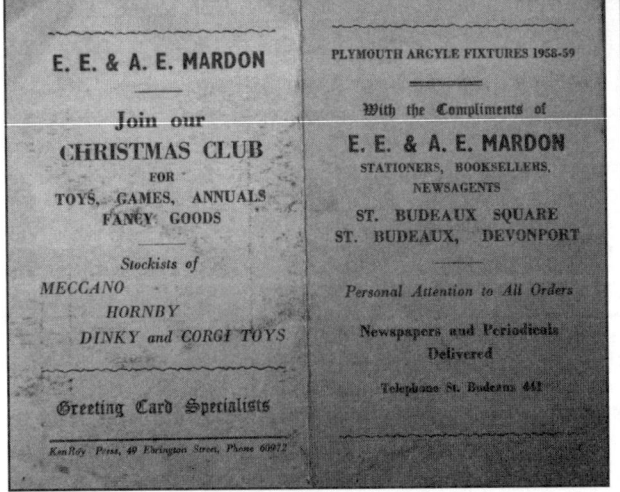

Pocket sized fixture cards were very popular. As well as the Supporters Club, local traders and public houses would distribute them as a form of advertising. Note the three digit telephone number for St Budeaux.

Fixture cards from the Colin Parsons collection

CHAPTER ONE

PRELUDE TO PROMOTION

1957-58 was the final season where the third tier of the Football League was geographically divided into Third Divisions South & North. The news of the amalgamation was first broken in February 1957. Despite voting in favour of an earlier proposal for such a change, when they were a Second Division side in 1954, Plymouth Argyle were now canvassing support to block the idea.

To an extent, the fears of the Board of that time were understandable. In February 1957, they were still not entirely safe from having to apply for re-election to the Third (South). Doubtless their thinking was that they could easily have been candidates for the new Fourth Division which the reorganisation would create. Although it was not widely known, the club was haemorrhaging money. The prospect of increased travel, with half the division formed of clubs from the north, would not have appealed. In the event, only Torquay, Newport and Exeter supported them. The motion was passed at the June 1957 Annual General Meeting of the Football League Management Committee.

The new Third Division was formed from the teams who finished in the top half of the old Third (South) and Third (North) in 1957-58. Those clubs in the lower half of each regional Division would make up the new Fourth Division. Failure to achieve a place in the new third tier would thus put the Second Division two promotions away. Argyle need not have worried. A top half finish was rarely in doubt and was easily achieved. It is unlikely that manager Jack Rowley would have survived had Argyle become founder members of the inaugural Fourth Division. Whilst the boss relished the opportunity to pitch his wits against some of the stronger teams from the north, he was a realist.

He could see that there would be an advantage; the new arrangements offered two promotion places from the new Third Division instead of one from the old regional set up. But he could also see the negative side. Four clubs would now qualify for relegation. Automatic promotion from the single slot available in the final Third Division (South) campaign remained his favoured option. In his first season as the full time manager, the team stayed in the 1957-58 promotion hunt almost to the end.

That was until Monday, 21 April 1958, when a controversial home defeat against Southend United saw their chances all but disappear. As they kicked off that on that Spring evening, the Greens were still clinging to a hope of filling that single place. Although the ground was dilapidated, the atmosphere at a floodlit evening game was, for some reason, better than on a Saturday. Many in the 22,000 crowd anticipated a routine home win against the Essex side, knowing that at the very worst it would maintain the pressure on the other teams in contention.

To get the full story, just mention the name "Pullin" to any Argyle fan born before 1950. You are guaranteed to hear the tale of that never to be forgotten April evening in 1958. The intervening 50 years have not diluted the anger and exasperation of those who were there – whether on the terraces or on the field of play. *Everyone* will tell you that many of the Bristol referee GW Pullin's poor decisions were, at best, appalling. Even today, Wilf Carter still shakes his head when recalling the official's bizarre judgements. "I wasn't the biggest fan of referees anyway, but this was the worst performance I ever saw from a man in black. "We had been two down. I scored twice to level the game, and then had another effort disallowed. To this day, I do not understand why he disallowed it. Southend then broke away and scored the winner. That was our slender hope of promotion gone really."

Feelings ran extremely high on the night. Folklore has it that Pullin was smuggled out of the ground in an Ivor Dewdney pasty van, to escape the mass of angry fans. A large, infuriated group had gathered outside the players' and officials' entrance, at the back of the main stand. The local press reported that the referee took police advice and cancelled his hotel booking at the Duke of Cornwall, finally finding a bed for the night in Torquay. Perhaps he should have gone for an Exeter hotel? For his contribution to such a costly Argyle defeat he might have received a complimentary room! Eye-witness accounts leave no doubt that had the crowd been able to get to him, Pullin would have come to serious harm that night. People who were there accept that there was a definite lynch-mob mentality.

Jack Rowley was famed for his aggression during the battle, but equally acknowledged as a true sportsman once the final whistle blew. On this occasion even he had to be restrained in the tunnel, where he had an angry exchange with the inept Pullin. Doubtless Rowley later had other concerns. Promotion was now dependent on the failure of others. He would have known that it was unlikely that the new Chairman Ron Blindell would give him more than another season to achieve promotion. Blindell seemed far less patient than his rather benevolent predecessor, Sir Clifford Tozer.

Blindell, about whom there is much more in chapters five and six, had made money as a successful shoe entrepreneur with a track record of year on year improvement. He would not tolerate failure in any venture of which he was in charge. For the time being, Blindell recognised that the side was heading in the right direction. He pronounced himself satisfied with the progress made.

As it was, Argyle failed to win promotion by a mere two points. The finish was tight, with Brighton topping the table on 60 points, Brentford were second equal on 58 points with third placed Argyle. Crucially, Brighton's goal average was 1.38 whereas Argyle's, thanks to their tight defence, was 1.39. Goal average was calculated by dividing the goals against into the goals for. Had Argyle won their fateful match against Southend, they would have overtaken Brighton and Brentford and been promoted by 0.01 of a goal! One can look at it more dispassionately 50 years on. Realistically, promotion was always going to be difficult, after a run of three 0-0 draws in early April. The free scoring Wilf Carter was missing for two of the goalless encounters – perhaps he may have made a difference?

There was also a heavy burden of expectation from supporters on Jack Rowley. As recently as 1952-53, Plymouth Argyle had finished fourth in the old Second Division, the season immediately after they had won the Third Division (South) title in 1952. That period, the nearest we have ever got to the Promised Land, left Argyle fans believing that fourth place in the Second Division was now the benchmark for the future. Undoubtedly it was that millstone of expectation that forced the resignation of the popular Jimmy Rae. He left in January 1955 as his ageing team struggled to stay in the Second Division. Later it emerged that the club was deep in debt, with money problems worsening every day. This must have limited Rae's ability to reverse the downward trend.

Jack Rowley's record thus far had been mixed. Arriving from Manchester United in the February of 1955 as player-manager, he saved Rae's team from relegation in 1954-55. However, that merely postponed the inevitable and they were relegated the next season. Worse was to follow when season 1956-57 saw Argyle have their poorest ever finish since they entered the Football League in 1920. Their dreadful start must rank with the worst ever – five consecutive defeats including a 6-0 home reverse to Reading, 4-1 defeats at Brentford and Newport County, a 3-0 trouncing at Loftus Road and a 2-1 home setback in the return game with QPR. After 20 matches they were 23rd out of 24 teams.

Rowley stopped the rot by recalling himself, but he had to play 27 games in a season where he had expected to play very few. He left himself out in February but, after three defeats in the next four games, the Board asked to pick himself for the forthcoming match against Bournemouth. He played in the next six fixtures, with the side losing only once. After a 2-0 win over Gillingham in mid April 1957, he never played in another competitive game. Just months from his 39th birthday, he formally announced that he would hang up his boots at the end of that season. By this time a new Board, with Blindell now firmly in charge, were keen for him to devote all his efforts to being solely the manager.

It was in late 1956/early 1957 that the true extent of the club's serious financial situation became public. The phrase "extinction is a possibility" was used by Treasurer RW Pengelly. Sir Stanley Rous at the FA, and the Football League Management Committee, were seeking assurances that the club would be able to complete its fixtures. Having formally named Jack Rowley as their full-time manager, the new Board backed him well in the summer of 1957. Blindell's injection of £30,000 stabilised the finances. The Board had agreed with Rowley a policy of buying experienced players, to properly fill the gaps left by the departure of high calibre players from the beginning of the decade, whose replacements had been substandard. Rowley was quick to point out that while he wanted to persist with a youth policy, he must also recruit a nucleus of tried men.

Blindell also announced that the policy of employing high numbers of part-time professionals would cease, as the club looked to improve the strength of the reserves. The more one reads of Blindell's ideas, the more perceptive and informed he appears. Jack Rowley was a shrewd operator in the transfer market. His acquisitions in the summer of 1957 all worked. The former

Manchester United legend used the knowledge he had gained during his playing career, raiding the reservoir of "nearly men" plying their trade in the Central League (North and Midlands) and the Football Combination (London and the South). These two competitions were full of powerful reserves leagues where sides could often contain 3 or 4 full Internationals.

Wilf Carter was a perfect example of how very talented players could be picked up relatively cheaply. Both Bryce Fulton and Tommy Barrett, brought in from Manchester United, looked as if they could play. Harry Penk showed particular promise. Penk's previous club Portsmouth, whilst perhaps on the wane, were still a decent First Division side. Penk had scored in two of his last three appearances for Pompey. Geoff Barnsley, signed from the Hawthorns immediately after the Carter deal, got a few games in 1957-58 when goalkeeper Harry Brown was injured and acquitted himself well. October saw Rowley uncover another gem, spending £6,500 to bring in Jimmy Gauld from Everton. The lightning fast newcomer quickly became one of the greatest crowd-pleasers ever to grace Home Park.

Not that the existing Argyle side was without talent. Quiet man Reg Wyatt had established himself at centre-half during season 1957-58. Originally an inside-forward, and then a full-back, he made the transition to defender towards the end of the 1956-57 season. After a successful 1957-58 term, where he became the first choice centre-half and missed only one game, he went from strength to strength. He was never going to be aggressive but covered for his perceived lack of strength with some skilful interceptions. Reg's close friend Peter Anderson (they played together in the same Plymouth Schoolboys side) had by now 105 appearances to his name, showing himself to be fully recovered from the broken leg he sustained against Stoke City in 1955.

Johnny Williams, who originally broke into the first team when still a part-timer, was now full-time and giving regular indications of what a powerhouse he would turn out to be. The manager, a great admirer of Williams, had converted him from an inside-forward to a wing-half. Williams relished the change to the number 4 shirt. Although the Bristol born Williams would be away on National Service for the whole of the 1958-59 season, Rowley knew he was a fitness fanatic who would keep himself in shape. Similarly George Robertson, for too long saddled with being the heir apparent to the legendary "Jumbo" Chisolm, was now settled at right back and playing very well. George Baker had been rewarded, having patiently waited for a regular place. Joining from Maerdy as a boy in 1952, for the genial Welshman 1957-58 was a defining breakthrough season. It ended with him winning a place in the Welsh 1958 World Cup squad and a call up to their under 23 team.

The men destined to represent Argyle during the 1958-59 season were now undeniably "Rowley's". With the departure of Pat Jones and the retirement of Neil Dougall, to take up a coaching post with the reserves, the only regulars from the 1954-55 side Rowley inherited were Robertson and Anderson. Often in the 1957-58 campaign the side had looked perfectly capable of promotion, falling away mainly when Carter was

Wilf Carter and his wife Margaret are welcomed to Home Park by Chairman Ron Blindell.

Photograph from Harley Lawer's 'Argyle Classics.'

Pictured in July 1957, from left to right are Geoff Barnsley and Wilf Carter from West Bromwich Albion, Harry Penk from Portsmouth and Bryce Fulton and Tommy Barrett from Manchester United. New Chair man Ron Blindell was determined that there would be no repeat of th poor showing of the previous season. Barnsley, Carter and Penk ha played in the First Division while Barrett and Fulton were regulars powerful Manchester United reserve side. *Courtesy Sunday Indepe*

injured. Third place was a vast improvement, and significantly they boasted the second best defensive record in the entire Football League. But there were still areas for improvement. Thus in the summer of 1958 transfer activity was almost as busy as the previous year. Four new players arrived. Gordon Fincham, a big centre-half arrived from Filbert Street to provide cover and competition for Wyatt. Argyle already possessed one wing-half called John Williams and Rowley signed another one! Arriving from Ninian Park after growing tired of waiting for a first team opportunity, he was referred to as "Cardiff" Williams. If the two were picked together in the same side they were listed as "JS" and "JL". With Tilley set to sign for Swindon Town, the former Cardiff reserve was seen as an ideal replacement. Eric Doughty, an Arsenal reserves regular at left back, was purchased for £1,000 to take over from the departing Pat Jones. Like John L Williams, to get Doughty Rowley had fought off strong competition from Norwich City. Goalkeeper Bob Wyllie was the final piece in the jigsaw, arriving from West Ham United to fill the gap left by Harry Brown. The Scotsman would start as cover for Barnsley.

The start to the new term was inauspicious. When pre-season training began on 14 July, Peter Anderson and Bryce Fulton were absent, both refusing the terms offered for the forthcoming season. (It was the day the King of Iraq was assassinated—turbulence in Iraq is nothing new) The players were not being offered the maximum wage, which now stood at £20 per week. Tommy Barrett, who had also been holding out for a rise, signed shortly before training commenced. New goalkeeper Bob Wyllie was excused attendance while he moved his family into his club house vacated by Harry Brown. Thus only 15 players reported for training, which was overseen by George Taylor and George Reid. The Brickfields and Bantham were the two main venues, as the players began to sweat off any extra pounds gained in the summer.

team through an intensive fitness training session
ʾrter and Jimmy Gauld lead the way.

Taylor, surely one of the finest servants Home Park has ever had, was a keen student of modern training methods. He had spent many hours at Lilleshall learning the latest techniques. The English game was in the process of modernisation inspired by the two still relatively recent international hammerings at the hands of the Hungarians. Much of the fitness training was now similar to that employed by athletes, with some military style exercises also being incorporated into the preparations. Blindell, quickly proving that he would not be a Chairman who would back off from advising his manager and training staff, had clearly been captivated by the Brazilian World Cup success that summer. His statements to the press on the topic, of which there were many, ranged from the bizarre to near genius, but he was anxious that his Argyle team should model themselves on the South American masters.

There was also the sad announcement that Jimmy Rae had passed away, at just 50 years old. Some felt he never recovered from his forced departure from Home Park. His passing was keenly felt at the club, for it was Rae who had given several of the playing staff their first start in the game. He had also given George Taylor his first appointment to the training staff.

Furthermore, Argyle found itself in conflict with the local Council, in those days rejoicing in the title Plymouth Corporation. They had taken the club to a Valuation Court to decide upon the net rateable value of the Home Park ground. Fortunately, the Chair of that Valuation Court was a Group Captain Pendlebury. He overruled the City Valuation Officer's request for £2,250 and set it at £550. Pendlebury had been close to the Club in the past. He was a Vice-President and former Director, connections which did not improve the mood of the Valuation Officer! The dispute made the national Press. The successful High Court appeal against the City Fathers was used as a precedent by many other clubs.

Argyle began to make improvements to facilities, befitting a club with ambition. On the 5 July Blindell announced that the floodlights were to be upgraded. Whether this had a bearing on the decision Rowley made about his future is not known. Seven days later it was reported that manager Rowley had turned down the opportunity to return to Old Trafford. Matt Busby had wanted him as a replacement for Bert Whalley, one of the victims of the Munich Air Disaster. During June Jack Rowley had returned to his old club, to try and engage the services of Ray Wood, the goalkeeper who had been injured in a clash with Peter McParland during the 1957 FA Cup Final. It was at that time Busby made him the offer to join the coaching staff at Old Trafford.

Supporters were also making their contribution. A report in the *Western Evening Herald* of 16 July stated that the construction of the Supporters' Club building, the one storey edifice just inside the players' entrance that still stands today, was progressing well. On the same day it was announced that the Supporters' Club had furnished the Club with a cheque for £4000, the amount required to modernise the floodlights (£68,000 at 2008 values).

Rumours abounded that Dave Hickson, the Everton centre-forward, was a transfer target and Blindell had agreed to pay what it took to sign him. The signing never came to fruition. Rowley's attention now turned to Colin Webster of Wolves, a member of that summer's Wales World Cup Squad and a former Busby Babe. In both cases the player's wife did not wish to move to Plymouth. 50 years on Paul Sturrock can sympathise with Jack Rowley's difficult task in attracting players to Devon.

Rowley began to get his team ready for the off. He asserted his authority over the players, showing a rare sign of anger when on 22 July he refused to let Wilf Carter, Charlie Twissell and David Downs play in a cricket match versus Plymouth CC, a fixture arranged as part of Harry Brown's benefit. The manager claimed that he had not been told early enough. Peter Anderson, still refusing to accept the terms offered, played. Jack voiced no objection to a subsequent fixture, an annual event against the Plymouth CC mid-week XI. Tommy Barrett took full advantage, scoring 93 not out in an unbeaten stand of 129 with "little" Harry Penk (36no).

In early August Argyle were given no encouragement as they pursued the return of Gordon Astall from Birmingham City. Fulton had still to re-sign. On 4 August Birmingham's attitude over Astall hardened. Despite some of their Board wanting to sell, manager Arthur Turner did not want to release him. Turner won the day. They turned down a £12,000 Argyle bid, with Chairman Blindell keen to emphasise that the transfer did not fail because of the terms offered to the player. With Anderson and Penk showing fine form on the wings, and Baker able to play there when needed, it is hard to see why Rowley was so keen to bring Astall back to the Westcountry. Another winger, Charlie Twissell, who had made 24 appearances and six goals during 1957-58, was rumoured to be unsettled and was clearly out of favour.

On the 8th Bryce Fulton re-signed and returned from Manchester to commence his pre-season training. The 13th saw Jack Rowley instructed by the FA to give a written undertaking that he would not repeat the misconduct which occurred after "that game" against Southend in the previous April. The club was also warned and was instructed "to post warning notices in prominent places around the ground and programme, for one month from 18 August." It says much for Pullin's performance that the FA did not seek to fine or punish Argyle further.

Despite the summer decision to avoid signing part-timers, on the 14th Truro City's Reg Jenkins signed under those terms. The Millbrook born forward joined Argyle while Geoff Peach, with 33 games in the Football Combination side in the previous season, made the reverse journey to Cornwall. Reg would wait some months before signing as a full-time professional, electing to continue his Shipwright Apprenticeship in the Dockyard.

14 August also saw the first public practice game. This was an era when pre-season friendlies were almost non-existent, the tradition being to play the first team against the reserves and the third team against the fourth. The main game was always dubbed Probables v Possibles and ended in a 3-3 draw, attracting 5,500 spectators. *Pilgrim*, the working name for *Western Evening Herald* reporter Ray Head, picked out 19 year old Reg Jen-

kins for praise, while also admiring Baker for running half the length of the field to fire home the Probables' equaliser. Carter and Dougall bagged the other 2 goals. For the Possibles Alex Garden also found favour with *Pilgrim*, who described the young Scotsman's contribution as "wonderful". Garden scored twice, the other Possibles' goal coming from Army trialist John O'Connor.

Mid August also saw an announcement from the Supporters' Club that they had donated £10, 647 to the parent club, with £9,500 earmarked for "specified purposes". There can be no doubt that the success of the Supporters' Club's money-raising ventures went a long way to keeping Argyle afloat at that time. In addition to the specified sum they had given £324 for the purchase of footballs, £48 for ball-boy kits, £310 for a new public address system. Amongst the monies raised during the previous season was £1,406 from programme sales, £570 from catering (a new venture in 1957) and £128 from the loan of cushions. Their annual financial report glumly announced that profit from dances and entertainment was down to just £19 – "due probably to the advent of television and other Saturday night distractions!"

The second public trial was held on 18 August, with the Probables leaving no doubt who was in charge. They won 6-2 with a hat-trick from Anderson and two from George Baker. Jenkins was again prominent and got both goals for the Possibles. On the same day the popular Billy Strauss returned to the club as Office Manager, a post he was dismissed from 18 months previously when the cash flow was at its worst.

Around the 19th the Argyle boss was seen in Cheltenham, speaking to Barry Meyer. He was one of a number of people back then who played both cricket and football professionally. Meyer was known to be out of favour at Bristol Rovers, having decided that cricket would come before pre-season training. Rovers were anxious to offload him; Rowley seemed keen to engage his services.

Although the Argyle manager would not confirm his interest in the Gloucestershire wicket-keeper, Meyer had an excellent scoring record and would be what Rowley felt to be the missing piece in his team jigsaw. To get him the club was prepared to break their previous record fee, the £6,500 spent on Jimmy Gauld in October 1957.

On the Friday before the season started, 22 August, the Supporters' Club AGM was held under the chairmanship of Fred Pring. The main point for discussion was the covering of the popular side, from penalty area to penalty area. The estimated cost would be £24,000 (£408,000 at today's rates). Blindell, in his pre-season address announced that "we have drilled our players to play football and to cut out any rough and tumble. We are aiming at the championship and not merely promotion."

Jack Rowley had been in the game long enough to know that, as of 23 August 1958, he was entering the last chance saloon. It was the start of a new era, not just at Home Park but throughout the Football League. It had become increasingly rare to see the words 'patience' and 'football manager' in the same sentence. Many of the supporters from those two roller-coaster seasons in the early 50s would still be regulars come the 1958-59 season. These days, most of us now go to Home Park more in hope than expectation. Not so then. With those perpetual successes still fairly fresh in supporters' minds, Jack Rowley was *expected* to win promotion. He had worked hard that summer driving many miles, in his own car, in search of new talent. He often based himself in the Midlands, where he was able to stay with relatives and save the club money. Blindell also frequently based himself in the Midlands, taking the opportunity to run the rule over his business interests in Leicester - and to preside over transfers.

So, the 23rd August was almost upon us. The players seemed ready, the manager had done his best to create a promotion team, the club had sold a record £9,000 worth of season tickets and the new Chairman was saying all the right things. Let battle commence!

A press advert for the first home game of the season. Look at those prices!
Courtesy of the Sunday Independent

CHAPTER TWO

PORT TO PORT –
FROM HULL TO SOUTHAMPTON

Any fair minded football fan would concede that Plymouth Argyle start every season with a major disadvantage, their travel itinerary. Not only is it a drain on finances, it is mentally and physically debilitating for the players and staff. Today, the players are often able to fly to away fixtures. Our 1958-59 men had no such luck. Road and rail were the only options. They spent long hours either on the national road network, or on the trains of the day. Odd pieces of the 50s national road infrastructure remain, almost as they were in bygone days. The old road which still runs past the Lyneham Inn is a fine example. It is difficult to comprehend that 50 years ago the Ridgeway at Plympton was the A38, the main road out of Devon.

The rail network is structurally little different – there is just a lot less of it. Railway carriages are significantly different, much more comfortable and open than they were. Nowhere on a late 50s train could a party of 14 sit together. At the end of the 1956-57 season, recognising the weariness caused by travel, the standard seats in the team coach were replaced with 18 second-hand aircraft seats from a retired Dan Air Dakota. The *Western Evening Herald* reported at the time that they were "very modern, with a push button recline system!" Though probably quite primitive by today's standards, for its time it was a very forward looking move by the club.

Because of a hangover from the petrol rationing of the immediate post-war years, and the subsequent Suez crisis, unnecessary long distance travel was discouraged in the late 50s. To comply with Government requirements, fixtures were arranged to maximise fuel consumption. For example, the 1958-59 season started with a northern tour. The opener, a Saturday fixture at Hull City, was followed by a Monday visit to Rochdale. For that first match of the season, at the old Boothferry Park on Saturday 23 August 1958, they initially travelled the 296 miles to Doncaster. It was a dreadful journey; 12 hours of storms and floods. August was an extremely wet and stormy month – no change there.

Moving on to Hull the next day, about 45 miles, *Pilgrim* was able to report a gallant point after a 1-1 draw, courtesy of a Gauld goal. The side fielded had a very 1957-58 look about it; Eric Doughty was the only new signing included in the line-up. The former Arsenal man replaced the retired Pat Jones in the number 3 shirt; Wilf Carter took over from Jones as skipper. Within half an hour of his debut Doughty suffered a dreadful knee injury. He showed the utmost courage in hobbling around for the whole of the second half, *Pilgrim* observing that he could hardly run or jump. A crowd of 14,318 paid the grand total of £1,463. In those days, after the home club had deducted their match day expenses, the visitors were entitled to a 20% share of the gate.

After the game the team moved across to Timperley in Cheshire. His

Manchester connections meant it was a part of the world Rowley knew well. They spent three nights there, beating Rochdale 2-0 on the Monday evening, their first ever visit to the Spotland ground. Carter and Penk got the goals, the latter having a knack of scoring in his native north. *Pilgrim* reported a routine victory in front of nearly 8,500. He marvelled at Carter's quick turn and shot for the first goal. He also noted how all of Rochdale's factories closed for the annual holiday, which meant that no programme had been produced. The teams were announced over the tannoy. Had there been a programme, Neil Dougall would not have been included. After Doughty's injury, and with 12th man John 'Cardiff' Williams nursing an ankle injury, Dougall's retirement was rescinded after just one game of the new season. He travelled to Timperley by train on the Sunday, and deputised for Doughty at Spotland. It was the only change from the XI who had taken a point at Hull. Argyle got back into Plymouth late on the Tuesday evening, satisfied with their three point haul.

Meanwhile, Secretary Bert Cole had been busy while the team was away. He was at Eastville on the Thursday prior to the season's opener, to tie up the transfer of Barry Meyer. Cole, highly respected throughout the game, was a personal friend and old bowling pal of his Bristol counterpart, Mr Gummow. The Bristol secretary had warned Cole to be in Bristol as soon as possible, as the city's other club were closing in and Cardiff City were also watching the situation. Rovers did not really want to do business with their rivals from Ashton Gate, but the Cardiff move appealed to the player. Cole caught an early evening train and was in Bristol just before midnight. He was on Meyer's doorstep by 9 o'clock the next morning. Argyle's John Timmins had also spent the night in Bristol, being valued at £2,500 in a deal which was worth some £7000 overall. Timmins had only joined Argyle from Wolves during the previous season, but he and his wife were unable to settle in Devon.

The two players were kept in separate Eastville offices, almost like criminals being interrogated, as the officials pushed the transfers through. Even when they went for lunch, they were taken to separate places. The deal was completed just before 4 pm. Meyer was soon telephoned by *Pilgrim* and the *Western Independent's Spectator*. The cricketer/footballer expressed his delight at being allowed to continue to combine the two sports.

At about the same time, elsewhere in Bristol, referee GW Pullin was opening a letter from the Football Association. The Bristol official, obviously still reviled at Home Park, read that he would not be officiating at the Plymouth v Rochdale game in early September. Plymouth Argyle had made it clear that this appointment, so soon after the Southend debacle, would not go down very well with the 20,000 plus expected to attend. Pullin's nominated replacement for that forthcoming home fixture with Rochdale was one Denis Howell, a Birmingham MP. A few years later Howell would be the target for a bottle-throwing Home Park supporter, an act which forced the FA to close the ground. Who would be a referee?

The first home fixture of the season, in front of an expectant 22,518, brought a fine 4-0 victory over Tranmere Rovers. Carter notched another two, with Baker and Gauld completing the scoring. Four days later Rochdale were beaten 2-0 with Carter scoring yet again, bringing his tally to four for the season. Nearly 27,000 saw Johnny Williams add a second. The *Western Independent* reported that season ticket sales had reached a record £9,000. An adult ground season ticket was £2, with a 50% reduction for under 16s and pensioners. 50 years ago the national average weekly wage was between £7 and £8. Clearly inflation in football has massively outstripped the rates elsewhere. The cheapest season ticket costs a lot more now than one third of the typical weekly wage. In *Pilgrim's* excellent *Football Herald* weekly round-up Ron Blindell came out in support of the PFA's initiative to outlaw time-wasting. Furthermore, the Chairman re-iterated that it would be Argyle policy that only captain Wilf Carter would be talking to referees.

Another long journey north beckoned, with the pattern of a Saturday and a Monday fixture continuing. A three night stay, and 18 hours on the road, saw a point gained from a 2-2 draw at Stockport on the Saturday. Penk (in the north again) and Gauld were the scorers. The short trip to Bury for the Monday fixture resulted in another draw, this time 1-1, courtesy of Anderson's goal in the final seconds of the game. There were 12,188 at Gigg Lane – how Bury could do with crowds of that size now. In the next home game against Reading, where Argyle came from two down, Carter and Penk netted in a 2-2 draw in front of 26,000.

The Thursday night return with Bury forced Rowley to give debuts to three players because of injuries. John 'Cardiff' Williams came in for the injured Barrett, the returning Alex Govan made the first start of his new spell in place of Anderson. Govan was given the captaincy for the night and Bury were swept aside 3-0 in front of 27,589. The Glaswegian had turned down moves to Cardiff City and Brentford, preferring a return to Home Park after an unsatisfactory six month spell at struggling Portsmouth Barry Meyer was the third newcomer, taking over from the injured Baker. Meyer opened his account with a brace after Gauld, with his fourth of the season had got the first, heading home a Govan free-kick. In his round up on the following Sunday John 'Cardiff' Williams was given the seal of approval by *Spectator*. At the Chairman's insistence, Barrett, Baker and Anderson were, unusually, kept on first team wages for the week. Being left out normally signalled a return to reserve or summer wage levels.

With an eight game unbeaten start, and top of the league, the team travelled to Colchester in good heart. Unchanged, they suffered their first defeat of the season, going down 2-0 in a lacklustre performance. Colchester was then a two night stay and they arrived back at Home Park early on the Sunday evening, with a home game against Doncaster scheduled for the Monday. Rowley treated the Colchester reverse as a blip and again named an unchanged side, a decision which was fully justified, as Doncaster were hammered 4-0. Carter got another two with Johnny Williams and Govan also scoring. Bournemouth & Boscombe Athletic were the next visitors and they were despatched 3-1, Meyer grabbing a goal against his home town team with Dougall and Wyatt adding one each. Strangely, neither of them scored again that season. Wilf Carter, one of

Alex Govan clearly looks pleased to be returning to Argyle after a nightmare six months at Portsmouth. Secretary Bert Cole and Manager Jack Rowley look on. *Picture courtesy Plymouth Evening Herald/Colin Parsons*

Gauld turns away after scoring the third goal against Tranmere Rovers in the opening home game. He latched on to a lob from Tommy Barrett and just ran through the away defence.
Picture courtesy Plymouth Evening Herald/Colin Parsons

the best and most consistent penalty takers ever to play for the Greens, missed not one but two in this game. The first hit the bar and the second bounced to safety off the post. After the game Carter told *Spectator* "I don't know what happened to that first one. I normally put them hard and low, with more emphasis on speed than position. That one just went up and up." *Spectator* noted that a section of the crowd were becoming impatient with Barnsley's preference for rolling the ball to a defender, by constantly calling "kick it." The journalist did his best to explain that the tactic was designed to keep possession and, in his view, was far more effective than the goalkeeper clearing his lines with a hopeful punt forward.

As October came the team embarked on their most difficult journey yet, taking in successive away fixtures against Doncaster Rovers and Norwich City. The Doncaster fixture was played on a Thursday evening at 5.30pm and proved eventful for Peter Anderson. On the journey there it seemed certain that the manager would retain the side that had trounced Doncaster 10 days previously and Anderson travelled thinking he would be 12th man. At the last minute the Plymouth born winger was told he would be playing and proceeded to score a hat-trick. Meyer, already looking like a shrewd buy, added two more and Penk confirmed his love of northern air by adding the final goal. Doncaster had led 4-2 at half-time. The manager was very critical at the interval but felt "that everything went right after that." Only 5,330 saw this thrilling encounter, probably because of the requirement of an early evening kick-off necessitated because Belle Vue had no floodlights at that time. According to reports, Gauld was a sensation in the second half and an inspiration to his team mates.

In an unchanged side, Carter scored at Norwich on the following Saturday, earning a 1-1 draw in front of 22,200 at Carrow Road. Added to the Doncaster success of a few days before, at the end of the season this would be seen as a very good point. The Canaries would soon set the nation alight as they embarked on an amazing FA Cup run – more of that in another chapter.

Whilst travel was a concern for the whole team, there was a particular worry for the effect it might have had on Johnny Williams. After the journey to Doncaster, and then on to Norwich, he returned to Plymouth in the early hours of Sunday morning, 800 miles in four days. After a few hours with his wife he caught a train to London, to meet up with the British Army XI. From London he took the sleeper to Edinburgh, where on the Monday evening, at Easter Road, he helped the Army beat Hibernians 6-1. He arrived back in Plymouth late on the Tuesday, in time to play in the Southend fixture on the Wednesday evening. A mid-week crowd of 25,349 witnessed a one-sided victory over Southend, with Williams showing no ill effects from his road and rail marathon. He and Gauld got a goal each, with the third an own goal from the visitors' defender Costello.

The following Saturday just over 26,000 turned up to watch their team beat Swindon Town 3-2. Carter, with a penalty and Gauld (2) were the scorers, with Baker having returned in place of the injured Meyer. Gauld was closely marked throughout. S*pectator* used the term "gaoler" to describe the tactics employed by Swindon manager Bert Head. But Gauld was in the form of his life. Towards the end, a large number of supporters had made their way to the exits, having settled for a draw. Our Jimmy had other ideas, and launched on one last run, displaying his usual mixture of skill and good fortune. On a pitch that was a sea of mud, it was a tribute to his physical condition that he could run from the halfway line, beating men on the way before finishing at the second attempt. His first effort had been blocked by visiting goalkeeper Burton but Jimmy slotted in the rebound. How many in the crowd that day took note of the skilful little Swindon right winger, one David Corbett? There was no place in the opposition for Rex Tilley, the Argyle wing-half who earlier in the season had transferred to the Wiltshire side.

The receipts from the two games amounted to £5,790. Southend's 20% share was £420 while Swindon pocketed £10 more. By modern standards these seem trifling amounts. However, in 1958 it was sufficient for each club to cover the basic week's wage of 21 of their professionals. The programme went up from 3d to 4d (to about 2p). The final two fixtures in October saw the team win twice. Firstly, a 4-1 away at Mansfield Town, Carter (3) and Anderson scoring. Carter's first (and only) hat-trick on an away ground took his season's total to 12. He was the Division's top scorer, with roughly one third of the fixtures completed. Gauld had seven and Meyer five in just seven outings. Then visitors Notts County were defeated by three clear goals, Baker, Gauld and Penk netting without reply. Almost 26,000 roared their team on to a fourth successive victory. Yet more programme changes followed with the price back down to 3d. This third version was completely different to its two predecessors, reflecting the rebuilding of the city with a picture of the newly constructed centre and a large legend "Make Plymouth Your Shopping Centre." (see page 31)

Williams was off to Newcastle the following day, where on the Monday he helped the British Army to another prized win at Newcastle – just a little matter of a 900 mile trek up and down England.   November opened with a hard fought win at Chesterfield, with Baker and Carter on the mark. At one time a goal behind, Carter's 90th minute effort sealed the two points. It was Carter's 13th of the season—lucky for some! Next up, Newport County were beaten 3-2 in front of 23,482 at Home Park. Gauld (2) and Baker, his third in successive matches, got the goals that mattered in an ill-tempered game. With the floodlights undergoing improvements the game, like that against Millwall Reserves the previous week, kicked off half an hour earlier than usual at 2.45pm.   If only that spirit amongst the playing staff could be replicated in the Boardroom. There were two Firework nights in 1958 – the Annual General Meeting provided the second one! On 6th November Argyle were top of the league. In the lead up to the Newport game, it was matters away from the field that had made the news. Argyle entered the week with Chairman Ron Blindell, seemingly well in control. It ended with Harry Deans in the Chair. It could only happen at Home Park. (The Boardroom squabble is extensively examined in a subsequent chapter).

Buoyed by a six point cushion at the top of the League, nearly 22,000 watched the home first round FA Cup tie against Gillingham, but were disappointed to see a 2-2 draw. Carter and Anderson scored but a run of six consecutive wins had come to an end. Ron Blindell was in attendance, though he sat away from other Board members. Could it be that the crisis in the Boardroom was affecting the playing staff? The replay meant a 520 mile round trip, a journey perhaps made more tolerable by a resounding 4-1 win. Meyer returned for the injured Carter and scored a hat-trick. This match was played on a Wednesday afternoon, as the FA still would not allow FA Cup ties to be played under lights. It is probably the last occasion upon which Argyle played on a weekday afternoon in the FA Cup. (The Manchester City match during the three day week was a League Cup fixture) Thanks to the Supporters' Club, British Railways ran an excursion to Gillingham for the game. It left Plymouth at midnight on the Tuesday and cost 38/- return (£1.90p).

With Argyle safely through to an FA Cup second round away tie at Coventry City, Wrexham were the next side at Home Park. Carter, with a badly cut eye, was absent for the game. It was the Welsh side's first visit to Home Park. Just over 21,000 saw Penk and Gauld score in a 2-2 draw. The Wrexham goalkeeper Ugolini was inspired, easily the man of the match. Centre-forward George Baker was married in the morning with fellow Welshman John 'Cardiff' Williams his Best Man. They were now unbeaten in 11. On the final Saturday in November they journeyed along the south coast to Southampton, at 154 miles a comparatively short hop for the League's most travelled team. The injured Neil Dougall, who had played in all of the 20 League and Cup games since his surprise recall at Rochdale, was replaced at left back by Bryce Fulton. It was the former Manchester United man's first appearance of the season. In another change, Carter returned for Meyer. Few of the 21,830 people packed into the Dell, where Argyle had not lost since the war, would have forecast that the inconsistent Saints side would thrash the league leaders 5-1. Carter got Argyle's solitary goal, his 14th in the League. A young Winchester-born right winger called Terry Paine gave Fulton a real chasing, while George Robertson fared no better against the flying Sydenham on the Saint's left flank. History shows that they would be the basis of the Southampton side which won promotion the following season, 1959-60. They have never returned to the third tier of the Football League, though they had a really good try in 2007-08. Within a few years Terry Paine would be part of the 22 man England squad which won the World Cup and Sydenham was regularly capped at under 23 level, as well as being a fixture in the British Army XI.

Until this trip along the South Coast it had been an excellent start. With the draining Christmas programme less than a month away, one could only hope that this was a temporary setback. It remained to be seen if Rowley would seek to recruit. Next was the second round of the FA Cup, an away date at Coventry which would provide an opportunity to regroup.

THE FOOTBALL HERALD '58 STYLE

A nostalgic reminder of what the broadsheet style *Football Herald* looked like 50 years ago. The copy above, from George Baker's large and varied scrapbook, reports the excellent 2nd round success at Highfield Road, Coventry (see story on facing page). In view of the week the players had undergone—the mauling at Southampton followed by the tragic news of George Reed's untimely death—the players showed great spirit in bouncing back.

The *Herald's* Argyle reporter Ray Head, who wrote under the pseudonym *Pilgrim*, had to lug a heavy typewriter around the country. He typed as the game progressed, before finding a phone box near the ground to phone his copy back to the Herald's offices. This *may* have been the first time he was able to dial the number himself.

The tie at Coventry was played on Saturday 6 December 1958. Only the day before Her Majesty the Queen had made the first ever dialled long distance call in Great Britain. From Bristol she telephoned the Lord Provost in Edinburgh. Prior to that every long distance call had been operator connected.

From George Baker's scrapbook

CHAPTER THREE

FROM DECEMBER TO EASTER

The first Saturday in December saw Argyle visit Fourth Division Coventry City in the 2nd round of the FA Cup. After the debacle at Southampton the experienced Dougall was recalled. The club was desperate to get through to the next round. Although the financial situation had improved, an attractive 3rd Round draw, preferably at home, would still be useful.

It had been a sad week at Home Park. Popular assistant trainer George Reed had been sent to assess Coventry's strengths and weaknesses. On the journey back, while running for a train, George collapsed and died of a heart attack. *Spectator* solemnly reported "The sympathy was prompt and practical, and typical of the sporting world." Secretary Cole immediately relinquished any claim to his testimonial when Argyle met the British Army XI on Monday; the players in that match each gave their £2 playing bonuses and later the entire playing staff gave £1 each. The funeral was attended by executives, directors, shareholders, supporters, local league and press representatives. *Spectator* informed readers that Argyle players acted as pall-bearers and that former 30's team mates of Reed – Bill Harper, now the Head Groundsman, Frank Sloan and Fred Titmus - were there to pay their last respects. Harper had just completed 37 years at Home Park.

As if in tribute to Reed, the team put the disastrous result at the Dell behind them. They won with a workmanlike performance against the Highfield Road outfit. Baker and a brace from Carter, including yet another penalty won by Gauld, ushered them to a 3-1 victory. Goalkeeper Geoff Barnsley, not too far from his Bilston birthplace, was inspired.

Johnny Williams was away again in the week, playing for the Army against a Scotland side. Amongst the Glasgow crowd was Manchester United manager Matt Busby, still recovering from the injuries he sustained at Munich. Busby remarked afterwards, "What a fine player the young man from Plymouth Argyle is." There is no evidence to suggest that Busby took his interest any further. Williams then missed his first game of the season, away at Bradford on 13 December. He was needed by the Army in Paris the day after, to play against the French Army XI. It was probably Williams' first competitive game on a Sunday.

Forgotten man Tommy Barrett came in for his first game in three months. He played solidly in a hard fought 0-0 draw at Valley Parade, only Argyle's second blank of the season. As *Spectator* reminded us, it was Argyle's seventh visit to the north thus far, and they were yet to taste defeat. *Spectator* continued "Geoff Barnsley took the honours on a tricky, frozen surface. Bradford had scored 16 in their previous four games, but Barnsley was equal to everything they threw at him. It was a point won rather than one dropped." The travel arrangements from Bradford meant that within 15 minutes of the final whistle the travelling party were in a coach heading for Leeds station. Once at Leeds they rushed on to an express train to London.

Rowley, still concerned at the manner of defeat at Southampton, elected to miss the Bradford game. He decided to watch a match in the south, instructing Secretary Bert Cole to watch another target. It is clear that Rowley implicitly trusted Secretary Cole's judgement of a player. It emerged after the weekend that Argyle now had first refusal on two Chelsea players. One was Len Casey, a powerful wing-half, who had made 21 First Division appearances the previous season, and 50 overall. The other was left-back Wally Bellett, who had made 35 appearances for the Chelsea first team, 20 of them coming in the 1957-58 campaign. Chelsea had won the League Championship in season 1954-55 and had a number of high quality players. Rowley, meanwhile, had been watching Mark Pearson. His bid was turned down by his old club, and the Argyle manager switched his attentions elsewhere. He told *Pilgrim* "the fees being asked are frightening."

The halfway point of the season, the 23rd league fixture, brought the visit of second placed Hull City, opponents on the opening day. It was a cold December afternoon. There had been talk of a new signing throughout the week leading up to the game. On the Friday evening before the game frantic activity saw Bellett and Casey signed from Chelsea. The club paid a record fee of £15,000 for the two players, albeit in instalments which would not finish until the Christmas of 1959. The Football League were notified by telegram, before the registration forms were posted off to Preston. The newcomers were welcomed by new Chairman Harry Deans.

The two players came straight into the side. Bellett replaced the injured Dougall. John L Williams was sacrificed for Casey. Barrett made way for Johnny Williams, an appearance which turned out to be the first in a run of 179 consecutive outings, a sequence that did not end until March 1963. Ted Drake, the Chelsea manager had proved to be a man of his word. Argyle's interest in Casey had alerted other clubs but Drake kept his "first refusal" promise.

Dougall had surely played his last game now. Only Barnsley, Robertson, Wyatt, Gauld and Penk remained ever present. Although Rowley had used 18 players, the overall consistency of his selections showed in the Hull match. Of the 11 chosen for the return, only new signings Bellett and Casey had not figured at Hull in the season's first fixture. It was a good indicator that before the season started he knew his strongest line-up. But for the injury to Doughty, there may well only have been a single change. One had to feel really sorry for Doughty. Still fighting back from that dreadful injury, it now seemed that any light at the end of his tunnel was blocked by the well-built Bellett.

Clearly that last Christmas shopping Saturday before Christmas was having an effect 50 years ago. A lower than expected 20,305 watched a 1-1 draw with fellow promotion contenders Hull, Carter grabbing his 15th League goal of the season. Govan was still injured and disappointed to miss this game, for the Tigers were managed by Bob Brocklebank, the man who five years before had taken him to Birmingham City. Bellett and Casey had sound debuts. *Pilgrim* noted in his match report that the crowd were asked to contribute to a collection for the late George Reed. In addition to Wilf Carter's goals, at the halfway mark Jimmy Gauld had weighed in with 11, with Penk, Baker and Anderson adding 15 between them. Meyer had looked dangerous when he played but could not get a decent run without injury. Furthermore, rumours were now circulating that he was unsettled and wanted a return nearer to the Severn. Some said he was already back in Bristol, training with his former club.

Unusually, there was no Christmas Day fixture in 1958. Boxing Day saw Queens Park Rangers beaten 3-2 in front of 30,036 people, a revised total after the 90 supporters in the ringside seats were included. Govan came in for Penk, who missed his first game of the season. Carter got his third in five games, with Jimmy Gauld getting the other two. Reg Wyatt made his 100th appearance for Argyle. The following day the return fixture was played in Shepherd's Bush. Rowley named an unchanged side, in a match which saw Argyle go down by the odd goal in three. Gauld was again on the mark. Referee Luty, based in Leeds, was the busiest man on the field in what, especially after the interval, was a physical encounter. Indeed, at one stage he fell over trying to keep up with play.

Gauld was frighteningly quick, and he seemed in the form of his life. Having scored twice in the previous day's encounter, he was a marked man. Gauld, the target of Petchey's violent tackles throughout the game, took it all with a smile. At the end he very nearly snatched a point with a fantastic run from deep in his own half. Another surging run into the QPR penalty area saw him pulled off the ball. *Spectator* was adamant it was a rugby tackle but referee Luty, perhaps mindful of the earlier crowd reaction, waved play on. At one stage there was a crowd invasion. Skipper George Robertson had stepped in to prevent Wyatt and QPR's Pearson coming to blows. He pushed Pearson who fell as if he had been hit by a heavyweight boxer.

For a team that were to travel nearly 11,000 miles by the season's end, a fruitless round trip of close on 600 miles was the last thing our promotion hopefuls wanted. Leaving Plymouth on Friday 2 January 1959, they travelled for a fixture with Tranmere Rovers. With four games in hand, Jack Rowley's side led the table on goal average. Despite another long journey their mood was understandably good. They travelled in the knowledge that Hull had been beaten at Chesterfield on New Year's Day. They left Plymouth by train at 10.30, arriving at their Liverpool hotel at just after eight that evening. There had been atrocious weather all the way; rain, sleet and snow, perhaps the reason they did not travel by road.

The next day, after their short trip through the Mersey Tunnel by local coach, they arrived at Prenton Park to find it looking like a lake. Tranmere had played Wrexham on New Year's Day. Many in the ground thought it unfit then. Given the perpetual bad weather, it was no surprise that referee Haworth, who had officiated at the recent Coventry cup tie, called off the match immediately after his 1.30 pm inspection. Some locals told the Argyle party that the pitch had been rolled immediately after the Wrexham game, effectively sealing the surface against drainage.

It was not even a consideration in those days for clubs to call for an inspection by a local referee. Only the match referee could decide, and he was not required to be there more than 90 minutes before kick-off. Argyle later complained bitterly to the FA and the Football League. FA secretary Sir Stanley Rous promised to introduce (and co-ordinate) an arrangement where a local referee could be called in to arbitrate. Perhaps today's system of early local inspections, to prevent players and supporters travelling unnecessarily, can be traced back to a wet, windy and cold day in Birkenhead?

As they left the ground to go and watch the Liverpool v Sunderland Second Division game at Anfield, winger Govan quipped to *Spectator* "Pity really, that was going to be my best game of the season!" Govan and *Spectator* also discussed news of Maurice Tadman, the cultured former Argyle centre-forward who had been a team mate of Govan. It had been announced that day that Tadman had cordially parted company with Distillery. He was leaving his manager's post to start a business in Belfast.

Two further problems emanated from this postponement. Reaching the third round of the FA Cup, a home tie with Cardiff City, had meant that next week's away fixture at Halifax Town was postponed. That would mean another long midweek journey to the north, with the re-arrangement of the Tranmere fixture now a further consideration. There was also the potential for another reshuffle. With Argyle and Accrington Stanley both still in the FA Cup, the forthcoming home fixture, scheduled for fourth round day could now be in danger. Even if Argyle lost to Cardiff, an Accrington victory would force the postponement of the Lancashire side's first visit to Home Park.

Moreover, the Argyle boss had been planning to experiment against Tranmere, ready for the impending Cardiff tie. Anderson was to be left out, with Baker moving to the wing and Meyer coming in at nine. With Govan recalled to the left wing spot at Christmas, for the first time that

A rare Argyle attack in the 3-0 home Cup defeat against Cardiff City. The grandstand was not as wide then as it is now. Note also that the terrace went right up under the stand. *Courtesy Colin Parsons collection*

season we would see an Argyle side without either Anderson or Penk on the flanks. The Welsh side were a mid table Second Division side, but only recently out of the top tier.

36,247 packed into Home Park, full of that special anticipation that any cup tie against opposition from a higher league brings. With Cardiff demanding their full allocation of stand seats, some home season ticket holders had to move. Secretary Cole called it an administrative nightmare, the like of which he had not seen before. In the event, the Ninian Park side won at a canter with three second half goals. Argyle never threatened them and Meyer's Gloucestershire cricket colleague, Cardiff keeper Ron Nicholls, was not troubled. The boss's experiment with Baker and Meyer failed miserably. The latter had his poorest game yet and Baker looked completely out of sorts, until he returned to his deep-lying centre forward role. Reg Wyatt, so dependable all season, had a nightmare game and was directly responsible for a couple of the goals.

An attribute of this Argyle side was that they always seemed able to bounce back after a setback. At no time in the season did they lose two in a row, though they twice lost two out of three. Stockport County were the next visitors to Home Park. Thanks to the continued bad weather, only 10,099 turned out for the game. In the only change Penk returned at the expense of Meyer, who was on the verge of a move to Newport County. Argyle, while not wishing to stand his way, wanted to recoup most of the fee they had paid. The Board felt they owed as much to the Supporters' Club. They had, after all, financed the deal bringing the player from Eastville only five months ago.

Govan and Baker scored in a 2-1 success, a match where Argyle ground out a result in very heavy conditions. In his match report *Pilgrim* bemoaned the fact that wingers Penk, playing on the right, and Govan were ineffective, despite the fact that they had the only decent parts of the pitch. It was rare to see such criticism placed at Penk's door, though many thought he was more effective on the left flank. With Accrington still in the FA Cup on fourth round day, Jack Rowley and Bert Cole moved quickly to bring forward a forthcoming evening away fixture at Southend. They had briefly considered a home friendly, with a Manchester United side that had surprisingly fallen at the first hurdle in the FA Cup. But fearing a fixture pile-up, and wishing to avoid a long midweek journey, they opted to bring forward the trip to Essex.

They drew 0-0 at Roots Hall, a round trip of 588 miles. Casey, back in his native Essex, was described by *Pilgrim* as "outstanding, and a real find as captain." Wilf Carter had begun the season as captain, but asked Rowley to hand the responsibility to someone else. George Robertson took over but, shortly before the Southend game, he asked to relinquish the job. After Reg Wyatt declined the opportunity to take over, Jack Rowley turned to the experienced Casey. A week later they went to Reading and won 2-0, Govan and Baker each scoring for the second time in three matches. Casey was again inspirational. Govan cracked the first and supplied the cross for Baker's effort. He was now beginning to exert some real influence in his second spell at Home Park.

Next came a disappointing 1-1 home draw against Colchester, in front of 22, 686. Fulton replaced the injured Robertson, the first change in five games. Neil Langman, the former Argyle centre forward, returned to Home Park. *Pilgrim* reported that Langman was given a generous welcome by the home supporters. Valentine's Day 1959 found them playing in the next county – a mere 258 mile round trip to meet Bournemouth & Boscombe Athletic. Govan hit his third in five games in a 1-1 draw. A higher than average crowd at Bournemouth, 15,107, was probably bolstered by a number of Plymouth supporters attending their 'local derby'.

Next was an attractive home fixture against Norwich City. Fulton retained his place at right back and, after missing five games, Anderson was recalled to replace the injured Govan. The Norfolk side, already through to

George Baker challenges Norwich goalkeeper Ken Nethercott as he takes a cross from the right. Harry Penk is on the right.
Photograph courtesy Plymouth Evening Herald/ Colon Parsons collection

the sixth round of the FA Cup, had remained unbeaten in 1959. Carter passed a late test, the manager having had Jenkins standing by for his debut if needed. Allcock silenced the 24,532 crowd when he scored for the visitors in a 1-0 victory. Reports of the game indicated that Norwich looked a fine side, moving the ball quickly. Argyle looked ponderous by comparison. George Baker was given a hard time by the crowd, booed every time he touched the ball. He looked low on confidence. Rowley admitted afterwards that "Baker was now a better player away from Home Park."

Despite Rowley's statement about Baker's away form, Reg Jenkins replaced him in the next game. The young Cornishman made his debut at the County Ground in Swindon. Anderson retained his place, scoring at both ends in a dramatic 4-3 win. Gauld, at his mercurial best, scored his first hat-trick for the club. It included yet another goal from an "impossible angle". It was their only win in February, a month marked by inconsistency. Baker, a recent target for the "boo-boys" at Home Park, asked to play for the reserves rather than travel to Swindon as 12th man. With a travelling reserve retaining his first team wages, it is clear that Baker was prepared to put monetary considerations aside, preferring to try and play his way back to form.

Incessant rain marked Accrington Stanley's first (and only) visit to Home Park. Only 12,022 turned out to brave the weather, to see Argyle comprehensively beaten in a match they were expected to win easily. Although it was their first league success since 27 December the emphatic 4-2 result did not flatter the Lancashire side. In his match report *Pilgrim* was quick to point out how well the two Accrington wingers used the flanks, the only part of the pitch where the ball would run properly. The two Stanley wingers were brothers, Harry and Jimmy Anders. The *Topical Times* Football Annual covering the 1958-59 season carried a picture of them both; each had become the father of twins.

Colin Parsons, a Basingstoke based Argyle supporter of more than 50 years, has a fine collection of Argyle memorabilia, including *every* first team programme home and away (except the Rochdale one!). He contends that the Accrington match programme is one of the rarer ones, as so many turned to pulp in the incessant rain that evening. If you have one in the attic, ensure it is well preserved.

There was real disquiet in the camp now, with the Board genuinely worried that all the good work before Christmas may now be undone. Promotion was no longer a cer-

Courtesy Sam Bailey

tainty. Games in hand had not been won. Two home defeats in a row had seen the crowd turn on the team. They could hardly blame Blindell now. A special Board meeting was convened to discuss the selection for the forthcoming Mansfield game, though Chairman Deans was quick to point out "that Jack Rowley will have the last word." Mansfield were one of the form teams of the Division.

Barnsley was left out for the first time, having had a bad time against Accrington. He, like Baker before him, had become a victim of the crowd. Wylie came in for his debut. Another debutant that day was Fincham, who replaced the injured Wyatt. It was a long awaited debut, with the former Leicester man having been in impressive form for the reserves. The injured Anderson was replaced by Govan and Baker returned for Jenkins.

The young man from Millbrook had not let himself down, but Rowley felt that "this is a time for an experienced hand on the tiller." *Pilgrim* was particularly concerned with Carter's form; he thought that the Black Country man had lost his edge and was trying too hard. He had not scored in nine games, his worst spell since joining Argyle in the summer of 1957. He was the talisman, and the Pilgrims desperately needed their top man to start scoring regularly again. Including the Cardiff Cup engagement, Carter had gone 10 games without a goal. For the Mansfield game, whilst the formation was the same, Carter wore the nine shirt rather than his traditional eight. Numbers were significant then so it was clearly a bid to change his luck.

If supporters had a hangover from the Accrington game, it was gone within 20 minutes of the Mansfield encounter. Argyle raced into a 3-0 lead. They had gone ahead after two minutes through a Swinscoe own

Swinscoe looks aghast as he puts through his own goal. Carter follows in but it was Govan (right) whose low drive caused the Stag's defence a problem. Swinscoe also scored a second o.g. at the end of the match.
Photograph courtesy of the Sunday Independent

goal. Wingers Govan and Penk increased the lead. Mansfield's Downie and Ripley then scored twice in three minutes before half-time. Within four minutes of the second-half it was back to 3-3, Downie grabbing his second of the afternoon. Having witnessed two consecutive home defeats, the crowd were not ready for a third. Once more they showed their fickle nature by turning on the team, an attribute which has, regrettably, lingered on for 50 years.

For nearly 15 minutes the game swung in the balance before Argyle stepped up a gear. Then five goals came in a fantastic 27 minute spell.

The previously angry crowd went to the other end of the emotional scale. In the 62nd minute Gauld scored a goal from an oblique angle. Three minutes later Johnny Williams fired in Argyle's fourth. Another 14 minutes went by before Carter finally broke his barren spell with a penalty. That change of shirt worked! Williams then added his second in the 88th minute, before the luckless Swinscoe finished as he began, with an own goal. It was amazing fare.

A week later, 14 March, Argyle won 2-1 at Meadow Lane. Notts County had been relegated from Division Two the season before. After a poor start they were beginning to find some form. In the 18th minute Gauld chased a through ball from Williams. He was heading away from goal. 17 year old Twigg, on his near post, watched as Gauld ran to the by-line. Expecting the Argyle man to square the ball, he suddenly saw it curled around him and into the far side of the net. It could hardly be a fluke; it was not the first time Gauld had scored from such a narrow angle. County goalie Dick Twigg was still bemused after the game. Gauld bagged both goals, while at the other end Wyllie caught the eye with some masterful goalkeeping.

Overall the visitors were the poorer side, the difference being the influential Jimmy Gauld. The referee was one Arthur Ellis from Halifax, later to become famous as the referee on the popular "*It's a Knock Out*" TV programme. *Spectator* wrote that "goals and points are all Argyle can be commended for – but what more do you want." There were now 11 games to go. To take the pressure off the players, Jack Rowley decided to stay in the north after the Nottingham fixture.

He organised a relaxing break in Southport. They were due to play the crucial re-arranged fixture at Tranmere on the Monday. It made sense to stay in the north. The sun shone for the entire time. In addition to the eleven picked for the Meadow Lane game, Wyatt, Anderson, Barnsley and JL Williams all travelled with the party. Johnny Williams had to return to his unit. Each of them was promised first team wages for the trip. Normally, only the nominated 12th man would get the extra few pounds.

The re-arranged Tranmere fixture was played on Monday, 17 March. Rowley, becoming something of a latter day "Tinkerman", moved Johnny Williams from wing half to inside forward, bringing in his Welsh namesake to wear the number four shirt. Wylie and Fincham were retained in the side. Although suffering a 2-0 reverse, it was commonly felt that it was their best display of football for weeks, a combination of skill and energy not seen for many a week. Fincham typified the fighting spirit which had been lacking. He stopped a ball right in the stomach. At first doubled up with pain, he angrily gestured the advancing trainer away, and immediately returned to the fray.

50 years ago there was no specific sports letters page in the *Western Evening Herald*. In his weekly round up in the Football Final *Pilgrim* would quote from letters received, either those sent direct to him or from correspondence received by manager Jack Rowley. It was then quite common for opposition supporters to write to praise the performance of a visiting team. The away game in Birkenhead prompted many letters, all of them exceedingly complimentary about the Argyle display. HJ Smith of Birken-

the arts and crafts of soccer." He continued "Many people who have watched Everton or Liverpool regularly were amazed by the heights reached in this wonderful Third Division game." And from Heswall, Cheshire a Mr. Howard Davies developed the theme. "I have been watching Tranmere for 40 years and have never seen a finer match." To manager Jack Rowley he said "I want to thank your boys for the part they played in this classic, which will be long remembered in these parts. You have a first-rate and sporting team and the class and gentlemanly behaviour of your boys on the field impressed us all." He finished by wishing the club "the best of good fortune for the remainder of this season." Honourable as it was, it was a bad time to lose their unbeaten record in the north of England. They had to get back to winning ways, or a season's work could be undone.

The travelling schedule for these two fixtures illustrated the durability required to be an Argyle player. They had set out from Home Park at 9am on Friday, 13 March. They stayed in hotels in Nottingham, Southport and Chester. During the journey they had meals at Bristol, Warwick, Knutsford, Gloucester and Taunton. They arrived back in Plymouth at 7pm on Tuesday, 18 March after spending a total of 30 hours on the road. On the following Saturday, in his weekly round up, *Pilgrim* paid tribute to coach driver Dick Williams. He wrote, "Spare a thought for the coach driver. He was off again on Wednesday morning with the reserve team, for matches at Northampton and Coventry!"

There were 10 games to play and they probably needed to win six to be certain of winning the league. More than ever they needed the support of the terraces. Too often, after a quiet spell in the game, the crowd had barracked the team. Messages were placed in the programme, asking for the crowd to get behind the team. Both *Spectator* and *Pilgrim* issued pleas for patience. Baker and Barnsley had been very badly treated, while Govan and Johnny Williams had attracted the occasional mistreatment too. Using his round-up column, *Pilgrim* published extracts of a letter received by the Argyle manager. Neither the journalist nor Rowley would reveal the identity of the writer. It was purported to be from "a man who knows what he is talking about (he has many connections within the game)."

Writing from West Park the mystery man said "I have watched football in all parts of the country and never come across a more unappreciative crowd." He felt that the word "rubbish" was the only word some supporters seemed to shout. He explained that what had really prompted him to write was the attitude of his workmates, after the recent 8-3 win over Mansfield. "After a hugely entertaining game I was amazed to hear my workmates running the team down." Mystery man, if you have survived these 50 years, keep off the various local message boards – things have not changed!

After the Tranmere match, the games in hand were gone, as had leadership of the league. Both Hull and Argyle had now played 36 games with Argyle trailing by a point. They were also looking over their shoulder at Brentford and Tranmere, the only other realistic promotion contenders. It was a neat symmetry – two teams from the south and two from the north, fighting it out to be promoted from this first ever combined Third Division.

There were recalls for Reg Jenkins and Harry Penk when Chesterfield were the visitors on 21 March 1959. Baker and Govan were injured and the experiment with Johnny Williams playing at inside forward was shelved. JL Williams stepped down. The attendance was a disappointing 17,334. Jenkins and Carter scored in a 2-0 win. The former notched his first goal, pouncing quickly when the young Chesterfield goalkeeper dropped the ball. That goalkeeper's name was Gordon Banks! It would be another seven years before Reg could appreciate the real significance of just who it was he beat to score his first League goal.

Argyle were destined to meet Brentford home and away at Easter, either side of a tricky away encounter at Newport. Would Meyer have a score to settle at Somerton Park? It was a worrying time for supporters. The team's skill and passion was still there, even in defeat. What was also needed was a continued mental toughness.

Half a century ago Easter was still a defining period for promotion and relegation issues. For the Greens, this spell of three games in four days could see a season's work undone, especially as two of the fixtures were against fellow promotion contenders Brentford.

George Baker takes the deep-lying centre forward role a bit too seriously in this home match against Notts County. Hopefully Johnny Williams was able to pull away as George fell. It was either that or a heavily bruised back. *Courtesy the Plymouth Evening Herald/ Colin Parsons collection*

MYSTERY PICTURE

Back Row (l to r): Anderson, Robertson, Barnsley, Wyatt, Dougall, JL Williams and Trainer George Taylor

Front Row (l to r): Baker, Gauld, Carter, Meyer and Penk

Courtesy Harry Penk, Margaret Callan and the defunct Daily Sketch

This photograph is puzzling. The eleven players pictured never took the field as a team. As the picture includes Barry Meyer it must have been taken between late August 1958 and February 1959, though Meyer rarely trained at Home Park after Christmas 1958.

There is only one recognised wing-half in the picture—John 'Cardiff' Williams. There are six forwards, the five at the front and Peter Anderson, standing at the extreme left of the back row. With Johnny Williams often away on National Service that could explain his absence. Also missing are Len Casey and Wally Bellett, which could date the photograph before December 1958. But for the first few months of their time at Argyle they still trained in London. Alternatively, as Neil Dougall was still one of the group, that would indicate it is prior to the Chelsea men arriving.

During the research and interview stage of this project this photograph emerged twice. Firstly, Harry Penk had a copy in amongst his extensive collection of cuttings. The other copy was sent to me by George Taylor's daughter Margaret. That copy provided the only partial clue. It was stamped *'Daily Sketch'* on the back.

CHAPTER FOUR

THE FINAL COUNTDOWN

On Maundy Thursday Argyle travelled to London by rail for an 11am kick off at Griffin Park the next day. The gates were closed on a near 30,000 crowd, with many more locked out. It was so crowded that some Argyle fans left at half-time, having found it impossible to see. Bellett, injured against Chesterfield, was replaced at left back by Wyatt. Alex Govan came in for Penk. The kick-off time rankled with some Argyle's supporters. However, with the team having to trek across country to meet Newport County the next day, the morning start suited the players very well. What didn't suit them was the 3-0 defeat. Brentford were unbeaten in 11, and they always looked like extending that sequence. It was another loss the Greens could ill afford, to a team still in with a shout of promotion. The return at Home Park was on Easter Monday. Argyle would have to play much better to get anything out of that.

They also travelled to Newport by train. Rowley rang the changes after the surrender at Brentford. Bellett returned for Wyatt, Wyllie's five match run came to an end and Johnny Williams was once more pushed forward to inside right, to take the place of Jenkins. Much to the confusion of the match announcer it was a John Williams who replaced Johnny Williams in the half back line. John Cardiff's mother and father came down from their Merthyr home to watch him star in a 1-0 win. This was yet another instance of a player doing well not too far from his roots. It was a small consolation for missing the Cardiff City FA Cup game. Carter was on the mark with a disputed penalty, his 19th of the season. In the event, Barry Meyer was injured and was not considered for selection by Newport. In view of his goals to game ratio when at Home Park, a fit Meyer could have proved a menace.

The next two home games ended in 1-1 draws. The Easter Monday encounter against Brentford attracted 27,073 supporters. The draw prevented Brentford from gaining ground on Argyle. By the time Halifax paid their first ever visit to Home Park, in early April, the attendance had fallen by 7,500. In both games the manager persisted with the side that had won at Newport County. Govan scored in the Brentford game with a superb header; for a small man he was still deadly in the air. Carter, on the score sheet for the 20th time, secured the point against Halifax Town. Overall though, scoring was becoming a real problem. It had been a decent display from the home team, except for putting that ball in the net. It meant that at the half way point of the final 10 game run in, the record stood at two wins, two draws and a defeat, with five goals for and five against.

Elsewhere Hull drew at Southend while Norwich walloped Brentford 4-1. A second point against Halifax would have made life more comfortable but promotion was still in Argyle's hands. Johnny Williams was hardly having the kind of football schedule best suited to a promotion run in. On the

Wednesday before Easter he represented the British Army against the Royal Air Force. He then joined Argyle for the three game Easter programme, playing for his Unit on the following Friday, before travelling back to Plymouth for the Halifax game.

On 11 April the team made their inaugural visit to the Racecourse Ground at Wrexham. A second successive 1-1 draw meant Wyatt once again came in for Bellett at left back, while Anderson returned to take Gauld's place. 13 proved unlucky for a disconsolate and angry Fulton – his run in the side came to an end with Robertson being recalled, after a 10 week spell out through injury. 8,817 were treated to a trademark Johnny Williams rocket, revelling in his return to inside forward.

A week later and Southampton came to the Westcountry. Wyatt continued at left back and Gauld returned for Anderson. It was a dour game, with Argyle prevailing by a single Carter goal. It was his fourth in seven games, proving he was back to his best. He was back to his best. Baker, who injured his knee at Wrexham the previous week, was in the wars again. He injured an ankle when he collided with the photographers behind the goal. The other winger, Govan, wrenched a thigh muscle, resuming for the second half heavily strapped. Baker only made it out after the interval with the aid of a pain-killing injection. Gauld wasn't entirely fit either. He left the field for a period in the second half, allegedly with a back problem. Carter worked tremendously hard to cover for his injured colleagues.

With Hull dropping another point it now meant that with three games to go, two away and the other at home, Argyle needed just three points to be certain of promotion. On the Sunday after the Saints game the players were off to Southport again. Neither Baker nor Govan was fit enough to travel. It was likely that a 13 strong party would set off for their northern retreat. It would contain Barnsley, Robertson, Wyatt, JL Williams, Fincham, Casey, Carter, JS Williams, Bellett, Penk, Jenkins, Anderson and Gauld, provided the latter was fit to travel. Tommy Barrett, the victim of a troublesome ankle injury, was celebrating the fact that he had earned a trial with Leicestershire County Cricket Club late April/early May. Because of football commitments, he was unable to take up the offer of a trial the previous year.

The team faced a tricky first ever visit to Halifax on the Monday, followed by a Saturday appointment at Peel Park, Accrington. If results went their way this final northern tour could see promotion clinched, on grounds that no other Plymouth Argyle side had ever visited. Prenton Park apart, the north of England had been a happy hunting ground from day one of the season. Penk and Anderson were recalled at the Shay, only the second time in 10 games that they had both played in the same side. He and Anderson were renowned for being able to switch wings and confuse the opposition. 50 years on both recall that it was not a tactic devised by the management; it was something they did when they felt it necessary to offer a different challenge to the full backs.

In front of 8,523 at the Shay, Anderson scored the crucial goal that secured perhaps the two most valuable points of the season. Just 16 days before Halifax had proved obdurate opponents at Home Park, and had not lost in their nine previous home fixtures. With the other results going favourably, just a point in the Saturday game with Accrington would be enough to secure promotion. The players recall it as a perfect week's relaxation. The weather was excellent. Harry Penk, not a million miles from his Wigan birthplace, took the role of tour guide. In hot and sunny weather he arranged for them to play golf at Birkdale, he took some to a Rugby League game at St Helens and a good time was had by all.

Poor Johnny Williams, the one who could have done with a week in the sun, was required by the Army back in Aldershot. He travelled north the day before the Accrington encounter. When it was time to journey to Accrington on the Saturday, the party were in fine fettle. Rowley named an unchanged side with Jenkins and Bellett the two to miss out again. After a run of decent weather, Accrington decided to soften up the hard and rutted pitch, hosing it all day on the Friday. And, of course, the weather then broke! The pitch was as heavy as any in the depths of winter, with the rain continuing right through the game.

It was a battling performance. Argyle had played up the decided gradient in the first half. Despite the pitch being like a black lake, both sides did their best to entertain. Penk, with his liking for the northern air, and against the run of play, scored after the home goalkeeper sliced a 15th minute clearance straight to him. They led until 12 minutes after half time, when Tighe pulled one back for the home side. It was fashioned after some good work by Jimmy and Harry Anders, the two wingers who had terrorised the Pilgrims' defence at Home Park in early March. Argyle battled to the end to ensure a season's work was not undone. It was the second gritty performance in a week from the Greens. Just as at Halifax five days earlier, Argyle had to defend well as Accrington probably had the better of exchanges. Robertson and Wyatt covered valiantly and Fincham was outstanding. Despite being on the receiving end for long periods, Carter and Anderson both missed chances they may have taken with a less greasy and heavy ball, while Johnny Williams operated a shoot on sight policy throughout.

This was the third time in Argyle's history that they had climbed from a third tier place to the Second Division. Remarkably, the 1-1 draw at Accrington meant that each of those successes had been achieved away from Home Park. In 1930 it was at Newport, in 1952 it was at Brighton and now it was in Lancashire.

Although Brentford beat Southend 6-1 it was too late for them. They were now out of it. Hull led on goal average from Argyle, both locked on 61 points from 45 games. Each had to play their remaining game on the following Wednesday. Argyle would entertain Bradford City; Hull had a tricky cross country trip to Wrexham... and they would be kicking off earlier.

Argyle returned to Plymouth via an overnight stop in Wolverhampton. On arrival in Plymouth they had completed 314 miles since leaving Accrington. This brought their League and Cup mileage for the season to nearly 11,000. Much of it was in their trusty motor coach, driven by Dick

Williams. Geoff Barnsley often joked that the players took it turns to go forward and talk to him – just to keep him awake.

The final 20 miles would prove to be the most enjoyable and colourful of them all. The Supporters' Club and Officials had chartered a bus to go and meet the team coach. They rendezvoused at a pre-arranged location on the other side of Ivybridge to decorate the team bus. It was expected that the party would arrive in the City Centre at around 4.45pm. The bus would make a circuit of Royal Parade before going on to Home Park to break open the champagne.

But there remained one goal. At the start of the season the then Chairman Ron Blindell had set the target of winning the Championship. Did anyone spare him a thought on this celebratory day, when the first part of the job was done? *Spectator*, to this researcher a very discerning and fair minded journalist, did not mention him in a long review of the 49 League and Cup matches played thus far. He was quick to introduce some realism to the joyful mood, pointing out inherent weaknesses in the side which had got more noticeable as the season progressed. He noted that he now felt justified in writing that he never wanted Argyle to have a successful FA Cup run.

He pointed out that in the 19 League games up to the second Saturday in November, Argyle took 31 points, suffering just one defeat. That was the Saturday before the FA Cup 1st Round was played. Thereafter, up and including the Accrington away fixture, Argyle played another 26 games but took the same 30 points.

50 years on, his account of matters is extremely interesting. But did he miss another important event? It was the Saturday before the first round FA Cup tie that Ron Blindell was removed from the Chair. *Spectator* didn't even think it worthy of mention. But it is an awful coincidence that the side was never the same after Blindell was ousted. Did it have an effect on the manager and the players? Was Blindell's vision, drive and enthusiasm an ingredient of the early season success? The surviving players look back and say no, they do not think it was a factor. I am not so sure.

Wednesday 29 April 1959 was a fine evening. 26,717 turned up to pay homage to their heroes. Although they formed the time-honoured guard of honour at the tunnel entrance, clapping the all conquering Greens on to the field, that was the last of niceties from Bradford City. They did not let their Yorkshire colleagues down, fighting all the way in a 1-1 draw.

Hull's final fixture at Wrexham kicked off earlier than Argyle's, possibly because of the quality (or lack) of the floodlights at the Racecourse Ground. Whatever the reason, Argyle knew at half-time that the point they were half way to earning was going to be enough. To a tumultuous roar, as Fulham based referee Mr A Bond blew the final whistle, Argyle became the first champions of the new Third Division of the Football League. It was, as *Spectator* observed, the strongest League any side had ever had to win to get Second Division football. It was good that they won it on home soil.

It was a wonderful night, where the jittery performances of the past few months no longer mattered. The 7pm kick offs of that era allowed sup-

cial explanation given by the Football League when they chose that particular time for evening games under lights.

Nothing had been heard from Blindell for a while. In mid April he had returned from a business trip cum holiday to the USA and the Caribbean. On leaving the Queen Mary at Southampton he declined to comment on Argyle matters. Perhaps he had purposely stayed out of the limelight, so as not to become a distraction? The Lord Mayor, Councillor GJ Wingett had accepted an invitation to the promotion buffet, to be held at the Continental Hotel the next day. Blindell was not invited, though he and his wife Kay were guests at the Supporters' Club promotion celebration. Their Committee felt it only right and proper that he should be there, a view not shared by either the new Board or the omnipresent Plymouth Argyle Shareholders' Association.

It had been a successful season on the pitch. The same could not be said for the Boardroom. The summer would see an unseemly battle for power, a dispute that would result in the Football Association being called in to arbitrate. Apart from the negative publicity it attracted, it rather took the focus off the preparations for an exciting new campaign to be fought in the Second Division.

BILL HARPER. Grand servant to Plymouth Argyle as player, trainer and head groundsman. Capped 11 times for Scotland. Came to Plymouth Argyle from Arsenal in 1932.

MALCOLM FERGUSON. Another "back-stage" member of the staff, to be seen resplendent in uniform, officiating at the officials and players entrance of the grand stand.

From the introduction of the more modern match day programme, it featured photographs of players and officials. Here from the 1958-59 season are two Home Park stalwarts. Bill Harper was a lovely man, always affable and cheerful.

Mr Ferguson had his work cut out keeping the kids with their autograph books away from the players' and officials' entrance at the back of the stand.

Photographs courtesy Plymouth Argyle and Sam Bailey

Mr. R. G. W. Pengelly
Chartered Accountant

The Argyle 'Cabinet' of Five

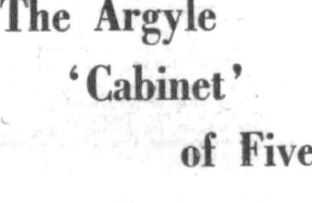

Mr. R. J. R. Blindell, the club's new chairman, head of a family boot and shoe concern. He with Messrs. Pengelly and Deans are the nominees of the £30,000 donor. Messrs. Crookes and James are the nominees of the old Board.

Mr. T. H. Deans, Joinery
Works director

Mr. C. W. Crookes, Holiday
Camp proprietor

Mr. David A. James, Dental
Surgeon.

"I got them from the Board-room at Home Park! The new B o a r d won't have
much time to sit down.

Picture and cartoon courtesy of the Sunday Independent

42

CHAPTER FIVE

THE BOARDROOM POWER STRUGGLE

Despite becoming Third Division Champions in 1958-59 season, the second half of the season was played out against a backdrop of conflict and strife in the Boardroom. There were angry scenes at successive Annual General Meetings and eventually the FA had to be called in to arbitrate. Many blamed the Chairman Ron Blindell, who was overthrown by his colleagues in early November 1958. *Thanks For The Memory* takes a detailed look at the saga which brought the club sustained publicity, mostly for the wrong reasons. To those not directly involved in the dispute, it seemed to hard to explain why such a gifted and successful man appeared to alienate so many people. What follows is the account of a period in Plymouth Argyle's history that arguably attracted more column inches in the national Press than at any other time.

Ron Blindell had been making overtures to the Plymouth Argyle Board from as early as 1953. He finally succeeded in gaining a place at the company AGM held on 16 August 1956. He had offered the club an interest free £3,000 loan, promising to leave it in the club even if he moved on. Some members of the Argyle Shareholders Association showed an enmity that evening which never fully went away. After Blindell was voted on to the Board by a 56-13 show of hands, a number of them demanded a poll vote, headed by director and major shareholder AE 'Archie' Cload. It is strange how that request was seen by the shareholders as their democratic right. In not much more than two years hence, they would judge a similar move by Blindell as abhorrent.

As well as the Shareholders setting a pattern of behaviour, Blindell showed a trait which was typical of him. His benevolence was a side to his character that was often overlooked, especially by his enemies and detractors in the Plymouth Argyle Shareholders' Association. Although at times he could be autocratic and domineering, there was a magnanimous side to him too. *Pilgrim* reported the next day that although Blindell "did not know what Cload had against him, he would be prepared to shake hands afterwards for the good of Plymouth Argyle." That kind of copy did not suit some of the Shareholders Committee, a group who did not always seem to act in the best interests of the club and were not averse to covert communication with local newspapers.

It was at the 1956 AGM that Chairman Sir Clifford Tozer became master of the understatement. He announced, "Unless we get substantial financial assistance in the very near future, the future of the club, to say the least of it, will be very precarious." Towards the end of January 1957 the local Press was full of speculation about a £30,000 buy out, believing it to be sponsored by Blindell. Rumours were circulating that if the reconstruction package was accepted Blindell would become Chairman, and the Board would reduce to four or five members. Blindell denied that it was mainly his money behind the refinancing arrangement, something he continued to do for some time afterwards. The club explained that the Board

WESTERN INDEPENDENT

Price 3d.   PLYMOUTH, FEBRUARY 24, 1957   20 PAGES

W BOARD TAKES OVER NEXT

NGED THE EME

Resign

"Sorry old boy, there's a camera over there!" Ron Blindell, cheque in one hand and cigar in the other. The cheque was handed to Chairman Sir Clifford Tozer just before a floodlit friendly with Grimsby Town, Blindell's home

king over to start the history of the it they start with ned !

ruction scheme was he general public But a leakage

in that is now unt in half of

over on t a small ony by Mr. ifford Tozer. ft drawn on branch of d made pay- of Sir

joint account, relieve Argyle e interest payable on overdraft. At lea

ing together with approval of the scheme

* * *

The Governors

Clearly the stage i well set for the governi to take over.

Here we have Mr. Bl a man in a substantial business with four fac and well over 100 shops footwear trade behind Mr. Pengelly, a ch accountant and part well - known lo of accountants; Harry Deans, in a joine and a leading man of the church.

Until last su prospective Blindell, unli leagues, was known and un mouth. He is mystery to th

He is now hold of leadi is seeking honours—in t like his fathe from an erra Alderma Grim Nati S fat w m

The camera catches Mr. R. J. R. Blindell, Argyle's prospective chairman, in an unusual pose. In his right hand is that £30,000 cheque just before he handed it to Sir Clifford Tozer, in his left a cigar; he is a cigar smoker. The cheque gave no clue to the Argyle "benefactor".

were merely looking at an offer of financial assistance 'from a Westcountry businessman', aid that would put the company back on its feet.

The key meeting took place at the Grand Hotel in early February. The sitting Board, minus Alderman Leatherby who was away on business, voted unanimously to accept the financial reconstruction package. Directors Cload and Gillin, who had voted against it at an earlier Board meeting, were now content to support it. They had tried to mount a separate financial rescue but could not raise sufficient funds. The package was then put before the shareholders at an Extraordinary General Meeting at the Continental Hotel on 16 April 1957 where Sir Clifford outlined the financial position. He explained that the club had commitments of £56,719, but on 31 March 1957 they had just £759 cash in the bank. Payments amount-

early June. This included debenture repayments of £8,450, a need to reduce the bank loan by £5,100 and sundry trade creditors amounting to around £8,000. The bank loan stood at £33,100, there was an overdraft of £1,995, an FA loan of £3,333, a £3,500 loan from the directors and the Secretary, the sundry creditors, debentures amounting to £14,300 and another debenture loan of £3,000. It was a sorry picture.

At the end of his presentation Sir Clifford came up with another priceless 'Tozerism'. Despite the irony, it was wonderful post-war English. He solemnly said, "The Bank is not desirous of giving further accommodation." Who could blame them? Even the shareholders had no alternative. Such was the financial position, there was an immediate need for a large sum of money to be injected.

The new Board would comprise RJR Blindell (Chairman), TH Deans and RGW Pengelly, billed as the nominees of the 'mystery backer', plus CW Crookes and DA James. Crookes, the owner of the Challaborough Holiday Camp and James, a local dentist, were the nominees of the old Board and were deemed acceptable to the sponsors of the reconstruction package. Sir Clifford Tozer accepted an invitation from the new Board to become the club's President. The last act of the old Board was to ask that all the directors with pre-war service should become eligible as Vice-Presidents which was accepted. Blindell personally stepped in to add that although Mr Cload had only been a director since 1946, he had worked so hard for the club in pre-war years that he too should become a Vice-President.

It was a thoroughly deserved accolade for a man who must be one of Argyle's best ever followers. As far back as 1923 he helped start the official Supporters' Club, he was a past Chairman and Secretary of that organisation and a former director. He was also a majority shareholder. Purchasing Argyle's Ordinary Shares was no more than an act of charity, if you like, a free loan. It was another example of Blindell's ability to forgive and forget. Not only had Cload tried to interfere with Blindell becoming a director, he had initially tried to counter the reconstruction too.

Some may question the financial prudence and business acumen of the old Board. But there was an iniquitous Entertainment Tax, which had cost the club £99,740 since the war. Admission prices were set by the Football League, so there was no question of increasing revenue to cover the tax. Set against debts of £62,000, it can be seen that without that levy they would probably have traded at a small profit each season. It was a stroke of good fortune for the new Board that Entertainment Tax was about to be repealed. It was not only football that had suffered – cinemas and theatres were struggling to pay it too.

Predictably, as the new Board took over there were a still a few questions asked by the Shareholders Association. Mr J Squire, their Chairman asked the new Board if the Articles of Association could be re-amended from 11 directors to six, instead of five, thereby allowing a space for Mr Gillin. Blindell replied that it was the old Board that had decided upon 5 and not the sponsors.

The new Chairman appealed for hard work and team spirit right through the club. With immediate effect, one thing was clear. Plymouth

Argyle was now run by Ron Blindell. Most statements in the Press came from him. The day after taking over he told the *Western Evening Herald* that, with immediate effect, Jack Rowley would no longer be player-manager. Blindell added that he had told Rowley 'in no uncertain terms' that he was dissatisfied with results and that the Board expected substantial improvements by next Christmas. The manager was to be relieved of any administration aspects of his job, and was told to concentrate entirely on team selection, training and coaching. Blindell assured readers that Rowley would be given an entirely free hand as far as the playing side was concerned. He added that training would be tighter and tougher than ever before.

What was not made public, until sometime later, was that when Blindell had warned the manager that things must improve, he also gave him a new package which included a £2,000 bonus for taking the team to the First Division, with staged bonuses for winning promotion from the Third and Second Divisions. That was a worthwhile incentive in 1957. Blindell also outlined his intention to talk to the Plymouth Corporation about reconstruction schemes for Home Park. The new Chairman also announced that "he had met all the players and staff at Home Park, and that altogether he had an agenda of 40 items for the Board to discuss".

In early May Blindell gave a resume of the new Board's first full fortnight. He told *Pilgrim* that "no Argyle Board had achieved so much progress in such a short time". Ron Blindell rarely understated any of his

The smiles didn't last. This photo was taken shortly before the 1958-59 season. Back row (l to r) Secretary Bert Cole, Directors David James and Cliff Crookes and Manager Jack Rowley. The front row (l to r) is Director Harry Deans, Chairman Ron Blindell and Hon Treasurer Bill Pengelly
Picture courtesy of Plymouth Argyle FC

achievements, though in fairness there were plenty of them. He explained to *Pilgrim* how Board members had now been given specific tasks. Pengelly was to be responsible for all administration matters, most specifically finance. Harry Deans was given the ground, buildings, equipment and club houses to look after, while Cliff Crookes was to be in charge of all travelling arrangements. Dentist David James was tasked with advertising, and subject to their agreement, would act as the liaison between the Board and the Supporters' Club.

The Chairman had a simple three point plan for the club, namely to attain a higher standard of football, to make improvements to the ground and amenities and to make the club free of debt. He had established a good rapport with the Supporters' Club, and was trying to build relationships with the Plymouth Corporation and with the Shareholders Association and their membership. He certainly struck the right note with the man on the terrace. The ordinary supporter felt that things could only get better under Blindell's leadership.

At first things went well. The initial target of avoiding re-election was achieved with ease, with the 1956-57 season finishing on a positive note. That was followed by a very successful first complete season for the new Board. Although the team did not finish in the single promotion slot, they showed enterprise and verve in finishing third, just one win short of promotion. The crowds were well up on the previous season, averaging around 18,000. There was the added advantage of a lucrative home FA Cup tie against First Division Newcastle United. Financially, things were on the up.

After supporting his manager in the transfer market in the summer of 1957, with the acknowledged help of donations from the Supporters' Club, he had pronounced himself pleased with the successful 1957-58 season, and the third place finish achieved. He backed Rowley again in 1958 and over the two summers around £20,000 had been spent on improving the playing staff. In return Blindell wanted them to win the new Third Division. Argyle started superbly in 1958-59, leading the table from the start. Blindell had spent the summer talking up the spirit and togetherness throughout the club.

There was an early season spat with the Shareholders' Association, with Blindell resigning from their organisation in mid August, after criticism levelled at the Board during the organisation's AGM. What infuriated Blindell was that the Association had met with the Board in July and expressed no adverse comment. Significantly, Pengelly and Deans, the other Board members who were also members of the Shareholders Association, separately announced their resignations. But they did not carry them through, preferring to deal with the matter by seeking assurances from the Shareholders' Chairman Jim Squire. That slight move away from Blindell's line did not seem important then, but it may just have been the first sign of a breakdown in relations on the Board.

By the end of September the two sides met and after a cordial meeting the Shareholders agreed that they would put points of conflict to the Board before making them public. *Spectator* shrewdly observed, "There is no question of both sides being out for the welfare of Argyle, but equally there is a strong measure of independence on both sides which probably more than anything was responsible for the initial clash." Blindell withdrew his resignation from the Association.

With the team in the ascendancy, in his column of 2 November *Spectator* looked forward to a routine company AGM. The sub-heading was 'No Sparks?' Normally there was little that went on at Home Park which remained undiscovered by *Pilgrim* or *Spectator*. Neither saw that stormy shareholders meeting on their horizon. Behind the scenes things were clearly not right, culminating in a dramatic week in early November 1958, after which Blindell would no longer be Chairman. In the day or two after Spectator's column was published it became clear that Blindell wanted a change to the Board, in that he intended to nominate Mr Richard Hughes as a director at the next Company Meeting, to be held on 6 November at the newly opened YMCA. But a Board Meeting prior to the AGM refused to second the nomination of Hughes. Some years earlier Blindell had picked out RD Hughes from his chain of shoe shops as the outstanding manager in the group. Blindell admired his drive and determination and he had risen to Assistant Managing Director of Blindell's businesses. Maybe he thought that it would give him someone 'on the inside,' someone who would ensure that things were being done as the Chairman instructed? Blindell clearly had a problem with the administrative side of the club, and it was widely known that he had issues with long serving Secretary Bert Cole, prior to pensioning him off.

Cole was actually serving his notice and the AGM would be his last official duty. Whatever Blindell's reasoning, it gave his enemies the perfect opportunity to hit back. Those who had nursed a grudge since the 1956 AGM were ready to exact revenge. Some thought his shareholding had allowed him to become a 'dictator'. That was definitely the shareholders' view, and that of the other directors. But as far as supporters were concerned, Blindell was delivering on all his promises. Finance was no longer a major discussion point, there were gradual improvements taking place around the ground and the team and attendances were unrecognisably better than when Blindell took the Chair. Unusually, it was the Board that wanted the Chairman out and not the fans.

It would take a separate book to report all of the proceedings of that November 1958 Annual Meeting. The turbulence started after Hughes had insisted on calling for a poll vote after Cliff Crookes, one of the retiring directors, had been re-elected on a show of hands. There were two votes against Crookes – that of Hughes and a Mr Sampson, Blindell's chauffeur! Director David James said, "We other four directors will withdraw and you will be left without a Board. We will refer the affairs of the club to the FA." At this juncture James called back fellow director Harry Deans, who was about to walk out. *Spectator* reported how, "Blindell had dented his gavel crashing it on the table to attempt to restore order out of disorder, but to no avail." For two hours the discussions raged. One senses that *Spectator* was a fair-minded and intelligent man. Without a trace of humour, he noted in his report "that there had been much intemperate behaviour in a place of temperance". He wrote eloquently, but solemnly, "So much had been said at the Annual Meeting of the Company – many remarks were left unrecorded by a discriminating and benevolent Press – to make one feel almost ashamed of one's fellow man. The meeting must go down as one of the saddest and most sullied chapters in Argyle's history – for which Mr Blindell could not be regarded as blameless."

Eventually it took a female voice to bring calm and reason, and to instil some order. Alderman Mrs LA Brock requested Blindell to withdraw his nominee, "in the interests of Argyle." Blindell and Hughes quickly adjourned to a corridor. Clearly Hughes was not one for turning the other cheek. After returning to the room he faced the baying throng and said, "Regarding criticism of a domestic affair at Home Park, I do not withdraw any statement I made this evening. It is only after very great pressure from Mr Blindell outside that I have decided to withdraw my demand for a poll. I have done this purely in the interests of Plymouth Argyle. I hope this will be a lesson to the directors and emphasise the need for loyalty and support to the Chairman."

There was clearly a cosy relationship between the Shareholders Association and those directors who had been around the club for some years. Blindell's decision to retire Secretary Cole was another major catalyst in the hatred that was engulfing him. It seemed that Blindell saw him as 'old Argyle.' Some important points got lost in the fury of the evening. Shareholders' Association Chairman Squire Secretary Charles Hill seemed to dominate their membership, without always being in accord with their members' wishes. After several angry exchanges with Blindell, Hill shouted, "There are plenty of eminent people in Plymouth ready to join the Board today". "And where were they 18 months ago?" retorted Blindell.

It is worth noting that in a letter to Mr Blindell, dated 17 April 1957, Charles Hill wrote, "*In your endeavours you can count on the goodwill of the Association's Officers and Members, and we trust in due course that the club and its numerous supporters will reap the benefit of your magnanimity which came at such a serious and critical time.*" Maybe that was provided that Blindell always acted in accordance with the way the Shareholders' Association wanted him too. After 120 minutes of complete bedlam the meeting closed quickly and quietly. Crookes and James, the other retiring director, were voted back by a show of hands. But the twists and turns were not finished yet. The battle was over but the war would go on for some time.

Within 48 hours of the AGM Harry Deans was in the Chair. Blindell was overthrown and, for good measure, publicly spurned by the other directors at the Saturday game at home to Newport County. He sat apart from them with his guests Michael Foot and RD Hughes. Just 17 months before Pengelly, Deans and Blindell were a united threesome, combining to save the club from extinction. Now the other two had helped to engineer Blindell out of the Chair. On the day after the AGM, Blindell tried to reconcile himself and the Board. Using Pengelly as an intermediary, he suggested that they meet for cocktails at 1200 on Saturday, before the Home

Park Board Meeting scheduled for 2pm. He further suggested that the Press should be invited "to witness us letting bygones be bygones". At 4.45 that day Pengelly phoned Mr Blindell to say that the 1200 Saturday date was off, adding that the other Board members were meeting at 9pm that night. Pengelly turned down Blindell's request to attend that 'private' meeting. Interestingly, Secretary Cole was about to return to the fold, now enjoying the title of Honorary Secretary.

Former player Bill Strauss, still the head administrator, confirmed with Mr Blindell that the 2pm Board Meeting on Saturday would go ahead. It was a strange affair, the meeting the previous evening had elected Deans to the Chair, with Blindell remaining as a director. The 'other four' had decided to take legal advice, with their main aim to challenge the altered Articles of Association, agreed at the 1957 Extraordinary General Meeting, which brought Blindell to power. Such was the speed of events during that tempestuous November week, it was Blindell who had originally called the pre-match Board Meeting, at the request of manager Jack Rowley. The manager wanted to discuss a list of potential recruits to give the promotion campaign a further boost. However, the new Chairman and his other three colleagues refused to discuss any matters concerning the playing staff.

It was easy to forget that all these politics were being played out against a burgeoning promotion campaign, built mainly on Blindell's money. According to *Spectator's* column the following Sunday, Blindell's view remained, "That if one has a fight at an AGM, win, lose or draw, that is the end of the matter". Unfortunately, it was not, and the next few months were littered with accusation and counter-accusation. By the following Monday most people thought that the smoke had cleared from the battlefield. However, Bert Cole had made a 'secret trip' to Blackpool that weekend. He had journeyed north to meet Football League Secretary Alan Hardaker. Unfortunately the London sportswriters had found out about the 'covert' journey, where Cole met Hardaker both at his Blackpool home and then at the League's Starkie Street offices in Preston.

Mr Hardaker was an important man in the late 50s. He was the Secretary of the Football League and was frequently quoted in the national Press. On this occasion he said "Mr Cole not unnaturally told me about what had gone in Plymouth since the AGM last Thursday, but it only cropped up in conversation. But the internal affairs of Plymouth Argyle are a matter which does not directly concern us at the moment. Mr Cole and I did not in any way discuss ways and means in which the Football League could interfere in what is purely a domestic affair of the club's. Any suggestion, whether it comes from the national Press or not, that Mr Cole has been to see me about buying Mr Blindell out of the club is entirely wrong." A *Western Evening Herald* reporter (presumably *Pilgrim* was by now lying in a darkened room somewhere, recovering from his amazing week) asked Hardaker that if it was not the current Boardroom crisis, just what did they discuss?

Never a man to use one word when three would do, Hardaker responded "It would be a breach of confidence to disclose the actual nature of Mr

Cole's business, but I can say he wanted to discuss a matter relevant to the Argyle club and the Football League. Mr Blindell was not discussed in this matter, nor is there any suggestion that Plymouth Argyle are in any trouble. Mr Cole made the trip because he felt he would rather see me personally than write a letter or make a telephone call." With due deference to William Shakespeare's Hamlet – methinks the League Secretary did protest too much. Bert Cole was considered a pillar of the football community, probably quite rightly so. But it would be interesting to know precisely who sent him to Blackpool and what his mission was. It is unlikely that he spoke positively about Ron Blindell. The new Argyle Chairman Harry Deans issued an unconvincing statement that it was "something to do with pensions".

A fact that was largely unreported was that when Blindell dispensed with Cole's services, the pension he was awarded was not too far short of his full salary. Positive interpretations of the Chairman's actions would not have suited the Shareholders' Association stance on Blindell.

The former Chairman resigned his directorship on the following Monday. His letter, sent via RGW Pengelly, is overleaf. At the time of the Boardroom coup, the team had suffered just one League defeat in 19 matches. The lowest home attendance had been the 22,518, in the opening home fixture with Tranmere. His tenure had been synonymous with success. The 1957-58 season had delivered a five figure profit, the first for many years. By 26 November every effort was being made to find buyers for Ron Blindell's shares, all of which he would make available at par. The Board were also seeking to appoint one of the old Board to replace Blindell, something dictated in the 1957 revised Articles of Agreement. New Chairman Harry Deans was in upbeat mood. He prefaced his 'state of the nation' statement with, "Democracy is an excellent system – provided there is no principal democrat." He went on to say that the present Board were pledged to normal constitutional control by a show of hands, adding that everyone must now be able to see that "the ownership of a huge number of shares by one person can create a privileged position".

At the beginning of January 1959, Ron Blindell, wife Kay and boys James and Ronnie embarked on the Queen Mary for a three month sunshine cruise to America and Jamaica. It would not all be leisure time, as before he went Blindell spoke of his wish to see his many business acquaintances in New York, and of his plans to invest in a hotel complex in Jamaica.

He arrived back in England on Monday 13 April 1959, looking tanned, fit and in good heart. *Twelfth Man*, Ray Head's deputy from the *Herald*, travelled to Southampton to speak to Mr Blindell. When asked if he was interested in returning to football, especially as Torquay had recently parted company with two directors, he simply laughed. With a distinct twinkle in his eye, he told *Twelfth Man* that he had no comment to make about football, claiming he would be a fool to say anything now with just two weeks of the season remaining. The *Western Evening Herald* man left Southampton with the distinct impression that he was far from finished with football in the Westcountry. As he climbed into his Rolls Royce, Blin-

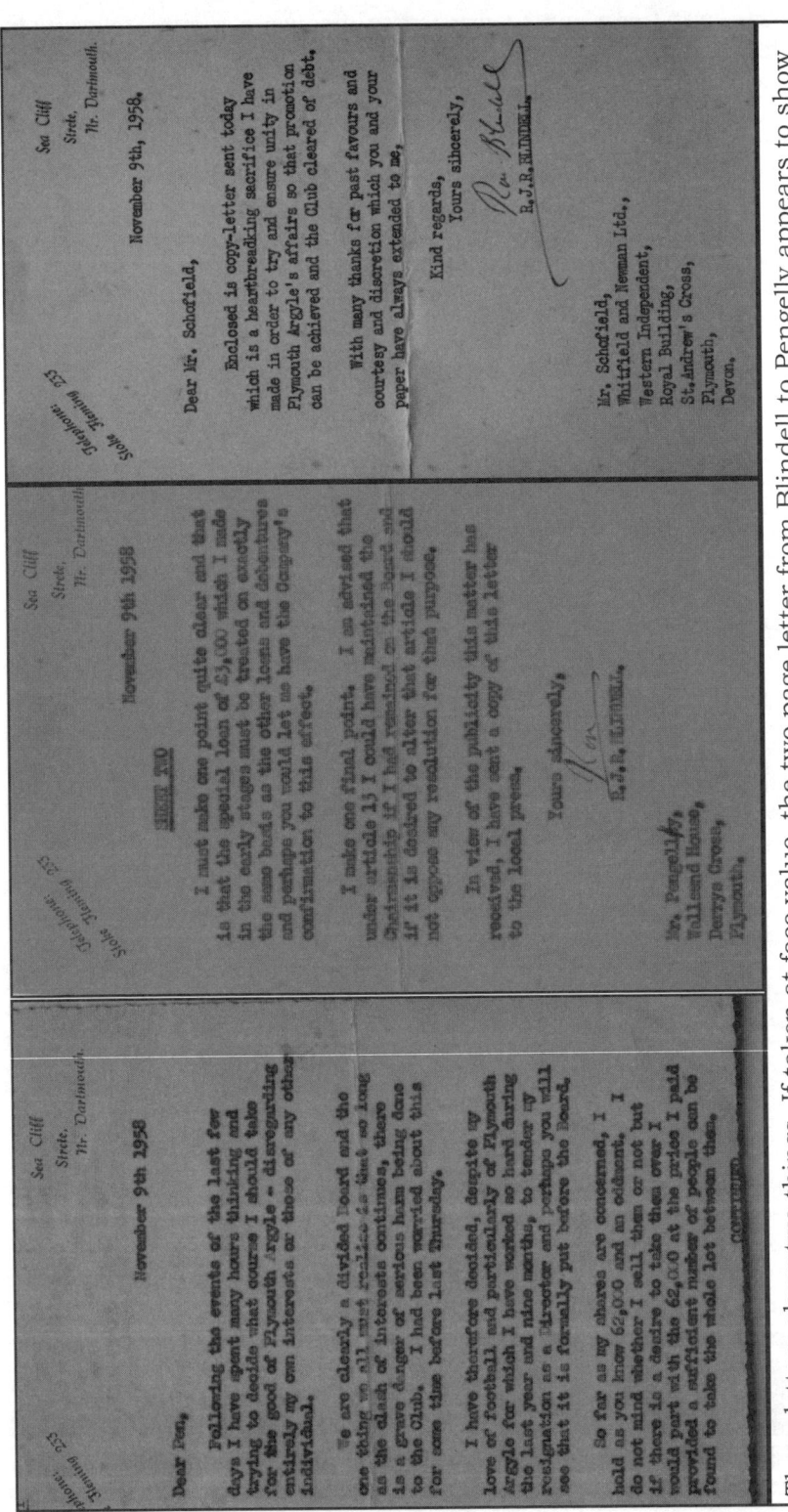

Sea Cliff
Strete.
Nr. Dartmouth.
Phone Stoke Fleming 233
November 9th 1958

Dear Ron,

Following the events of the last few days I have spent many hours thinking and trying to decide what course I should take for the good of Plymouth Argyle – disregarding entirely my own interests or those of any other individual.

We are clearly a divided Board and the one thing we all must realise is that so long as the clash of interests continues, there is a grave danger of serious harm being done to the Club. I had been worried about this for some time before last Thursday.

I have therefore decided, despite my love of football and particularly of Plymouth Argyle for which I have worked so hard during the last year and nine months, to tender my resignation as a Director and perhaps you will see that it is formally put before the Board.

So far as my shares are concerned, I hold as you know 62,0-0 and in element, I do not mind whether I sell them or not but if there is a desire to take them over I would part with the 62,0-0 at the price I paid provided a sufficient number of people can be found to take the whole lot between them.

CONTINUED

Sea Cliff
Strete.
Nr. Dartmouth
Phone Stoke Fleming 233
November 9th 1958

SHEET TWO

I must make one point quite clear and that is that the special loan of £3,000 which I made in the early stages must be treated on exactly the same basis as the other loans and debentures and perhaps you would let me have the Company's confirmation to this effect.

I make one final point. I am advised that under article 13 I could have maintained the Chairmanship if I had reminded on the Board and if it is desired to alter that article I should not oppose any resolution for that purpose.

In view of the publicity this matter has received, I have sent a copy of this letter to the local press.

Yours sincerely,
E.J.R. BLINDELL.

Mr. Pengelly,
Willond House,
Derrys Cross,
Plymouth.

Sea Cliff
Strete.
Nr. Dartmouth.
Telephone Stoke Fleming 233
November 9th, 1958.

Dear Mr. Schofield,

Enclosed is copy-letter sent today which is a heartbreaking sacrifice I have made in order to try and ensure unity in Plymouth Argyle's affairs so that promotion can be achieved and the Club cleared of debt.

With many thanks for past favours and courtesy and discretion which you and your paper have always extended to me,

Kind regards,
Yours sincerely,
E.J.R. BLINDELL.

Mr. Schofield,
Whitfield and Newman Ltd.,
Western Independent,
Royal Building,
St. Andrew's Cross,
Plymouth,
Devon,

These letters show two things. If taken at face value, the two page letter from Blindell to Pengelly appears to show that he had a genuine affection for the club. But the third letter to the *Spectator* of the day, Arthur Schofield, shows how the *Western Independent* (now the *Sunday Independent*) was often caught in the crossfire. Both sides of the divide regularly tried to the use the newspaper to air their views, often in a covert manner.
All three letters are from the Colin Parsons collection

dell called over "You can take it from me that I hope Plymouth Argyle gain promotion."

None of his 62,000 shares had been sold during his absence. He still effectively 'owned' Argyle and could, at any time, out vote anyone else currently involved. Without being able to speak to any of the personalities involved, it is difficult to form an accurate view. The indications from some of the correspondence are that Blindell deliberately went to ground, so that he would not prove a distraction. But that would not last much beyond the end of the season. The Third Division title was secured on 29 April 1959. By 3 May Ron Blindell was beating the drum that would signal his return to the Chair at Home Park. Despite correspondence between the Board and Blindell there was no progress. There was a definitive statement from the new Board that they could see no way that they could ever work in harmony with Blindell. It was his final attempt at trying to heal the rift.

As he turned up the heat, Blindell's first target for scorn was Mr Charles S Hill, the Secretary of the Plymouth Argyle Shareholders' Association. He accused Hill of behaving undemocratically, referring to a statement issued after a meeting of the Officers and Committee of the Association. Blindell was kind in calling it a statement – there have been shorter Queen's Speeches! Hill's pronouncement called for "the Plymouth Argyle Football Company Limited to resist, by all constitutional means, the return of Mr Blindell to the Board." For his part, the former Chairman felt that Hill should have called for a meeting of all shareholders, and not just Committee members. Hill also came under fire from Ron Lucas, Honorary Secretary of the Supporters Club. In his statement Hill had implied that the Supporters' Club was concerned with getting Mr Blindell back on the Board. 50 years on, when one reads the cuttings, Mr Lucas's anger was well placed. It is patently clear for anyone to see how impartial the Supporters' Club were. They had but one interest – for Plymouth Argyle to be successful.

Lucas, a man of the utmost integrity, comprehensively explained that he and Fred Pring had acted only as intermediaries to bring the warring parties together – the current Board and the former Chairman. Once a time and venue was fixed they withdrew from the scene. Lucas added that "he and his Chairman had cleared all of their actions with the Committee, who backed us 100%." Meanwhile dockyard worker Stan Cullis of Weston Mill had started a 'Bring Back Blindell' petition, and had quickly got 1,000 names. Cullis and Blindell were swapping correspondence, with the former Chairman expressing his deep gratitude.

The following day the dispute dominated the front page of the *Western Evening Herald*. The lead article contained extracts from a letter to Blindell from the Boards' solicitors, Messrs Bond, Pearce, Elliott and Knape. The crux of it was that the current Board would abide by a majority decision at a Shareholders' meeting, but not through a poll vote. If that course of action was not acceptable the solicitors were offering two other alternatives. Firstly, they asked Blindell to honour his decision of 8 November 1958 to sell his shares. Secondly, that "in accordance with FA Rules, the

Board would request the FA to appoint an investigating committee, as a matter of urgency, to see if it is in the best interest of the club for you to return to the Board." The letter added that it would have to be a pre-condition that both the current Board and the former Chairman would accept the decision of the investigating committee.

Meanwhile Ron Blindell was in Kingsbridge, addressing a meeting of the workforce at his building firm, JW Scoble and Son Limited. He was angry and upset and threatened 'those four will go if it is last thing I do'. He was also cursing the loss of business ally Richard Hughes, who had decided to leave the Westcountry. He paid an emotional tribute to Hughes, reminding everyone that Richard had risen from the shop floor to be his right hand man. "It is a loss to me personally, and a serious one for the business. It has been brought about by a chain of damnable events and I will never forget last November." He reiterated that he had wanted to bring Mr Hughes on to the Board to put the club's administration right. "But some people had to delve and uncover facts regarding Mr Hughes's past life. We have all made mistakes at some time or another in our lives. If we have paid for them I say that they should be left alone."

The gloves were now well and truly off! This was the bitterest outburst yet by Blindell and it was clear he meant business. In terms of a come-back it was now time to substitute 'when' for 'if'. Towards the end of May Blindell played a major trump card. He announced that the new Board he was putting together would include Mr Fred Pring, 53, now in his fourth year as Chairman of the official Supporters' Club and a member since 1933. This man was 'Argyle through and through.' It was a huge coup for Blindell. His committee were unanimous in endorsing Pring's nomination. One can only imagine how Charles Hill took the news. Blindell had already 'recruited' Saltash solicitor Peter W Skinnard, aged 30 and a self-confessed Argyle fanatic, plus Jimmy Hall, a 35 year old director of Sugdens newsagents who had shops in Cornwall Street, Frankfort Gate and Notte Street. It was significant that both Skinnard and Hall were in their thirties – Blindell had always preferred younger people when looking to propel his businesses forward.

Blindell explained that a fifth nominee would be added later, but for the moment he could only nominate himself and three others. In *Spectator's* column in the *Western Independent* of 31 May Blindell challenged the Board to, "Go now and stop the damage". He clearly held all the aces and challenged Harry Deans "to tell the public what the current financial position was, compared to when I was removed from the Chair". The paper also reported that in the city and in various other districts, "Sign for Blindell" campaigners were collecting thousands of signatures of support. The beleaguered Deans (although that term did not seem to accord with his view of things) spoke about another reconstruction, with the creation of another share issue to increase the capital by another £15,000.

Deans kept saying that the matter was with the company lawyers and he could not make further statements. As Blindell pointed out, these were just delaying tactics. With his shareholding, Blindell would have to en-dorse the resolution on fresh capital – something he clearly wouldn't do.

Deans also took time out to deride the petitions in favour of Blindell. There were now 10,000 signatures with Cullis part of a six man committee collecting signatures as far afield as Cornwall and rural Devon.

Spectator was as always impartial, reporting the facts as he knew them, rarely voicing his own opinion. However, in a piece penned in early June 1958 he reflected that under Blindell there was the best flow of information the local Press he had ever known from Home Park. He also pointed to the fact that the players, in return for success, were being paid on a par with First Division players, something that was not the case throughout the lower Divisions. The journalist went on to say that he could see little hope for the current Board; legally speaking he felt their position to be untenable. "Mr Blindell may lose on a show of hands but he will simply demand a poll." Other than the FA intervening, the *Independent's* reporter could see no opportunity for Deans and company to survive.

The crucial Extraordinary General Meeting was set for 27 July. The question was where? What auditorium would be large enough for this gladiatorial encounter? *Spectator* reported that over 500 hundred people were showing an interest. A routine turn out would have been about 60 to 100 people. If the meeting in the previous November was fiery, what was going to happen at this one? 8 July brought more bad news for the Board. Former director Archie Cload, the largest independent Ordinary Share holder, announced that he had sold the bulk of holding to Mr Blindell. He said he had taken legal advice and also consulted with long standing friends, many of whom had been associated with Argyle for years. Having been a hard working member of the Supporters' Club there is little doubt that he consulted them. For sure, he would have had known Pring very well. Cload, who made his money as a fishmonger, said that he had feared that the dispute could rumble on for more than 12 months. He finished by saying that he had sold his shares to Mr Blindell at the same price he paid for them, with no conditions. Although he said at the time "Anyone could have bought them" it did seem like a clear endorsement for Blindell. Or perhaps the new Board could not raise the cash?

Added to this, the highly respected Edgar Dobell voiced his doubts about the current Board's ability to understand Company Law and, in particular, the 1957 change to the Articles of Association. In an eloquent and detailed letter to the *Western Evening Herald* he left no doubt that Mr Blindell was acting perfectly correctly under the terms to which all the current Board were signatories. Dobell was an eminent legal practitioner and for many years was the Court Registrar. Letters to the editor ran at about 3:1 in favour of Blindell's return, including one from the delightfully named 'Two Bob Ender'.

One thing was for sure. Blindell already owned all 60,000 Preference Shares; now it was thought that with those Ordinary Shares he now owned, plus proxies, he was now in control of 32,000 of the 60,000 Ordinary Shares. Clearly the Board was now between a hard place and a much harder place. The *Western Independent's* column continued to be balanced and detailed. *Spectator* wrote that he had been in touch with both parties and had finally discovered common ground. Both camps were "tired of the battle but equally, were not prepared to give any ground." In his inimitable way, he pointed out that "for all his interest in petitions and shares, the man who pays his two bob on a Saturday afternoon cares only about the eleven men in green and black who take the field. Neither the Board nor the proposed Board will score the goals or win the points." He finished with a suggestion that maybe they should all walk away and let new people came in, reminding everyone "that by the time the EGM was held the players would be back training for the new season, the crew of a now rudderless ship."

23 July saw the official Promotion Celebration Dinner at Dingles' Dartmoor Restaurant. Blindell was not invited, a point made by Chairman Harry Deans at every opportunity. It was a timely reminder that Plymouth Argyle was actually about winning football matches, rather than victories in poll votes. The Meeting of 27 July, with an estimated 600 squeezed into the Continental Hotel, was as rowdy as predicted. At the time it was held Britain was in the grip of a national newspaper strike. The *Western Independent* did not publish again until 2 August and the *Western Evening Herald* was an A4 affair produced on a duplicating machine. Harry Deans opened the meeting 30 minutes after the scheduled start time. He immediately sprang a surprise by saying that all those present should know that the FA would be visiting the club 'within days' to investigate the affairs of the club. Was this Deans's way of saying "Do your worst tonight Mr Blindell?"

Attempts had been made to find an independent Chairman, but the sides could not agree. Because of the newspaper printers' strike, and the tremendous public interest, a small booklet was produced containing a blow by blow account of the meeting. Colin Parsons, a major collector of Argyle memorabilia, owns a copy and it makes interesting reading. As it stretches to 17 pages, it is far too detailed to be repeated here.

In summary, Ron Blindell was beaten on a show of hands at each stage of the voting. Despite an estimated 600 attendance, no vote counted more than 349 hands. As each resolution was defeated so Blindell's solicitor Malcolm Collinson called for a poll vote. On page seven there is a bitter indictment of Charles Hill. In a long statement by Collinson, the solicitor reminds the audience that in 1954 greatly respected former vice-Chairman Edgar Dobell resigned with a despairing statement, "It is best I go and leave the club in the hands of those prepared to fall in with the secretary of the Shareholders' Association". Dobell had voted against a bid to raise more capital, proposed finance which was believed to be coming from Messrs Cload, ...and Harry Deans and RGW Pengelly. Dobell's objection seemed to be that if the new shares were issued Deans and Pengelly would be in a position to dominate voting! Elsewhere in his statement Collinson informed the meeting, "It ill becomes the Shareholders' Association to accuse Mr Blindell of dictatorship. It should not be forgotten that the Shareholders Association has 645 members. That is roughly one quarter of the number of shareholders."

The next three pages were filled by a long reply from Hill. He did not miss any opportunities to discredit Blindell. Early in his statement he said

"I wish to present to you a statement which will debunk all the wonderful things Mr Collinson has described about Mr Blindell. Looking back at the records, it is difficult to see Hill as someone who worked solely for the good of Plymouth Argyle. The suspicion is that previous Chairman had rather bowed to his Association – Blindell neither did not nor would not. Finally the Chairman announced that matters would be decided by a poll to be conducted at Home Park on 17 August 1959. He confirmed that this would be the only intimation of that poll. He outlined the reasons why a poll could not be taken that evening. If only they had listened to one of the opening speakers, a Mr W Rowe. He had wanted to postpone the AGM until after the poll vote, but he was shouted down. There were some in the audience that had travelled long distances to be there – an adjournment after five minutes would not have improved their mood.

In amongst the midsummer madness there was a ray of hope for Blindell. His nominee and Saltash solicitor Peter Skinnard was afforded a good hearing by both sides, giving notice that he could turn out to be a valuable asset to any future Board. For a comparatively young man, he spoke with a wisdom and authority beyond his years. However, even when reason was in the air, there was one dissenter, a Mr Ken Cooke, who felt Skinnard was unqualified for the job because he went to a school which only played rugby and hockey. Cooke was constantly shouted down, at one time being invited to stick his head in a bucket. Did the Continental Hotel leave the bar open perhaps?

But on an evening where recrimination was the watchword, Cooke eventually brought some humour to proceedings. He asked who was going to run the club once Blindell was in Westminster, a clear reference to Ron Blindell's nomination for the forthcoming General Election, where he would represent Labour in Truro.

Fortunately for all concerned, before the date of the poll vote was reached, the much forecast intervention by the Football Association took place. Their investigation team comprised Sir Stanley Rous, the FA Secretary, with area representative Frank Adams and staff member Mr D Howes. They arrived at Home Park on Wednesday 5 August 1959, almost nine months to the day when the current Board ousted Blindell and voted Deans into the Chair. Within 330 minutes they had 'solved the crisis and united the two factions'. Sir Stanley made the following statement, prior to announcing a seven point peace plan. "On the evidence examined there appear to be no irregularities which require further investigation, but the confidence of the supporters of Plymouth Argyle FC, which in recent months may have suffered by adverse publicity tending to bring Association Football generally in Plymouth into disrepute, must be restored."

Clause 1 of the agreement was that the current Chairman and directors should continue in office, at least until the November AGM. The next point was that they be joined by Messrs Blindell, Skinnard, Hall and Pring, with the latter having no vote until Clause 4 was approved. The third item of agreement was that Blindell was to Chair the new 'united' Board. Clause 4 was that the Articles of Agreement should he amended at the next AGM to allow eight directors. The fifth was that Mr Blindell should, over a five

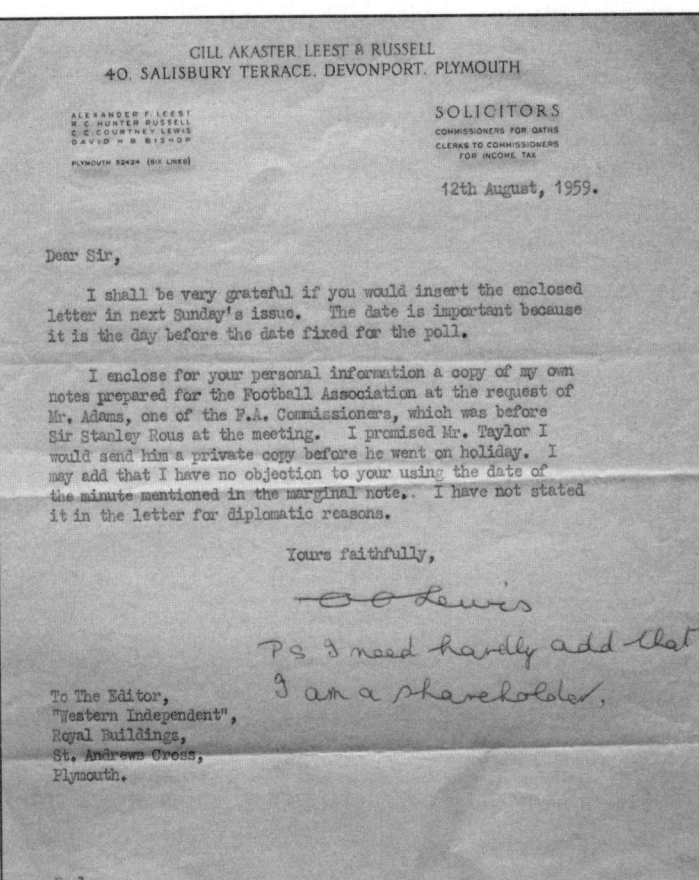

GILL AKASTER, LEEST & RUSSELL
40, SALISBURY TERRACE, DEVONPORT, PLYMOUTH

ALEXANDER F. LEEST
R. C. HUNTER RUSSELL
C. C. COURTNEY LEWIS
DAVID H B BISHOP

PLYMOUTH 52424 (SIX LINES)

SOLICITORS
COMMISSIONERS FOR OATHS
CLERKS TO COMMISSIONERS
FOR INCOME TAX

12th August, 1959.

Dear Sir,

I shall be very grateful if you would insert the enclosed letter in next Sunday's issue. The date is important because it is the day before the date fixed for the poll.

I enclose for your personal information a copy of my own notes prepared for the Football Association at the request of Mr. Adams, one of the F.A. Commissioners, which was before Sir Stanley Rous at the meeting. I promised Mr. Taylor I would send him a private copy before he went on holiday. I may add that I have no objection to your using the date of the minute mentioned in the marginal note.. I have not stated it in the letter for diplomatic reasons.

Yours faithfully,

C C Lewis

P S I need hardly add that I am a shareholder.

To The Editor,
"Western Independent",
Royal Buildings,
St. Andrews Cross,
Plymouth.

Encls:

Gill Akasteer wish to make it clear that this letter did not represent the views of the firm. Though written on company notepaper it was quite clearly expressing the private opinion of one of the partners.

The letter (left) is an example of the way both sides tried to use the *Western Independent* as a clearing house for their arguments.

Below is a section from the notes.

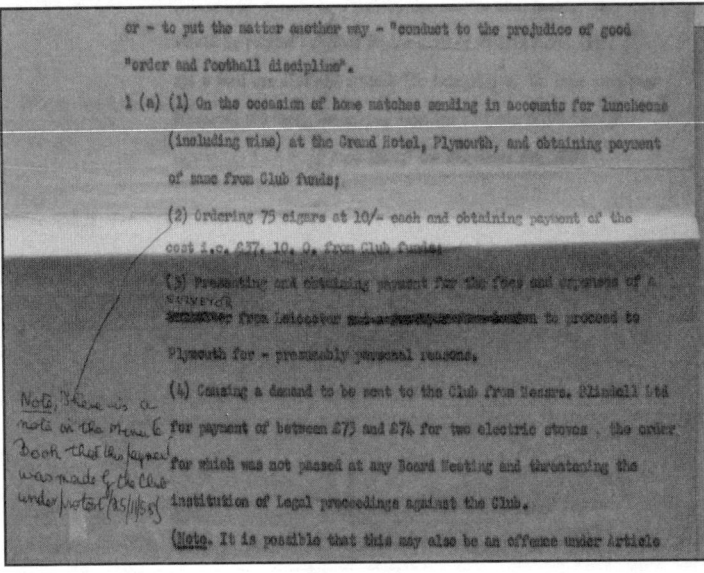

or - to put the matter another way - "conduct to the prejudice of good "order and football discipline".

1 (a) (1) On the occasion of home matches sending in accounts for luncheons (including wine) at the Grand Hotel, Plymouth, and obtaining payment of same from Club funds;

(2) Ordering 75 cigars at 10/- each and obtaining payment of the cost i.e. £37. 10. 0. from Club funds;

(3) Presenting and obtaining payment for the fees and expenses of a surveyor from Leicester and ... to proceed to Plymouth for - presumably personal reasons.

(4) Causing a demand to be sent to the Club from Messrs. Blindell Ltd for payment of between £73 and £74 for two electric stoves, the order for which was not passed at any Board Meeting and threatening the institution of Legal proceedings against the Club.

(Note. It is possible that this may also be an offence under Article

Note. There is a note on the Menu £ for payment of ... Book that this payment was made £ the Club under protest 25/11/58 ...

This is a sample from a long set of notes by Mr CC Courtney Lewis, which accused Ron Blindell of a long list of misdemeanours. Despite all of the efforts of Lewis and those like him, history shows that the FA sided with Blindell and found no fault with the club.

MR. Ron Blindell, who put £25,000 into Argyle nearly two years ago, resigned after being voted out of the chair last November, and now bids a "come-back". Mr. Blindell, 54 years of age, was formerly the head of a £1,000,000 company — mainly a family affair, with its main interest in shoe manufacture and retail sale, comprising over one hundred shops and factories.

Some months ago he sold the business as is now the principal of a building contractor's concern at Kingsbridge and owner of several hotels; he plans a luxury hotel in Jamaica, which he recently visited.

MR. Fred. T. Pring (53), now in his fourth year as chairman of the Argyle Supporters Club, and a member of the club's committee since 1933. Says he has been an Argyle supporter all his life; he joined the Supporters' Club 25 years ago.

In the past two years, the influence of the club has advanced remarkably by reason of finance provided by the Green and Black Club. — a football pool run by Mr. Ron Lucas, organising secretary of the Supporters' Club, and Mr. W. Jutson. Argyle have been helped by £25,000 from the club in the last eighteen months.

Mr. Pring is a printer by trade, in business with his brother.

MR. Peter William Skinnard, a "fanatical" follower of Argyle since the war, 30 years of age, for seven years a solicitor and a partner in the firm of Messrs. Blight, Broad, and Skinnard of Saltash and Callington. He is married and has two children. He qualified as a solicitor in 1952 and is a bachelor of law of London University. Served in the Royal Air Force, a member of Saltash Borough Council; chairman of Saltash Tennis Club; has played cricket for Saltash and Callington and hockey for O.P.M.'s — he was educated at Plymouth College.

MR. James William Hall, director of Sugden's (Newsagent's) Ltd, of Cornwall Street, Frankfort Gate, and Notte Street. Plymouth born and bred, 35 years of age. National newspaper representative. When a boy, had trials for Plymouth Schoolboys and in the Army played for representative Army teams.

After being invalided out of the Service, he became a referee in the Kingsley League, North Devon. A member of Plymouth Junior Chamber of Commerce; member of Plymouth Special Attractions Committee; local secretary of the Old Bens Newsvendors Benevolent Trust.

These were Blindell's nominees with whom he wanted to oust Deans, Crookes and company. In the event the Rous peace initiative precluded Pring from joining the Board. Later he withdrew due to his loyalty to the Supporters Club. *Courtesy Sunday Independent*

Chairman Ron Blindell welcomes local Dentist David James to the Board. Extreme left is Colonel RV Hunt, Peter Skinnard (centre) and on the right Jimmy Hall. It was the first time Blindell could really trust those around him. *Photograph lent by Peter W Skinnard*

year period and in equal instalments, agree to his holding of 15, 000 Preference Shares being redeemed by the company. There was an added rider that the nominal capital be reduced accordingly, this to be reflected in the Articles. Point 6 was that Messrs Hall and Skinnard should accept a responsibility to the Bank for the same sum as the other directors. The final criteria for agreement was that "the provisions of this settlement were agreed by all concerned and it is unlikely that the poll agreed for 17 August will now take place. The resolutions for that meeting will now be withdrawn."

It strikes this writer that all the while the official Shareholders' Association had a voice, this peace treaty would be about as successful as the partitions of India in 1947, and the one in Palestine a year later. And, so it was - on Sunday 9 August Mr Charles S Hill issued a statement via the *Western Independent*. He had been the shareholders' representative during the FA talks and described the settlement as palliative, claiming that the FA representatives gave no deference at all to the very convincing show of hands against Mr Blindell at the recent AGM. Hill felt that a prerequisite of any agreement should have been the appointment of an independent Chairman, at least until the next company meeting. He went on to say that whilst all concerned hoped for success, a final and lasting solution could only come through the goodwill of the shareholders' themselves. Almost menacingly he added "Unilateral agreements will not satisfy this elementary demand." He failed to mention that with the decision for Fred Pring to have no voting power, the voting strength of the unified Board favoured vice-Chairman Deans and his old Board. He also failed to acknowledge the clause which called for the redeeming of the Preference Shares.

Not unsurprisingly, Bert Cole asked to go as soon as he possibly could. As a temporary measure, new director Peter Skinnard became Secretary, impressing everyone with his organisation and thoroughness. Although manager Jack Rowley was seen by some to be at odds with Blindell, neither made any public statement to that effect. There were no significant public utterances from the Board. Blindell was said to be away on his Falmouth based yacht and Harry Deans made no statements. The unified Board was scheduled to meet for the first time on 10 August.

Nothing of importance happened for a couple of months. But in November the first public weakness in the armistice arose, with RGW Pengelly announcing that he would not be standing for re-election at the next company meeting, scheduled for December. Pengelly's move strengthened the current Chairman's position, for already it was clear that David James, although one of the 'Deans's four', had now aligned himself to Blindell. There was no word as to whether Deans would follow Pengelly and not stand for re-election.

The battle weary shareholders assembled again on 12 December, this time in the YMCA. This was to be the last contest of the 1958-59 era. Whatever was agreed with Rous over poll votes, it was a call for a poll which lit the fuse again. Former Chairman Harry Deans was overwhelmingly returned by a show of hands and Blindell nominee Jimmy Hall lost.

Peter Skinnard was elected on a show of hands, but by this time Charles Hill had ordered his members to tear up their ballot papers and boycott the votes. The traditionalists accused Ron Blindell of sponsoring the new association, an accusation made with no tangible evidence. Blindell, who in July had been beaten on a show of hands by a 260-64 had now closed the gap to 125 against him and 102 in support.

When the poll result was announced Deans was gone and Hall was in. Blindell also won the poll by a landslide. At this point, Cliff Crookes, who was not up for re-election, resigned in protest. As he left the stage he shouted "Nobody knows what Harry Deans has done for this club; far more than Blindell ever has." *Daily Express* reporter Roger Malone reported that "to a mixture of boos and cheers 400 mixed-up Plymouth supporters disappeared into the night." Charles Hill claimed afterwards that his Association would have backed Blindell on a show of hands, had he not called for the pernicious poll vote to defeat Harry Deans. What is one to believe?

The final announcement from Blindell that evening was to tell the audience that he had decided to waive the £825 dividend due on his Preference Shares. He was back and in full control. Who was right and who was wrong we will never know. It was just good to know that we could all now concentrate on trying to lift our team struggling at the wrong end of the Second Division.

'That booklet.' The minutes from the battle at the Continental Hotel 27 July 1959. It was an extraordinary Extraordinary Meeting!
From the Colin Parsons Collection

RONALD JAMES RAE BLINDELL
1905-1969

There has never been a more controversial figure at Home Park than Ron Blindell. Despite saving the club from almost certain extinction in 1957, there were a group of people in and around the club that sought to discredit him at every opportunity. Blindell was a brilliant businessman and, for his time, an extremely radical thinker.

He was removed from the Chair by his fellow Board members in November 1958. Although he returned as Chairman in August 1959, after intervention from the Football Association, the club never recaptured the impetus he had initiated when he took the Chair in 1957. He was later credited with saving Brentford FC from going out of business.

CHAPTER SIX

CHAIRMAN RON BLINDELL

Dan McCauley's recent time as Plymouth Argyle's Chairman may have seemed turbulent and, of course, it is relatively fresh in the memory. As will be seen from the preceding chapter, the controversy during Mr McCauley's time was nothing as compared to the years when Ron Blindell was associated with the club. There are definite parallels between the two men. Both were extremely successful in business. Each of them wanted the club free of debt and to be run in a business like way. Neither of them could be faulted for the effort they put into trying to make Plymouth Argyle a success. Perhaps the most important similarity is that if it were not for Ron Blindell and Dan McCauley, at separate times we may have been left with no club at all. Yet despite their role as saviours, both attracted fierce criticism, often when they believed they were doing the right thing.

But why did Blindell attract so much flak? He was successful, he was very wealthy and he wanted Plymouth Argyle to punch their weight. Some who were at the club at the time saw him as a visionary. No one could ever question his ability to make a company profitable. But throughout his time at Home Park there were people around the club who were constantly questioning his motives and trying to discredit him. As you will have seen in the preceding chapter, Blindell spent almost seven years as Chairman of Plymouth Argyle, which was split into two spells. It is fair to say that his original spell as Chairman, from April 1957 until November 1958, was his most successful period. There can be no dispute that, initially, he transformed the way the club was run and helped turn a struggling, loss making football club into a profitable success. Although he returned to the Chair in August 1959, after intervention from the Football Association, his second spell never got close to achieving the accomplishments of the first. After the second coming, apart from a successful 1962-63 campaign, Blindell oversaw some pretty average times. After years of acrimony and confrontation off the field, and generally poor results on it, he resigned his position on 14 July 1964. Apart from penning his resignation letter, his final act as Chairman was to welcome manager Malcolm Allison to the club on 7 July 1964.

Business apart, it is clear that Blindell's other passion was football. He served on the Boards of Torquay United, Plymouth Argyle and (famously) at Brentford and was a vice-president of Reading Football Club. In 1956 he turned down the opportunity to join Crystal Palace. He was for some years the President of the South Western League and is credited with helping that organisation through some troubled times.

Mainly for health reasons he moved to Torquay in the early 1950s. Although he was rarely seen without one of his trademark cigars, he was asthmatic. His doctors clearly thought the Devon air would help the condition, doubtless thinking that it was easier to persuade him to move than to try to stop him smoking. It was just after his move to the south west that he joined the Board of Torquay United. Setting aside local rivalries, it is a fact that Plymouth Argyle has always been seen as a bigger club than either Torquay or Exeter City, whatever position they occupy in the League. Of the three options, Blindell would have seen Plymouth Argyle as the best opportunity to help steer a club into the First Division of the Football League. He may well have been driven by the fact that he was 14 years the junior of Grimsby born Arthur Drewry, a hugely successful fish merchant. A Grimsby Town director and Chairman, Drewry was also President of FIFA and President and of the English Football Association. It is almost certain that Drewry was something of a role model for Blindell. Certainly, Blindell was always keen for Argyle to do well against his home town team. In the week before any match against the Mariners Blindell would keep reminding the Argyle management staff of the importance of the game. The press cutting on page 68, provided by former Argyle director Peter Skinnard, indicates just how passionate Blindell was about games against Grimsby. The last two paragraphs are important. It is a perfect summary of the man. Indeed, when I spoke to Johnny Newman recently, he laughed about the incident and maintained that he had "great respect for Mr Blindell." Former director Peter Skinnard, was always an ally to Blindell and genuinely liked the man. Skinnard accepts that Blindell could be awkward and combative. "But he was quick to apologise and forgive and forget. "His bark was most certainly worse than his bite."

Ronald James Rae Blindell was born in Grimsby on 20 May 1905. At 14, after a normal elementary education, he joined the family boot and shoe business. He was given no choice, despite his declared preference to join the Royal Navy. The business was run from Oaklands, a large house cum company headquarters in Laceby, near Grimsby. At the time he went to work for his father the company had two shops in Grimsby and four in other small Lincolnshire towns. From such humble beginnings he became one of the most successful businessmen of his time. He was, perhaps, the 1940s and 50s version of Sir Alan Sugar. Like the man who built the Amstrad brand, Blindell did not see business management as a popularity contest. A further similarity was that both wanted success in football, while trying to run their football clubs along business lines.

In a 1929 by-election, his father James was elected as MP for the Holland with Boston constituency in Lincolnshire, a seat he kept until his untimely death in 1937. Blindell Snr started as a Liberal, overturning a Conservative majority of 5,000 to beat the Tory candidate by 3,706 votes. It was the last Liberal victory in a by-election until they famously took Torrington in 1959. Later, representing the National Liberal ticket, he retained his seat in the 1931 and 1935 General Elections with enhanced majorities. At some stage in his time as an MP he was knighted and led the Treasury.

Tragically, on 10 May 1937 Sir James and Lady Blindell were involved in a car accident at Stickford in Lincolnshire. Their chauffeur, Marshall Woodhall, braked and swerved to avoid two dogs fighting in the road. Sir James sat at the chauffeur's side died instantly from severe head injuries.

The date is significant, inasmuch that it was the day before the Coronation of King George VI. Some sources say that Sir James and Lady Blindell were on their way to the Coronation. On 11 May *The Times* coverage of the accident reported that the couple were being driven to a Hospital Carnival in Boston. There is insufficient evidence to prove it one way or the other.

But one thing is for sure, at 32 years of age, Ron Blindell assumed control of Blindell (Boot and Shoe) Company Limited. At that time the company still had no more than ten shops, two in Grimsby and others in various Lincolnshire and Nottinghamshire towns. It was a viable business but by no means immense. It was a challenging time for him. The nation was on the one hand emerging from the Depression of the late 20s and early 30s, while simultaneously looking over its shoulder at the threat of Hitler's Third Reich. Sir James' eldest son did not fail him. On 4 September 1958 Ron Blindell was the guest of the Grimsby Rotary Club, where he had been inducted in 1934 as their youngest ever member. That is probably a clear sign that he was already running his father's business while Sir James concentrated on Westminster. Indeed, records show that it became Blindell's (1934) Limited.

When the business was eventually sold in the late 1950s Ron Blindell had created a shoe empire as great as any in the land. There were three factories near Leicester, one each for men's, ladies and children's shoes and more than 120 retail outlets. Blindell's Shoes was a market leader. Documentation tracing the amazing growth of the business is rare. A company report dated 23 May 1949, and published in the *Times,* shows a thriving balance sheet and speaks of "progress and expansion, leading to a pre-taxation profit of £202, 881, compared to £142,390 the previous trading year." It is clear that long before the term became fashionable,

Blindell was quick to see the advantages of 'merger and acquisition'. After expanding in Lincolnshire and to Nottinghamshire and Leicestershire he looked further south in the Midlands, buying businesses in Coventry and Birmingham. The ultimate prize was when he acquired a shop and offices in Regent Street.

He had a near miss when he sold the shoe business. It had been for sale for a few years and major entrepreneurs of the day (Charlie Clore and Isaac Wolfson were two) looked without buying. Eventually it was sold to two men by the name of Grunwald and Jasper. Seemingly respectable businessmen with a nose for buying and selling businesses, it eventually emerged that their empire was built on fraud. Blindell had got the price he was asking and, fortunately, the cheque was met. It was one of the last transactions the fraudsters made before being found out and jailed.

The *status quo* was never enough for Ron Blindell. He never seems to have considered the easy option. As well as developing his successful businesses, Blindell found time to fight three times for a seat in Parliament. His second wife Kay, who he married on 4 November 1953, smiles as she speaks of his aspirations to be a Member of Parliament. "I know he desperately wanted to do it" she said, "but whether he would always have accepted the Whip is a completely different matter!" First, in 1945 he stood as a Liberal in Nottingham South. He then fought as a Conservative-Liberal in the 1952 Wellingborough by-election, before he failed to be elected as a Labour candidate for Truro, in the 1959 General Election. Three election campaigns, each time representing a different Party and he failed to win a seat. There is not much that Blindell went for that he did not get but a Parliamentary seat was one of them. There are few reports of his first two election campaigns, but his work in the hustings at Truro drew national Press attention. What attracted the national papers was this great entrepreneur who constantly smoked expensive cigars, stepping each day from his 55 foot yacht into one of his two Rolls-Royces to canvas *Labour* votes. Blindell being Blindell, he gave as good as he got. Indeed, as he spoke at various meeting halls in the Truro constituency area he encountered a regular heckler. After one meeting Blindell offered the heckler a lift to the next.

He had moved first to the Torquay area, to the beautiful Rock House in Maidencombe, once leased by Rudyard Kipling. The house was on the market in 2007 for some £2.5 million. After marrying for the second time, he moved to the tranquillity of Mawnan Smith, near Falmouth. There he purchased a house called Trehuncey Vean. With his new wife and young family, his yacht *Blue Finch* moored in Falmouth, life for Blindell could not have been better. There was nothing ordinary about Ron Blindell. Like many aspects of his life, the *Blue Finch* was not just any yacht. She was originally named *Bluebird* and was built for Sir Malcolm Campbell, once holder of both World land and water speed records. A stipulation of the sale by the Campbell estate was that the name *Bluebird* could not be used.

In the late summer, early autumn of 1958 his commitment to Plymouth Argyle was shown by the fact that he moved to Sea Cliff, a beautiful house in Strete near Totnes. The property had been owned previously by Eric Williams, the famous author whose best known book was *The Wooden Horse*. Ron wanted to reduce the amount of time taken to travel from Falmouth to allow him more time to devote to the club. The omnipresent critics forced him to issue denials about the cost of renovations, dismissing it as something any man would do for a beautiful wife and young family. But what was it to do with them anyway? By this time he already owned the Seymour Hotel in Totnes, the Albion in Kingsbridge and the JW Scoble building firm in Kingsbridge. He had not lived in the South Hams for long when he was overthrown by the other Board members. Although his wife Kay took no part in the football side of his business ventures, she looks back and wonders what possessed her late husband to ever get involved in Plymouth Argyle, especially after the coup by his fellow Board members and the constant carping of the Argyle Shareholders' Association. She has no doubts whatsoever that it played a part in his relatively early demise. She declined to comment specifically about some of the personalities involved with Plymouth Argyle during the major falling out of 1958, and I did not want to press the issue. Suffice to say that mention of some names made her bristle more than others. In common with many other people, a name that stuck with her, for all the right reasons, was Peter Skinnard.

No one knew Ron Blindell better than Kay. She readily acknowledges that he could be 'difficult' but points out that he was frequently frustrated if people around him could not think and act at the pace he did. "He was so full of ideas; he had a brilliant mind and he wanted people to seize the moment." I spent several hours at her Berkshire home, with the Thames flowing past the end of the garden. She was quite clear that the man she knew and loved was nothing like the figure often portrayed by his critics. "Half of his trouble was that many people could not think or act at the pace he could. He had big ideas and until his health started to fail he mainly delivered. I also believe that he trusted too many people and was often more generous than he should have been." When I asked if she could shed any light on the reason why he stepped in to save Brentford Football Club, the only comment she made was that, "it was something of a surprise to me after he died to find that he had borrowed the £104,000 he used at Brentford, against the value of our house at Ascot".

Looking back he was hugely successful. He owned some of the finest homes in the land. At the time of his death, on 10 January 1969 (the same date on which Kay's father had died some years before), he owned Tittenhurst Park, a large Georgian Manor in Ascot. He had purchased the property in 1964 from another man who, coincidentally, had been a well known figure in Plymouth. It was Peter Cadbury, who had founded Westward Television in the early 60s. Kay recalled, "The house was far too big for me and the boys and it was sold—to John and Yoko Lennon." I later discovered that it was at Tittenhurst Park that Lennon wrote and recorded the now iconic 'Imagine'. Shortly after he acquired the house, Lennon added a recording studio. Anything credited with being recorded at Ascot Studios would have been produced at the former Blindell home. The

ELEVEN weary Argyle players felt reasonably happy as they slumped on to their dressing room bench and threw off their boots after holding Grimsby Town to a 1-1 draw.

Indepent 6/2/72

The match had been played in a howling gale, which made the final result even more satisfying. Any point away from home is a point worth having.

But this was Grimsby, the birthplace of Ron Blindell, and there was no town in England where the Argyle chairman liked to savour the fruits of victory more.

As the fixture drew near each season, Blindell would urge his training staff to make sure everyone was fit for the big day.

"This is one we have got to win," he would remind them.

Blindell didn't travel to many away games but he always made the pilgrimage back to Grimsby in the hope of seeing Argyle put one across his home town team.

And, although Argyle hadn't succeeded in their mission on this particular occasion, the players thought Mr. Blindell wouldn't be too disappointed when he made his customary appearance in the dressing room afterwards.

He might even manage a smile, they thought. But there wasn't a trace of a smile as Blindell thundered in and castigated them for letting him down.

Peter Skinnard, who was the director-in-charge of the team that week-end, was just going in as the red-faced Blindell stalked out.

"Where are you going?" asked Blindell. "To say 'well done' to the lads," Skinnard replied.

"I shouldn't do that," snapped Blindell. "I have just told them how rotten they were . . ."

Peter Skinnard returned to the boardroom and waited until everyone was ready for the long haul back to Plymouth.

But, when the message came to leave, the team bus was still half empty and the few players on board were strangely silent.

Asked what was wrong, Johnny Newman, the skipper, said the players felt very bitter over Mr.

Blindell's attitude and some were in a "rebellious mood."

Skinnard returned to the boardroom and reported the trouble to Blindell.

And it didn't take him long to decide to go out to the rebels, crack a few jokes and apologise for his hasty outburst.

THE story, in many ways, sums up the Blindell character. If the players were doing well he would give them the earth but if they failed him, he found it difficult to hide his disappointment.

Someone had to feel the lash of his tongue, yet he was often quick to forgive and forget and many could tell similar anecdotes about his attitude in defeat.

Cutting reproduced by courtesy of the Sunday Independent

Blindell gives up his Argyle monopoly

SELLS 75% OF HIS SH/
THREE 'TAKEOV

Crowds jeer story of Blindell's £30,000

ttle for power at Plymouth Argyle
board, chairmaned by Harry Dea
ex-chairman Ron Blindell, l
"dictator," "Krushche..," l
was an extraordi

Blindell is chairman of Argyle again

DEANS STAYS ON BOARD

MR. RON BLINDELL, the wealthy Westcountry businessman, is once again chairman of Plymouth Argyle
Football Club. Under him
rectors which includes
his chairmanship.
announced
ball Ass

POLL VOTE WINS ARGYLE FOR BLINDELL

Ron Blindell was no stranger to headlines during his stormy reign as Chairman

famous accompanying video, where Lennon is seen at the white piano, was shot in that very house. So, there is a link between Plymouth Argyle and John Lennon's greatest work—albeit a rather tenous one!

The Blindells had a box at Ascot once owned one of the few horses ever to beat Arkle. Although the great horse was giving away 35 pounds, history records that Blindell's grey Stalbridge Colonist won the 1966 Hennessy Gold Cup and beat Arkle into second place. Ron and Kay and their boys were regulars on the Queen Mary, though Ron died before they could make a planned trip on the QE2 shortly after it came into service.

The couple had honeymooned in Jamaica and eventually bought some land on the north side. They had intended to build a house there and he was also in a consortium that planned a hotel complex. Unfortunately, with his health now failing, neither project ever came to fruition. Squatters moved in and ultimately the whole investment was lost.

Towards the end of his time in the shoe business, and certainly afterwards, he diversified into printing, furniture, hotels and building. A former employee with Stones the printers, who wished to remain anonymous told me that in 1962 Blindell laid on a coach to take 55 staff from Banbury to the 1962 Argyle v Tottenham cup tie. He added that they were treated to lunch and dinner at the Seymour Hotel in Totnes and in between they had ringside seats at Home Park. Another member of staff there, Les Chapple, recalled Blindell having the Hennessy Gold Cup paraded around the printing works. Neither Fyne Lady furniture, which at one time provided quality desks for the House of Commons, nor the printing arm of the business made money for Blindell. His health prevented him working as hard as he had done in the shoe business. After he died Sunningdale solicitor Neville Avens helped Kay stabilise the printing business. With her boys Ronnie and Jamie too young to run it, she agreed with his two daughters from a previous marriage that it should be sold.

During my conversation with Kay Blindell she could not have been more frank or open. She made a powerful case for her late husband, illustrating her defence of him with clear examples of his kindness and generosity. She did acknowledge some of his shortcomings but I came away convinced that this man was not the ogre some people in Plymouth had made him out to be. I was told Ron looked after those members of his family in difficulty and was a devoted son to his mother.

It was clear from our conversation that Blindell attracted great loyalty from people in his businesses. Richard Hughes and solicitor Collinson we heard about in the previous chapter. In addition to them there was a man named Eddie Stockwood, who followed the Blindells from the north and stayed loyal to his boss until the very end. Kay laughed when she mentioned 'Stocky' - "Poor man, Ron did give him some stick but he remained fiercely loyal." Would people stay so loyal to a man of the sort that some of the Argyle Shareholders' Association described? I think not.

The Blindell's eldest son James has lived in Australia for almost twenty years — after initially going there temporarily. The second son Ron was at one time the youngest ever director of a football club, when he served on the Board at Brentford. A former lawyer, he now lives in the Hungerford area, travelling to meet up with Kay as often as he can.

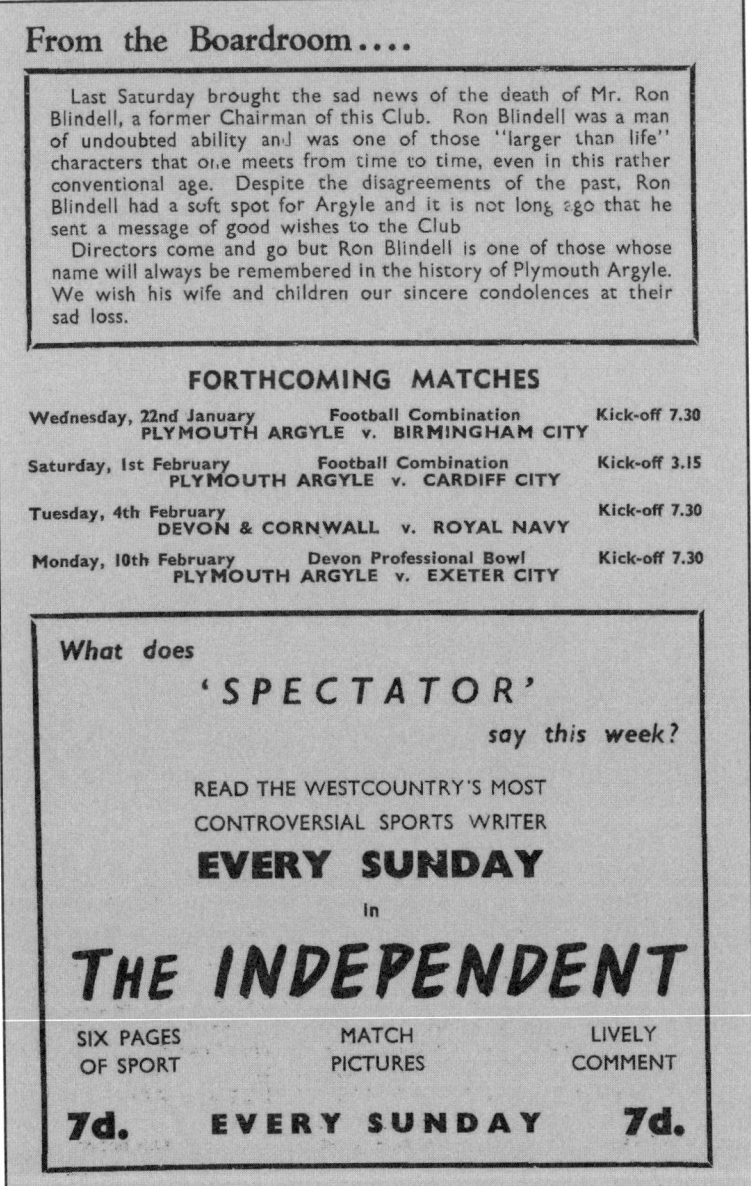

From the Boardroom....

Last Saturday brought the sad news of the death of Mr. Ron Blindell, a former Chairman of this Club. Ron Blindell was a man of undoubted ability and was one of those "larger than life" characters that one meets from time to time, even in this rather conventional age. Despite the disagreements of the past, Ron Blindell had a soft spot for Argyle and it is not long ago that he sent a message of good wishes to the Club

Directors come and go but Ron Blindell is one of those whose name will always be remembered in the history of Plymouth Argyle. We wish his wife and children our sincere condolences at their sad loss.

FORTHCOMING MATCHES

Wednesday, 22nd January   Football Combination   Kick-off 7.30
PLYMOUTH ARGYLE v. BIRMINGHAM CITY

Saturday, 1st February   Football Combination   Kick-off 3.15
PLYMOUTH ARGYLE v. CARDIFF CITY

Tuesday, 4th February   Kick-off 7.30
DEVON & CORNWALL v. ROYAL NAVY

Monday, 10th February   Devon Professional Bowl   Kick-off 7.30
PLYMOUTH ARGYLE v. EXETER CITY

Above is the obituary to Ron Blindell which appeared in the programme for the home match v Barrow on 18 January 1969. The crowd of 5,558 was a quarter of the size of the average crowds that flocked to see the 1958-59 promotion side. Note the price of the Sunday Independent! And the reporter was still *Spectator*.
Courtesy Plymouth Argyle FC & Trev Scallan of Greens on Screen

CHAPTER SEVEN

MANAGER JACK ROWLEY

With Argyle struggling at the foot of the Second Division, Christmas 1954 was not the happiest of times at Home Park. After the heady days of a fourth place finish in 1952-53, the Board were unable to invest in the players needed to mount another drive for First Division status. 53-54 was a struggle and 54-55 was worse. In January 1955 the likeable and very popular manager of the day, Jimmy Rae, paid the price for the Board's lack of financial support. Enter Jack Rowley, erstwhile Manchester United centre-forward and a key figure in their recent Cup (1948) and League (1952) triumphs. Peter Shilton apart, Jack Rowley is probably the most famous and successful player ever to join the Home Park staff.

Rowley came to United's notice in 1936. He had been one of the "Buckley Boys", a group of outstanding youngsters brought together at Wolves. As a Wolverhampton lad, he was disappointed not to make the grade there. After being loaned out to Cradley Heath in the Midland Combination League, he was given a free transfer in February 1937. Major Frank Buckley, the Wolves manager of the day, was seen as a football visionary who was at the cutting edge of sports science and famed for his eye for a player, but his judgement of the young Rowley proved to be a big mistake.

Snapped up by Bournemouth and Boscombe Athletic, Jack was an immediate success. At the start of the 1937-38 season, he notched 11 goals in 10 games. Scott Duncan the Manchester United manager moved quickly to invest £3,000 in the young man, a considerable sum in those days for a virtually untried youngster. United were then in the Second Division and were not by any means a rich club. Jack repaid their gamble in bucketfuls, while within a few weeks Duncan left to manage Southern League Ipswich Town.

The day after signing Rowley made a quiet debut for United in a 1-0 home win against Sheffield Wednesday on 23 October 1937, 16 days past his 19th birthday. Initially he found the step up in class difficult and asked to be left out until he found his feet. Weeks later he was back, hitting four goals in a 5-1 defeat of Swansea. A shooting star was born! He finished the 1937-38 season with nine goals in 29 League and Cup outings and the team won promotion to the First Division from second place. After being something of a yo-yo team, United concentrated on consolidating their top-flight status. They finished 14th in 1938-39, with Jack bagging ten goals in 38 League and Cup outings.

If it had not been for World War II Jack Rowley might have been the greatest goal scorer these islands ever saw. War was declared a few weeks before his 21st birthday. Like many other great players of the day, it was a severe blow for him. He lost seven full seasons, spanning his early and middle 20s when he was entering into his prime. Although he played regularly throughout the war, his huge goal return in the various wartime competitions does not count in official records. It would be the 1946-47 season before he could pit his wits against the best in an official League game.

Once the War League was established in 1940-41, he was as prolific as anyone in the country. On 8 March 1941 he played in the last United home game before Old Trafford was severely damaged by heavy enemy raids on Manchester, on the nights of 11 and 12 March. Jack and United captain Johnny Carey each scored hat-tricks in a 7-3 win. History does not record their opponents that day. The team would not play another home game there until 1949, moving their headquarters to Maine Road. On Easter Monday 1941 they repaid Manchester City's kindness with a 7 – 1 hammering, Jack Rowley weighing in with four goals. At the start of the 1941-42 war season United opened their North Regional League pro-gramme with a 13-1 drubbing of New Brighton in which Rowley hit the target no less than seven times. In a 2-2 draw with Liverpool in November 1942, Jack scored twice, but the match was special for him as his 15 year old brother Arthur played on the left wing.

In the Second World War, unlike the First, when professional football was suspended, the government believed the game had a vital role to play in keeping up morale and fund-raising. But Jack Rowley did his bit for the war effort as a footballer and a soldier. Initially joining the Militia, on 15 February 1940 he enlisted in the South Staffordshire Regiment, going on to spend six years in the Army. He was promoted to Corporal Rowley on 17 January 1941. In 1944 he landed in France a few days after D-Day, and was wounded during heavy fighting around Caen. He reverted to Pri-vate in 1945 and became a Physical Training Instructor.

A feature of the War League was that clubs could enlist the aid of guest players. Although a player's club held their registration throughout the War, it was accepted that they could 'guest' for a team near their unit. Someone like Jack Rowley was in popular demand. The system was often abused, with registered players at a club being overlooked in favour of 'star' players who had been posted locally. Jack also turned out for Man-chester United as regularly as military commitments would allow. Be-tween 1941 and 1946 he played 78 times for them, scoring 100 goals. In addition he guested for Aldershot, Wolverhampton Wanderers, Tottenham Hotspur, Walsall, Folkestone, Shrewsbury and even Belfast Distillery.

Whatever team Jack Rowley turned out for, goals were almost guaran-teed. He played just the once for Aldershot, but got a goal. For Walsall he scored 24 times in 14 outings during season 1940-41. For Wolverhamp-ton Wanderers, the team that rejected him as a boy, he made eight ap-pearances across five different seasons, hitting 17 goals in the process. Two virtuoso performances stand out. Against Derby County in 41-42 he hit all eight in an 8-1 rout. He must have been pleased to have starred at Molineux, the very ground where he had suffered an early rejection. In the 1943-44 season he hit the target seven times in a game for Tottenham Hotspur, where overall he played 22 games, averaging a goal per match. By far his best war time season was the 1941-42 campaign. He scored 42 times in 23 games for Manchester United, including a staggering 15 in the first three games. He then played twice as a guest for Wolves and hit seven in two appearances.

One of those games was an 11-1 win over Everton. Jack had only turned up to watch, but when a player did not make it to the ground he volunteered to play. He scored five, though Everton with two players injured played much of the game with nine fit men and a passenger. Clearly, with players' availability affected by travel difficulties and military commitments, some defences he plundered were not the best. However, you can only beat what is put in front of you. It still takes a very good player to score so prolifically.

His goal getting efforts did not go unnoticed and it led to his selection for the Football League against the Scottish League at Bloomfield Road, Blackpool. The match took place on 11 October 1941 and was billed as an RAF Benefit match. The inside trio for the Football League side was Wilf Mannion, Jack Rowley and Peter Doherty. (What would they be worth in today's transfer market?) Each scored a goal in the 3-2 win. It was the only representative game played under the Football League banner during the War.

International matches were much more frequent but Jack played in only one War International, a 2-0 victory over Wales at Ninian Park on 6 May 1944. He did not score. This time the number 8, 9 and 10 shirts were filled by Raich Carter, Tommy Lawton and Rowley, another powerful threesome. At centre-half was Stan Cullis of Wolves and England, who went on to lead the Black Country side to three post-War League titles and the 1960 FA Cup.

Just before the War ended Rowley was chosen as part of a powerful FA Services side. In the party with Rowley were, amongst others, Joe Mercer, Matt Busby, Tommy Lawton and Frank Swift. They were dubbed the 'Vera Lynns' of football, offering entertainment to troops all over Italy in the summer of 1945. Things did not go according to plan for Jack. After a flight to Naples the group climbed out of an ancient Warwick transport plane. While the rest contemplated a night under canvas, Rowley was taken straight to hospital with dysentery. He was later to say to his family "they say see Naples and die – I bloody near did".

When the war ended, Jack was nearly 28 years old. He came out of the post-war blocks firing on all cylinders. He was strong and robust, a hard but fair striker who never complained about strong tackling defenders. Matt Busby, United's untried new manager, had spent the 1945-46 unofficial season preparing for real thing. During the next nine seasons the club would not finish lower than eighth, a renaissance in which Rowley played a huge part. In 1946-47 United finished second in the First Division and Rowley hit 28 in 39 appearances. In 1947-48 they were runners-up again, but won the FA Cup. Jack was on the mark on 28 occasions, playing in 39 League games and six FA Cup ties.

In every cup round United had been drawn against First Division opposition. In the third round they were a goal down to Aston Villa after 11 seconds, before a United player had touched the ball. But this was a

Above is the 1948 FA cup winning side, with Jack second from right in the centre row. Below are the 1952 League Champions, who also won the Charity Shield that year. He is second in from the left in the centre row. *From Susan Watson's (Jack's daughter) scrapbook*

special and very powerful team. By half-time the Villa Park scoreboard read 5-1.... to United. They eventually won 6-4. Although their fourth and fifth round draws gave them 'home' ties, their temporary home at Maine Road was unavailable. So they beat Liverpool 3-0 at Goodison Park and then Charlton 2-0 at Leeds Road, Huddersfield. Including the Final, United scored 22 goals in six ties, with Jack Rowley getting five of them. That 1948 FA Cup Final against Blackpool is regarded by many as one of the best ever. Rowley twice brought United level with goals in the 28th and 69th minutes. United eventually won 4-2. Just as they would 21 years later in their poignant European Cup win, United wore a blue change strip for that 1948 Wembley success.

The following season United were runners-up in the League for the third consecutive time, Rowley scoring 20 times in 39 League Games. In the FA Cup, he hit nine goals, including five in a fifth round 8-0 trouncing of non-league Yeovil Town. The crowd at Maine Road that day was an incredible 81,565. John Russell, a life-long Red, was there. He described how Alec Stock's brave non-leaguers were cheered off the field at the end. Although United won easily, after each goal he remembers that the players quietly returned to their own half for the restart. At the end of the game every Yeovil player queued to shake five goal Rowley's hand.

The League title still eluded United, indeed the next two seasons were something of a disappointment after the high expectations Busby's side had generated. In 1949-50, United could only finish fourth, though Jack's 23 goals in 44 League matches was another good return. He could not match this in 1950-51 and amassed his lowest total since he became established in the side, with 'only' 15 from 42 appearances in all competitions. But the team was back in second place. 1951-52 was a triumphant season for both Rowley and his club. Although dumped out of the Cup at the first hurdle, they changed their status from nearly men to title winners. Rowley scored 30 in 40 League outings, smashing Stan Turnbull's 40 year old club record. After seven games Rowley had netted 14 goals, including hat-tricks against West Brom (3-3) and Middlesbrough (4-0) in the opening two games and three more in a 4-0 win over Stoke City. In April 1952 Arsenal travelled to Old Trafford with a very slim chance of taking the title. Although in second place, they need to win by seven clear goals, an unlikely scenario, especially after early injuries to two Arsenal players, including goalkeeper George Swindin. Jack Rowley ended the season as he began it – with a hat-trick. It helped United to a 6-1 home win, in front of 53,651 delighted United supporters. Busby now had his second major trophy and United their first League title in 41 years.

The seasons which followed were not as successful for United or Jack. In 52-53 Jack sustained the only major injury of his career and made only 26 League appearances as United finished eight. He managed another four in the Cup and finished with 14 goals in all. The following season United finished fourth, but Jack Rowley was not now as prolific. He scored 12 goals in 36 League games, but to accommodate Tommy Taylor he was frequently employed wide on the left. Rowley's last season in Manchester was 54-55. He was the final member of Busby's first great post-war side to go. His role as the link between the old guard and the new kids on the block came to end on 22 January 1955, in a 1-1 draw with Bolton Wanderers. In less than a month he would become player-manager of Plymouth Argyle.

* * *

Rowley's close bond with the emerging Busby Babes would bring him great grief when eight were killed in the Munich air disaster of 1958. Not only did he play with all of the young players who perished in the February snow. He had watched them grow into the fantastic players they were. Also killed were Walter Crickmer and Bert Whalley, who had coached him in his early United days. He had never known an Old Trafford without them. Frank Swift, by then a journalist, was an opponent and friend. It affected him greatly and he grieved for weeks.

* * *

Make no mistake, Jack Rowley was one hell of a footballer. He was highly instrumental in leading Manchester United back to the highest contours of the football map, thanks to his venomous left foot! It was said that when Jack Rowley came to town people behind the goals took out extra personal insurance. Those who saw him in his prime will tell you that no one hit a ball harder. His powerful left foot earned him the nickname "The Gunner". It is difficult to tell precisely where the nickname came from. He had only had two seasons at Old Trafford before his time as an anti-tank gunner in the South East Staffordshire Regiment. To have made a national reputation in such a short time may not have been possible. There is every chance that during the War people linked his military service and his hard shot.

His 11 career hat-tricks are still the best return by a Manchester United player. Only Sir Bobby Charlton, with 199, heads Rowley's total of 182 League goals for United. In the FA Cup he notched 26, second only to Denis Law's 34. In all competitions he is third with 208. Charlton had a total of 247 and Law 236. His 30 League goals in the 1951-52 season, equalled by Law in 1963-64, has only ever been beaten twice by a United player. Munich survivor Dennis Viollet hit 32 during the 1959-60 season and in 2007-08 Cristiano Ronaldo got 31. Only van Nistelrooy has a superior goals per game ratio. Capped by England in four forward positions, he was clearly more than just a goalscorer. As he proved when he became player-manager at Plymouth, he had a range of accurate passing that was almost unequalled. Not only did he score a lot of goals, he provided just as many for his colleagues. The Morris, Delaney, Rowley, Pearson, Mitten forward line, assembled by Matt Busby after the war, put fear in the heart of the best defences in the land. Although he was originally seen as a left winger, Rowley quickly took to the number 9 shirt. Being predominately left footed was no disadvantage to him.

Rowley was unlucky to be born in an era when England had a surfeit of talented centre-forwards to choose from. Tommy Lawton, Nat Lofthouse (who both went to the same secondary school) and Ronnie Allen of West Bromwich were all of the same generation. Their presence, and the War, meant that Jack Rowley made only six peace-time appearances for

England, scant reward for sucha huge talent. The only forward position he did not play for England was at outside-right. He scored at an average of a goal per game.

His first cap came against Switzerland in 1948, where he scored once in a 6-0 win. Four others followed in 1949. They included a four goal haul in a 9-2 World Cup qualifier victory against Northern Ireland, played at his 'home' ground Maine Road. He scored a stunning long range effort in a 2-0 victory over Italy, at White Hart Lane. The newspapers reported that "the Italian goalkeeper could only wave at it". Surprisingly over-looked for the 1950 World Cup party to represent England in Brazil, his place was given to the emerging Roy Bentley of Chelsea. England had not competed in the 1938 World Cup. The tournaments of 1942 and 1946 were lost to the war so he knew, at almost 32 years of age, that 1950 probably represented his last opportunity to take part in a World Cup tournament. Rowley's intense disappointment was probably tempered by the infamous 1-0 defeat against the USA which he missed!

There was another consolation. While England prepared for South America, Manchester United embarked on a North American tour. They opened in Toronto on 10 May and finished in Chicago on 20 June 1950. The penultimate match of the tour saw United play the English FA XI (the World Cup team preparing for the tournament in Brazil) in Toronto. Watched by the then record Soccer crowd in Canada, 24,809, the match finished 2-2. Rowley scored United's second.

His outstanding form in 1951-52 led to a recall for the 1952 Home International with Scotland. It was his final appearance in an England jersey. He was at outside left in a forward line that included his club colleague Stan Pearson. In front of 134,504 at Hampden Park, with Pearson scoring twice, England ran out 2-1 victors to enable them to share the Home Championship with Wales.

Was Rowley perhaps immortalised in the *Tiger* comic? Roy of the Rovers first appeared in 1954, just 2 years after Jack broke the Manchester United scoring record. Rowley had averaged almost 20 goals a season since football re-started after the war. Is it a coincidence that Roy was described as having "a left foot like a rocket?" Maybe for Jack Rowley we should read Roy Race and for Manchester United read Melchester Rovers? Who knows? The comic book hero must have had some basis in fact, though from the look of him it is more likely he was based upon Ronnie Allen of West Bromwich.

Busby had gradually made changes from the 1948 Cup winning side. Once the 1952 title winning season was over, he realised that further surgery was needed. By 1954-55 only Rowley and centre-half Allenby Chilton were left from the great post-war sides (see photo on page 81). Chilton had become prone to mistakes and had Mark Jones breathing down his neck. Rowley had to permanently return to his original outside left spot, to accommodate the talented Tommy Taylor.

As 1955 dawned, Matt Busby had made it known that he would release Jack Rowley on a free transfer, provided the right opportunity to go into management occurred. For his part, Jack Rowley was clear that he did not want to be a player-manager. In the *Western Evening Herald* of 11 February 1955 *Pilgrim* reported on an interview he had conducted with Rowley, one of five on the short-list to replace Jimmy Rae. He said "I am not prepared to become a player-manager, but if the need arose I would be prepared to help out the club for a month or so, on the strict understanding that at the end of that period I would revert to manager. I feel I have a definite future in club management. Since the War I have taken a great interest in coaching schoolboys and juniors and I am a qualified coach." In case the point had been missed, he reiterated, "I am not keen on a player-manager post, but any executive position that would allow me to continue coaching would be very acceptable". The Argyle Board must therefore have been very determined when they interviewed him as they reached an agreement that he would play on for one or maybe two more seasons. They challenged him "to put some devil into the team".

Busby was keen to reward the 36 year old Jack Rowley for the phenomenal service he had given Manchester United. Despite the fact that only months before Arsenal had wanted to buy Rowley as a player, where a fee of several thousand pounds would have been involved, the United manager gave his blessing for Rowley to play for Argyle. And Manchester United was not a rich club at that time; it was a generous gesture. The United manager told *Pilgrim* "Jack has been with us for 18 years. He has been a wonderful club man and a great help to us in bringing on the many youngsters on our books. We want to show just how much we appreciate what he has done for us, and he is completely free to play for Plymouth whenever he wants. There is a lot of good football in him. After all, he has been more or less a regular for us and we could have got a good fee for him."

On 16 February 1955, after his interview in Plymouth, he returned by train to his home in Sale, Cheshire. He trained at Old Trafford for the last time on 18 February 1955, before catching an express to London. He then completed his signing as a player with Argyle Secretary Bert Cole, before meeting his new charges for the first time. Rowley would make his debut at Craven Cottage the next day, buoyed by a contract which would pay him as manager *and* player. He later recalled to *Pilgrim* that he even got the £10 statutory signing on fee, joking to Secretary Bert Cole that he hoped the cheque would not bounce. A close friend of Jack's wrote to *Pilgrim*, "Argyle have got a grand chap. He is a tee-totaller and a non-smoker as well as being a real family man". He would be moving his wife and three children to Plymouth at the earliest opportunity.

Somewhere between leaving Plymouth after his interview and meeting up with Cole in London, Rowley had contracted food-poisoning. He told *Pilgrim* that he had seen a doctor and taken some pills, adding that he would see the Manchester doctor again on the Monday. He already had a long term nasal problem, but eschewed treatment for that to commence his mission to save Argyle from relegation. It did not take Rowley long to get a response from the struggling team. Second from bottom, Argyle were 2-0 down to Fulham after 23 minutes, but Rowley then began to run the show from the inside-left position. Reports of the day remarked that although his customary powerful shooting was not a feature of his play, he was the ace exponent of the sweeping pass. *Pilgrim* described how "the ball arrived at the toe of the intended player with precision accuracy and it is danger ahead every time this happens". Rowley had shrewdly decided he could have more influence in a deep lying, playmaker inside-forward role.

Eric Davis and Malcolm Davies drew Argyle level and Peter Anderson secured the first away win of the season with his 61st minute goal. *Pilgrim* remarked upon Rowley's "supreme confidence" and marked him down as "one of those people who are at their best when at the helm of a sinking ship." It was a good day for the Rowley family. Elsewhere in London, Jack's free-scoring brother Arthur had hit the target at Highbury to secure a 1-1 draw for Leicester City. The brothers celebrated over dinner that evening. Arthur still remains the highest ever Football League goal scorer. He netted 434 goals in 619 games, a record which is unlikely ever to be beaten. Almost eight years younger than his brother, the war was not so damaging to his career. Both were predominately left-footed and shared an ability to hit the ball with tremendous power. It is generally accepted that Jack was the better player. Although Arthur scored nearly twice the number of goals, he never achieved the stature of his brother. When they were growing up, one can only wonder what damage they did to their Wolverhampton back garden! Jack's daughter Susan recalls her Dad saying that a third brother, Albert, would have been a better player than either Jack or Arthur. Unfortunately injury curtailed his career.

Argyle may have been a sinking ship but there was a new man on the bridge now. Gradually results improved. Jack Rowley played in 13 of the remaining games, scoring twice. Prior to Rowley's arrival they had 17 points from 29 games. They finished with 31 from 42 games and Second Division football would be played at Home Park in the 1955-56 season. It was not to last. The flow of water into the sinking ship had been stemmed rather than stopped. A lack of money was still a problem and little or no investment was made in the summer of 1955. There were too many amateurs and part-timers on the books, few good enough for the reserves let alone the Second Division of the Football League. Relegation was inevitable and Jack Rowley would now sample life in the third tier of the English League for the first time in 18 years. In that utterly forgettable 1955-56 season Rowley played 16 times and scored on six occasions. The rest of Rowley's time as manager at Home Park has already been covered in earlier chapters. Like many great players before him, as a manager Jack Rowley never quite hit the same heights, though overall, his managerial record bears comparison with many other former United players. In his first job, at Argyle, he suffered relegation in 1955-56, but then led them to promotion in 1958-59. The next season saw him sacked after a run of poor results. But he was soon back in work, joining Oldham Athletic in July 1960. 1960-61 and 1961-62 saw mid-table finishes but he steered them to promotion from the Fourth Division at the end of the 1962-63 season. Amazingly, after a superb 6-1 victory over Hartlepool in the final match of the season in front of 12,283, three days later Boardroom

Jack Rowley, where he was happiest, with his children Susan and John. Judging by the age of his children, this picture probably dates from the early 50s. *Both pictures lent by Susan Watson.*

This picture was taken after Rowley returned to the north. His wife Vi is on the left, with John, Susan, Rowley himself and Linda on the right.

Season 1954-55 and one of the last photographs of Jack Rowley in a Manchester United team. Only he and Allenby Chilton now remained from the great post-war sides as the Busby Babes came to the fore. The original picture is typical of the era—a hand-tinted black and white photograph.
Back Row (l to r):Roger Byrne, Don Gibson, Bill Foulkes, Ray Wood, Jackie Blanchflower and Duncan Edwards
Front Row (l to r): Johnny Berry, Tommy Taylor, Allenby Chilton, Dennis Viollet and Jack Rowley
Picture above lent by Cleeve Carter, the ones below by the Rowley family.

Jack Rowley—the player, the international and the manager

politics led to his dismissal. Ken Bates had just arrived at Oldham, though there is nothing to connect him with the dismissal of the manager! Rowley then had a season abroad with Ajax, taking them to fifth in the table but was keen to rejoin his family in Lancashire. He had a spell out of the game, which gave him chance to help in his thriving shop and Post Office at Shaw, near Oldham. But football lured him back and in January 1966 he was appointed as manager of Wrexham.

He took over a struggling Wrexham but failed to prevent them having to apply for re-election. Once reprieved he set about bringing in some experience in the form of goalkeeper John Schofield, Don Weston and ex Wolves man George Showell. In a dramatic turnaround Wrexham finished a creditable seventh in the Fourth Division. He left Wrexham at Easter, having delayed his departure for Bradford until Wrexham were out of the promotion reckoning. Jack knew all about young footballers. During his time at Wrexham he called the players together during a visit to the ground by his daughter Susan. He introduced her. "This is my daughter." he told them, "if any one of you as much as looks at her the wrong way you will have me to answer to!"

In April 1967 Rowley took over at Bradford (Park Avenue). It was not the best football move he ever made, but he needed to be closer to the business in Oldham. Bradford were in freefall and he could do nothing to get them away from consecutive re-election applications. They finished 23rd and then 24th in his time there, though they were re-elected each time. It clearly wasn't all down to him as 1968-69 they again finished 92nd in the League. In October 1968 he was persuaded to return to Oldham. The side were bottom of the Third Division but he was unable to reverse their fortunes. They were relegated and by the next Christmas they were struggling two points from the foot of the League. Following a run of 5 defeats, including an FA Cup exit to a non-League side, he was dismissed and thereafter never returned to football.

For a short while he took a job with Osram, the light bulb manufacturer. During his time there some 'clever souls' loosened the handlebars on his bike, causing him to fall off and into the road. City fans perhaps! Susan was told afterwards that 'it was just a bit of a laugh.' One cannot help making a parallel with the modern game. Will the present United centre-forward ever need to work at Osram – and would he ride a bike there?

Jack still had his successful business in Shaw and in later years he turned to watching rugby. He was often seen as the guest of local Rugby League club Swinton and he also watched the local Rugby Union team in Shaw. In his customary blunt style he explained that while he was still interested in soccer, he found it convenient to walk down the road to watch the rugby. He felt that he identified with the player's attitudes. He liked the way they took the knocks, shook them off and then had a drink together afterwards.

No matter what Jack Rowley achieved as a footballer and as a manager, he was first and foremost a family man. He was never happier than when he was with his beloved wife Vi and children John, Susan and Linda. He had his grandchildren to dote on; Gillian, Jason, Nicola, Christian, James and Edward. They in turn have provided him with nine great-grandchildren, though Jack did not live to see them all.

His daughter Susan spoke at great length about her father, and 10 years after his death she still had to fight back the tears. She talked of an idyllic and secure childhood. "Dad brought us such love in a protective kind of way." Despite his success and fame she loved how unpretentious he was.

She can just remember him at United, and a visit to the ground to see his peg in the dressing room. She recalls sitting on Tommy Taylor's knee; the player briefly lodged with her maternal grandmother after signing from Barnsley. When Jack was still playing she and her brother would inspect his 'wounds' when her Dad arrived home, extracting an explanation of how each cut and scratch had occurred.

The children loved their time in Plymouth and the lovely house called "Shandon" in Seymour Road, not too far from the BBC. Susan can recall starting school at Hyde Park Juniors on her seventh birthday. While she was there the famous radio puppet Archie Andrews paid a visit. Through his ventriloquist partner he asked the children what they wanted to be when they grew up. One young man volunteered that he wanted to be a dancer – his name was Wayne Sleep. She spoke about wonderful holidays at Challaborough; those holidays of our youth when the sun shone every day. When Jack went away each summer looking for players the family went with him. They stayed with his parents in Wolverhampton, the journey full of games of I-Spy. Dartmoor was a favourite place, though when Jack showed his children the prison – and told them he had played football inside – they were rather scared.

Though Jack, George Taylor, Alex Govan and their wives spent many a Saturday night at the Glenholt Country Club, the family made many friends outside football. The ones Susan particularly remembers are a Jewish family, the Solomons. They were in textiles and she recalls how she enjoyed seeing their traditions and eating their food.

There was also the 'Ackers' family, who lived in a detached house not too far from "Shandon." Susan recalls that Mr Ackers was manager at the Co-op and she remembers that every Christmas a window dresser would come and decorate the house. Gwen and Peter Davies were other friends of the family. "We loved going there because they lived next to a big park. Gwen made her own ginger beer and a single sip would blow your head off." It seems so strange that a famous footballer and manager had such a normal life away from the hurly burly of the professional game. "Shandon" was clearly a happy time in the Rowley family's life. There were two big events every year. Jack was heavily into bonfire night and always tried to make a big thing of it. And at Christmas the sliding doors between the dining room and lounge became the curtains of the Palace Theatre. Each Christmas the Rowley children would put on a family panto for their parents and friends. Unfortunately, as far as Plymouth was concerned, the perfect life did not last.

When in March 1960 he lost his job there were no secrets in the Rowley household. He sat the children down to explain to them that Daddy no longer had a job and things would be a little bit tight. Susan, brother John and little sister Linda left the room, returning with their piggy-banks. The shame is that while those three kids were trying to help the family budget, most Argyle fans were burying their head in the *Western Evening Herald,* to see who was on the short-list to take over! Most would not have given Jack the family man a single thought.

His children and grandchildren speak with one voice. This was a man they loved dearly. It would seem that he watered down his own mother's rather Victorian intolerance, replacing it with a strict but fair code of conduct. Whatever he did, it must have been successful. It is now 10 years since he passed away, but Susan still finds it difficult to speak about him without a tear or two.

An e-mail exchange with his granddaughter Nicola embellishes the picture her mother Susan paints. Nicola and her brother Christian spent a lot of time with Jack and Vi, including most school holidays. She wrote *"My Grandfather was the best any child could have asked for, a patient, caring man who always had time for each and every grandchild. My brother and I in particular spent a lot of time around him at his home in Shaw (Oldham), as my parents were divorced and my Grandparents played a very big part in bringing us up.*

"My Grandad was a very modest man and rarely talked about his time as a footballer; he would only ever talk about it to us when we asked him about it. Even then he played down his importance. Grandad was always very keen to see what the local boys could do on the field. He would spend many hours watching the local football and, in particular, the local rugby team, playing on the local playing fields. A very keen gardener, he spent many hours in his own garden or in the greenhouse, growing fruit and vegetables for the family, which I would pinch out of the garden, the moment his back was turned. He knew full well who it was, but he never chastised me. At school, people would come up to us and ask if it was true that my Granddad was Jack Rowley, and that he played at Manchester United, managed Plymouth Argyle, Ajax, Oldham Athletic etc. etc.. At the time it meant very little to me. He was just my Granddad, a man I loved very dearly and was very proud of; for being the man he was and not the footballer he had been. My children have spent many hours asking about him and my mum and I have spent many hours reciting tales of his life."

Not only was this man a great footballer, he was someone who fought for his country and he was a decent football manager. More importantly, he was a great man away from all that. John (Jack) Frederick Rowley was born in Wolverhampton on 7 October 1918. Many Manchester United web-sites show his year of birth as 1920, but his family and his Army record confirm that it was 1918. Suffering from Alzheimer's Disease, he died in Ashton in Lancashire on 27 June 1998, just over four months short of his 80th birthday.

He passed away the day after England had beaten Colombia 2-0 in their final group match in Lens. Son John and daughters Susan and Linda had been with him in the nursing home. They had got him a World Cup wall chart and kept it updated, despite the fact that he did not always understand. Susan recalls them telling him that England were safely through. Despite being in the grip of that terrible disease, on that occasion he seemed to be aware that he could now safely depart. Clearly it was a sad time for the family. Around the time of her Dad's death Susan remembers seeing Sir Alex Ferguson on television, as a World Cup summariser in France. The next time she saw him was at her Dad's funeral. He had interrupted his television work to fly back to Manchester. He returned to France immediately afterwards.

Sir Alex was well qualified to recognise greatness when he saw it. 43 years had elapsed since Jack Rowley had last kicked a ball for United. Despite the galaxy of stars that had trodden the Old Trafford turf in the meantime, United have never forgotten one of their finest sons.

Plymouth Argyle should similarly treasure his memory.

Jack and daughter Susan on a day out to a famous landmark. There are not too many visitors to the Coronation Street set who are more famous than the cast they are visiting. Jack Rowley is one exception.

Picture lent by Susan Watson

George Taylor (with ball) as he is best remembered, instructing the players. From right to left are Wilf Carter, Harry Penk, Jimmy Gauld, Reg Wyatt, Peter Anderson, Geoff Barnsley , George Baker. The number 3 was not recognised. The photo was probably taken prior to the start of the 1958-59 season but it could have been taken any time after October 1957 when Jimmy Gauld signed.

George Taylor the player, photographed not long after he joined the club in 1948 from Aberdeen. He had been instrumental in bringing the first major trophies to Pittodrie before moving west four days prior to the start of the 1948-49 season.

Both pictures courtesy George Taylor's daughter Margaret Callan

CHAPTER EIGHT

TRAINER GEORGE TAYLOR

No story concerning post-war events at Plymouth Argyle could be complete without mention of George Taylor. He served the club from August 1948 until February 1966. He was signed as a player in 1948, before becoming an assistant trainer. He went on to become head trainer. In addition to the trainer roles he was at various times a scout, caretaker manager and, for a short period, co-manager of the first team with Neil Dougall. He finally left the club in March 1966, quite shattered by his sacking.

George was born on 9 June 1913 in the village of King Edward, Banffshire (now Aberdeenshire) on the north east coast of Scotland. After playing as a centre-forward for shipyard team Hall Russells (the same junior side as Jimmy Gauld was to play for some years later), in 1937 Taylor signed as a professional for Aberdeen. At 24 he was late coming to the professional ranks. He made his Dons' debut in a 1-0 defeat at Queen of the South towards the end of the 1937-38 season. He had one more full season prior to the outbreak of World War II. In October 1944 he was selected as travelling reserve to the Scotland side to play England at Wembley. His favoured left-half berth was occupied by Matt Busby, still a year away from becoming Manchester United's manager. With Scotland losing 6-2 George may well have been glad to have missed it! He was to be a reserve for three further internationals. Although he never made it into the full international side being so close was a sign of how much ability he had.

11 May 1946 was Southern League Cup Final day in Scotland and Aberdeen had fought their way to a Hampden Park final tie with Glasgow Rangers. It was to be one of the greatest days of George Taylor's life. Entering the final minute, with the score locked at two apiece, the 135,000 crowd prepared to savour another half an hour of exciting end to end football. Outside right Alec Riddie launched one final Aberdeen attack. His cross was only half cleared and George Taylor pounced to blast the ball home off a post. Aberdeen's forty year wait for their first trophy was over. The thousands of Aberdeen supporters roared their approval, many recognising the fact that Taylor was the only north-easterner in their side. In addition to the Aberdeen Cup success, they finished the 1945-46 season in third place in the Scottish First Division.

At the end of the following season, when the Dons again finished third in the League, they made two further visits to Hampden. On 5 April 1947 they appeared in the Scottish League Cup Final but were hammered 4-0 by Rangers. Electing to kick against a gale force wind they were three down at half-time and never recovered. A fortnight later they were back in Glasgow for the Scottish FA Cup Final , winning 2-1 against Hibernian. Football is such a great leveller. Unlike the previous year's last minute glory, against the Easter Road side George experienced first minute disaster. Because of injuries he had to play at left back, an unaccustomed role. Early in the game he tried to find goalie George Johnstone with a back-pass. It slipped past the keeper, allowing Hibs' John Cuthbertson to nip in and score. Fortunately, goals from Hamilton and Williams ensured the Cup went north to Aberdeen.

The 1947-48 season was a less successful campaign for the Pittodrie club. Four days before the start of the 1948-49 campaign Aberdeen supporters were shocked to find that George Taylor, by now their captain, had been lured south to join Plymouth Argyle. After 82 appearances and six goals he was transferring from the most northerly British professional club to the most southerly.

He played in roughly half of Argyle's first team games in the 1948-49 term, with the side only just avoiding relegation. The next season proved worse and they slipped into the Third Division (South). His first team days were over, after sustaining a knee injury in a scoreless draw at home to Blackburn Rovers on 18 February 1950.

In the summer of 1950 he was appointed assistant trainer. In addition to his 48 first team appearances he had played a further 23 times for the reserves, several of them after the knee injury that prevented further appearances for the chiefs. George had clearly been planning for some years to stay in the game. When he joined Argyle he was two years into a three year chiropody and physiotherapy course at the Glasgow Foot Hospital. He completed that course in Plymouth. He also attended every conference he could on fitness training and the treatment of injuries. Each summer found him at Lilleshall increasing his knowledge of the trainer's job. It is clear that he loved meeting up with other managers and coaches, swapping ideas, tactical viewpoints as well as the latest developments for treating injuries.

It should be remembered that when George Taylor held the post of Head Trainer in 1958-59 his tasks encompassed almost all of what Kevin Summerfield, John Blackley and Paul Maxwell do today. Until Malcolm Allison arrived at Home Park in 1964 Argyle managers had rarely been seen on the training ground. During the 1958-59 promotion campaign, his workload was increased when his good friend, Assistant Trainer George Reed, tragically died of a heart-attack while returning from a scouting mission. It was some months before Neil Dougall took up that appointment full-time.

During the research for *Thanks for the Memory* I asked respected former Argyle skipper John Newman how he rated George Taylor's training. Newman had served under several great managers before coming to the south west and after leaving Home Park had held several managerial roles himself. He was quick to pay tribute to Taylor. "George Taylor put on some very well structured and interesting sessions. For that time they were as good as anything else I had seen." The views of the 1958-59 group of players varied. Many respected George but one or two of the younger ones found him to be a hard taskmaster. All agreed that he knew his stuff when it came to fitness training.

For my part, as a ten year old autograph hunter I was scared to death of

George! He had that air of a Drill Sergeant. However, looking back, I think it was a parental thing – when he shooed us away it was because he wanted us out of earshot when he was about deliver one his time honoured bollockings! In the 1950s adults rarely, if ever, swore in front of children.

George Taylor served seven different managers in his 16 years on the training staff. Often, when the manager left, he would apply for the post. Indeed, when Jimmy Rae was sacked in 1955 he was one of six people interviewed for the post, prior to Jack Rowley being appointed. It is to his eternal credit that he then stayed and worked for Jack, often impressing him with his knowledge and skill on the training ground and in the treatment room. .

When George Taylor was dismissed in February 1966, for some reason the club chose to release a statement which indicated that he was "sacked for the future good of Argyle". He was justifiably embittered by such an epitaph for 18 years loyal service and hard work. At the beginning of March he wrote a series of articles for the *Sunday Independent*, recalling some of the characters of his time at Home Park and the trials and tribulations of his time there.

Taylor's major point was that he felt Plymouth Argyle had been badly served by the constant publicity about off the field events. By the time he left the club there had been almost eight years of constant Boardroom wrangling, including the well-documented 'Blindell years'. He made it very clear that he felt that the blame for Argyle not having reached the First Division lay more with some of the Boards he served, rather than with the managers he worked for. He wrote that he had lost count of the number of managers who arrived with high hopes and bright ideas, but eventually floundered due to interference and indecision from above.

He was, for instance, part of the backroom team that nearly led Argyle into the top tier. They finished fourth in 1952-53, a season after running away with the Third Division title. Taylor is convinced that had they bought at Christmas 1952 the team would have been promoted. He wrote, "There was an inherent weakness in that side, which worsened during as the season progressed". Whilst it looks to the layman that Taylor is right, in the interest of fairness, it could be that in that Jimmy Rae era, perhaps George was not told how bad the finances were?

His articles in the *Sunday Independent* said very little about Jack Rowley's tenure, simply describing him as "a very down to earth man with the fiercest will to win I ever saw". He suggested that perhaps Rowley suffered as much as most from Boardroom interference, something of a surprise when Rowley developed a reputation for being too blunt with some of his employers.

When Rowley was sacked Taylor and Neil Dougall were handed the job on a joint basis. They successfully steered the club away from relegation and started very well in the 1960-61 season. It was re-wind to 1952 for Taylor, for at Christmas he and Dougall urged the Board to make funds available. The only signing made by the twosome thus far was experienced Leicester goalkeeper Dave Maclaren. Taylor's view is that apart from Welsh international Bill Shortt, the Scotsman was (at that time) the club's best post-war goalkeeper. Both Dougall and Taylor was certain that two more decent players could see the team win promotion.

Former Argyle man Jimmy Buist had spotted a couple of young players at East Stirling and wrote to Taylor recommending them. George Robertson's father, himself a former pro, lived in Stirling and was sent to run the rule over the pair. He endorsed Buist's view, urging Argyle to act quickly. The Board refused, and within a year Chelsea paid £10,000 for the duo – Eddie McCreadie and Tommy Knox! McCreadie went on to become a great player at Stamford Bridge as well as winning international honours. Knox, who also had spells at Newcastle, Third Lanark, Mansfield and Northampton, flattered to deceive and never really fulfilled his undoubted talent. But at £10,000 for the two, it was a justifiable gamble.

Although they were reasonably successful on the field, it is clear from Taylor's story that neither he nor Dougall enjoyed the interface with the Board. Any problems with players, be it an amateur, part-timer or professional, had to go before the Board. Taylor was often admonished for protesting that these were decisions for football men and not for the directors. The worst single incident he described was when players George Kirkby and Jimmy McAnearney were approached by a Board member, without the knowledge of Dougall and Taylor, and asked to write down all the training methods used when they were with Sheffield Wednesday. Taylor was beside himself with anger and let the Board know exactly how he felt.

The partnership also grew tired of Monday night Board Meetings, privately referring to them as 'music night'. It seems that it was demanded of them that they name the team for the following Saturday. "Despite the stupidity of it you weren't allowed to argue with them," wrote Taylor. "It was as daft as it was impossible. Neil and I had not had a proper chance to analyse the previous game and we didn't know what injuries would interrupt our plans." George made it clear that whilst he had no time for most of the Board, he greatly admired Callington solicitor Peter Skinnard – "Mr Skinnard was the only one with the guts to stand up to Blindell. He often took the side of me and Neil". Eventually the Board decided to appoint a new manager and towards the very end of the 60-61 term Vic Buckingham was appointed. He stayed only long enough to prepare the retained list before accepting a post with Sheffield Wednesday.

George tells one amusing story, almost against himself. "I felt that with Jack Rowley gone I was having to pick the team, train the lads and administer treatment of injuries, it was time I had a pay rise. I asked to see the Board and they listened intently. I was asked to go outside for a while before being called back in." The Chairman explained that for the partnership with Neil to work properly we must be on an equal footing. "I stayed on 20 quid a week and they upped Neil's money from £15 to the same as mine!"

The Board then chose to go with Neil Dougall as manager and Taylor returned to his trainer's role. Dougall did not last long in the manager's chair – it simply wasn't for him - and Ellis Stuttard came in. The team's form was transformed and they finished a creditable fifth in 61-62 and 11th in 62-63. But 1963-64 was a disaster for Stuttard and Andy Beattie was brought in, with Argyle looking like certainties for relegation.

Although he greatly admired Rae, the man who gave him his first non-playing role, it is clear that the Argyle manager George Taylor most admired was Andy Beattie. The Scot replaced Stuttard for the remainder of the 63-64 season and gradually steered the club away from trouble. Taylor recalled, "Just before he arrived I had been made chief scout. "It wasn't a job I wanted and within a day of arriving he had appointed me as reserve team manager. "We finished second in what was a strong Football Combination League."

George always referred to the manager as 'Mr Beattie.' Strange really – George was actually a couple of months older than Beattie. Their close bond maybe explained by the fact that Beattie was born in Kilmore, Aberdeenshire, just 30 miles from the village of King Edward where George Taylor was brought up. "He used to sit down with the staff – me, Pat Jones and Neil Dougall – every morning and over a cup of tea would discuss the forthcoming day's work. He would then leave us to it. His success was that simple." Taylor expressed the view that Beattie's departure in June 1964 was a great blow for the club on and off the field. "He seemed to be able to unite all the warring factions in the club and that showed in results on the field. He was a remarkable man."   Looking back it seems significant that Beattie never sought to dispense with the 'caretaker' tag. It was as if he was some kind of relegation avoidance consultant who came in, did the job in hand and then moved on.

In view of the apparent difference in their life styles, it is perhaps surprising that Taylor rated Beattie's successor Malcolm Allison very highly. In his *Independent* memoirs he was unreserved in his praise for Argyle's first 'tracksuit manager'. Despite Allison attracting a reputation for champagne, cigars and women Taylor saw him as the hardest working manager Argyle had in his time. "If Malcolm had a fault, it was that he pursued tactics and team plans which were not compatible with the talent we had." That the two men gelled so very well confirms just how forward-looking George Taylor was. Allison's playing career was littered with clashes with managers who were not prepared to embrace a more modern approach. He would not have tolerated a man who was 'old football'.

Significantly, Taylor's articles completely ignored the period Derek Ufton was in charge. It was during Ufton's unsuccessful tenure that George was dismissed. After deciding to turn his back on the game George and his wife took a pub, the Penguin in Ashford Crescent. He proved to be a popular landlord but it wasn't what he wanted to do. He then developed Parkinsons' Disease and eventually died after a bout of pneumonia.

When paying tribute to or discussing other managers or coaches Harry Redknapp often uses the term - "He is a proper football man". It is difficult to think of a better accolade for George Taylor, surely one of the finest servants Plymouth Argyle has ever had. He was indeed a proper football man.

George Taylor (second right) receives the hearty congratulations of his Aberdeen team mates after his last minute winner at Hampden Park. *Lent by Margaret Callan*

A rueful George Taylor sits at home after his surprise dismissal in 1966. Few can have worked harder for the good of Plymouth Argyle. He was with the club for 18 years. *Courtesy of the Sunday Independent*

Having been born in 1913 George Taylor survived two World Wars. In the second he was a member of the Home Guard.

He was a bricklayer by trade and he was excused military service as many jobs in the construction industry were considered 'Reserved Occupations.'

A SUPPORTER'S STORY
Jeremy Wills

Eight year old Jeremy Wills was excited every time he went to Home Park. Boarding the train at Okehampton, it would cross Dartmoor passing through places like Bridestowe, Lydford and Brentor before calling at Bere Ferrers. There Jeremy felt the excitement really started to mount, with many people joining the train bedecked in their team's colours. After the short ride to St Budeaux (Victoria Road) it was up the ramp to catchy the waiting Football Special to the ground.

In an e-mail Jeremy recalled a match against Newport County on 8 November 1958, a day that was to become a very special for him. *"Like so many supporters, Dad and I had our usual match-day rituals. After picking up our Ivor Dewdney pasty we would buy a programme, which cost 3d (1½p). In those days the team printed in the programme was normally the team that ran out onto the pitch, so we eagerly checked who was playing. First name to look for was the legendary Wilf Carter – as long as he was playing I was happy! Next was to buy a match ball ticket – would it be my lucky day THIS time? I sat in Row D seat number two. The cost then was 5/-(25p). I know because I've still got the ticket! There was no pre-match warming up but time dulls the memory and I don't remember much about the game, other than we won 3-2 with goals from George Baker and two from Jimmy Gauld. I remember Dad telling me that County had a good player in Alf Sherwood, who had been Welsh international captain. My main memory surrounds the announcement of the winning ticket for the match ball. I couldn't believe it! I'd won a football that Wilf Carter had kicked. Believe you me, that's exactly my first thought! I've still got the ball and no it wasn't one with the lace on it! Post match meant catching the 'Football Special' bus into town for a look around Woolworths – always a treat for an Okehampton boy! We would look around the shops until the Football Herald Special came out. We'd wait outside Lawson's, then next to the Western Morning News in New George Street. The street seller there got first delivery from the speeding vans coming out of Harmsworth House. Then we made our way back towards North Road station but not before calling into a little café, whose name I've forgotten, for a tea of sausage, eggs and chips – lovely!"*

Jeremy at Okehampton station in 2008 to celebrate the 50th anniversary of winning his prized match ball.

Photo sent in by Jeremy Wills

Wilf Carter, Plymouth Argyle's highest post-war scorer and a true legend, outside the main stand at Home Park in 1958. In the inset, taken during my visit to his home in February 2008, he looks at a team photo taken at the end of the successful 1958-59 season.
Old photo courtesy Cleeve Carter. Inset by the author.

CHAPTER NINE

WILF CARTER

Wilf Carter arrived at Home Park on 28 May 1957, shortly after the curtain had come down on Argyle's 30th season in the Football League. It had ended with their worst placing since they were admitted to the competition in 1920. The 23 year old had been on the West Bromwich Albion transfer list for a while. He made his debut at 17, in a First Division game at Fulham and scored in his second against Chelsea. He played 54 League games for the Midlands club, scoring 12 goals. An added attraction when signing Carter was that he had already completed his National Service. Professional footballers were not exempt, unless they had a medical condition which would affect their suitability for military service. As far as the clubs were concerned it was a necessary evil; something they understood had to be done, but a frustration when trying to work out tactics, travel plans and fitness regimes.

Trooper Carter had been in the 12th Royal Lancers, attached to the 67th Training Regiment RAC based at Carlisle. His conscription had run from 1952 to 1954, a vital time in his career as a professional footballer. It is impossible to be sure, but it may have been that interruption which prevented him from becoming a fixture in the West Bromwich first team. Britain's military was engaged in Kenya where the Mau-Mau terrorists were keeping the army fully occupied. When he received a posting notice to Kenya in 1953, although he came to make a reputation as a sharpshooter on the football field, Wilf wasn't so keen to employ his marksman skills against the African dissidents. His reluctance did not stem from fear - far from it. Rather he was concerned that his football activity would be severely curtailed, both for his unit and his professional club. It was not unusual for footballers to seek rescinding orders. But Wilf had a problem – the regimental sergeant major. Warrant Officer Hilary had an absolute hatred for footballers and all things associated with the round ball game! Fortunately, Captain Clark, the depot Adjutant, had a soft spot for Wilf. Eventually a sensible compromise between Clark and the management team at West Brom led to him remaining in Carlisle.

Captain Clark had long wanted Wilf Carter to take charge of training and lead the depot football team. Indeed, to give the young man some authority he had him promoted to Lance Corporal. It was a job Wilf took to well, and one where he helped shape the destiny of the 1966 World Cup! Wilf smiles as he recalls the lanky, tousle-haired young lad who pitched up for a practice match, probably sometime in 1953. "Where do you play, son?" Wilf enquired. "I'm a centre-forward" the kid replied, "and I am on Leeds United's books." After the game Wilf sought out the newcomer. "Look son," he said, "there is no kind way I can put this. As long as your arse points downwards you will never be a centre-forward. But I reckon you may have half a chance at centre-half." Laughing, Wilf expresses regret that neither Don Revie nor Sir Alf Ramsey ever acknowledged his important input to Jack Charlton's career!

On 4 March 1961 Jack Charlton and Carter met again, when Argyle beat Leeds United 3-1 in a Second Division fixture at Home Park. It was an afternoon of contrasting fortunes for the two former soldiers. Carter hit a hat-trick while Charlton ended up as a passenger on the right wing, his right arm strapped inside his shirt. A little over five years later Wilf would be plying his trade at Bath while Charlton was winning the World Cup. As Jimmy Greaves so famously said "It's a funny old game".

But to return to Wilf Carter's arrival at Home Park. With their first re-cruit able to fully concentrate on football, the new Argyle Board hoped that their first signing would be a success. There is success, and there is great success. Many players get to the threshold of the door marked "True Legend". Few gain admittance to that special place, where qualifying stan-dards are extreme. In the era the young Carter joined the Argyle payroll, the number of past players with that iconic standing probably numbered no more than three or four.

First amongst them was the late, great Sammy Black, a true 24 carat legend. With 491 games and 185 goals to his credit, the quiet Scottish left winger is still a yardstick for greatness today. That is an opinion that en-dures 74 years after he played his last game. Few now remain who actu-ally saw him play; to that exclusive group he is still the best forward ever to grace Home Park.

Jack "Jumbo" Chisolm is another assured of life-long adoration by the Argyle faithful. In his case, to say he was "large than life" seems almost an understatement. Braveness personified, the former Sheffield United and Tottenham man was an inspirational leader; the man who led Argyle to their highest ever league position, fourth in the 1952-53 Second Division. That was immediately after he had captained them to fourth (1950-51) and first (1951-52) in the Third Division (South). In the 20s Moses Russell was a legend, a teak hard man who won 23 Welsh caps.

Doubtless each supporter could find six other names to add to the list. Everyone has their special favourite, but there is an intangible 'something' which separates the very good from the very special. That indefinable 'it' factor that only very, very few are blessed with. Little did we know that in exchange for just £2,500, the young man from West Bromwich would quickly give notice that he was destined to be extra special; a player who would *never* be forgotten by those who saw him. To the discerning watcher, the signs were there. *Spectator* felt at the time Wilf signed, that his First Division record (12 goals in 54) was unspectacular. However, it must be remembered that at least a quarter of his first team appearances came at full back. But, as ever, the *Western Independent* man presented a wise and balanced argument, commenting that Carter's tally of 76 goals in 126 reserves games, in the very strong Central League, was extremely impressive. 0.6 goals per game was some indication of his quality.

It should be remembered that several Central League sides were packed with high quality players. For Football League fixtures, with clubs only selecting eleven, plus a twelfth man who was cover for last minute injuries or illness, there were good players available to play for the reserves. This meant that some Central League sides would often field two or three internationals. With that kind of scoring record, in that kind of company, it is little wonder that Lincoln City, Derby County, Shrewsbury Town, Swindon Town, Port Vale and Walsall had all been taking an interest in him. Each of those clubs was closer than Plymouth to the player's Midlands base, but luckily an all expenses paid trip to Devon clinched the deal.

After meeting Chairman Ron Blindell at Home Park, shortly before a four hour Board meeting, Wilf and Margaret were given a tour of the city, and a look at potential accommodation. They arrived back at the ground just as the meeting broke up, with Margaret pronouncing that she was "crazy about Plymouth. "I think it's a wonderful place." Wilf signed there and then. It was a big move for the player and his young family. Wilf had travelled on football and military duty. But as a family, they had rarely if ever gone far from their Black Country roots. 51 years after his own first visit to Plymouth, son Cleeve can still recall the wonderment of seeing the sea for the first time. His little sister Helen shared his excitement.

Other factors, like the Plymouth sunshine and the long-standing friendship between managers Jack Rowley and Vic Buckingham, played a part, but nothing was more important than the fact that Margaret Carter saw Plymouth as a wonderful place to bring up her family. It was a feeling she never lost. The club owned several houses in those days, houses which were let to the players. In 1957, renting was more traditional than ownership. Club houses were fairly customary throughout professional football. Players could quickly move their family to the new location, making the move much less stressful for all concerned.

The Carter family were allocated a pleasant house in Langhill Road, Peverell and settled in very quickly. They still have fond memories of their neighbours, Mr and Mrs Crispin and, more than 50 years after the move, Margaret recalls that the Crispins "were like family to us, lovely, lovely people. The kids was always round there." The family loved Plymouth, walking on the Hoe, exploring Dartmoor and visiting the shiny new City Centre. They liked the Cinema, swimming at Tinside and Central Park was right on their doorstep. Daughter Karen was born after they came to the city.

Wilf recalls that, "the Director Mr Crookes had us all round to tea, and he would let us have a caravan at Challaborough in the summer. "He was a nice man – even left a shilling for us to put in the electric!" Margaret Carter hoped that they would never have to leave. "But football is not like that. "When it was time to go it was time to go, we had no real say in the matter." Wilf was quick to add that "We loved Plymouth and we loved the people there".Off the field he was a quiet family man, enjoying the occasional game of snooker at the Hyde Park Social Club or a visit to the greyhounds at Pennycross Stadium. Once on a football pitch he was an extrovert, focused and confident in his ability to score from anywhere around the penalty area. Whilst he was no giant, he was solidly built. Athletic and good looking, he quickly became the favourite of almost every supporter. 50 years on, Wilf Carter is still revered. Jack Wild, a long term supporter now exiled in Norwich, wrote, "You can keep your Peles, Maradonas and

Cruyffs. Wilf was the best I ever saw!!" A slight exaggeration perhaps, but a testament to the great admiration he earned from those who saw him. Most of the other players interviewed for this book named him as the best player during their time at Argyle. Dozens of fans, answering appeals for their memories of the 1958-59 promotion season, picked Wilf as their favourite.

The manager, Jack Rowley, knew a thing or two about scoring goals. He clearly reckoned that Carter was the man to fire Argyle back to Division Two. What a shrewd judge he was! Argyle had seriously flirted with re-election in the 1956-57 season. Rowley, who had now dropped the "player" tag, was free to concentrate on team management not a moment too soon. With a new, forward thinking Chairman, a buying policy had been agreed. Rowley would only pursue players with previous experience in the First Division. Carter was the first to arrive under the new criteria.

Born in Wednesbury, Staffordshire, in 1933, Wilf was the youngest of six children. His father died at 42, when Wilf was just four years old. Whilst he recalls a happy childhood, the poverty was unrelenting. He remains full of admiration for his mother; our conversation evoked memories of how she worked and worked to provide for her family at a time when there was no Welfare State. In the War she toiled at a munitions factory close to their home. Amongst his childhood recollections is climbing the stairs at the side of a Billiard Hall in Church Street, Wednesbury. He remembers the glow in the sky over Birmingham, barrage balloons, bombers, continuous anti-aircraft fire and hunting for shrapnel – "some of it still hot!"

Wilf remains grateful to Joseph Brighton, a teacher at St Bartholomew's Secondary Modern who recognised and encouraged his football talent. He was selected for the South East Staffordshire under 15s, a side that also included Norman Deeley and George Showell, who made it to the very top with Wolves, and Gordon Wills who turned professional with Leicester City. For four of an eleven strong under 15's side to make it as professionals is a testament to the strength of Midlands football at that time. Success at representative level led to Wilf joining West Bromwich on leaving school in 1949. As was the way then, he first combined his football education with an office job at the club, as well as sweeping the stands and cleaning first team players' boots. He was also detailed to help groundsman Harry Powell, who also offered coaching advice.

Wilf signed as a full-time professional in 1951. During his time at the Hawthorns he regards himself as so fortunate to come under the influence of the late Billy 'WG' Richardson, as well as trainers AG Fitton and Harry Ashley. This was one of the best periods in the history of the Midlands outfit. Amongst Carter's contemporaries at the club was a young full back called Donald Howe. He went on to play at international level, eventually moving to London to join Arsenal. He turned out to be better working as a coach or as an assistant manager. Until recently he still wrote an excellent weekly tactical analysis in the *Daily Telegraph*.

Another player on the Albion staff was destined for long and glittering career in management. When Bobby Robson came from Fulham in March

WEST BROMWICH ALBION : Back row — Millard, Williams, Dudley, Barlow, Sanders, Brookes, Kennedy. Front row — Griffin, Carter, Allen, Nicholls, Lee and mascot John Tremans.

A West Brom team photo from circa 1955, with Wilf Carter second from the left in the front row. To his right, behind the mascot John Tremans, is the great Ronnie Allen Like the one above, many pictures from the 40s and 50s were given a curious part photo/part painting look by hand tinting. *Picture lent by Sam Bailey*

1956 for a club record £25,000, he was already an England regular. Despite the presence of Howe and Robson, Carter recalls that the driving force, and the man he thinks was the best he ever played with, was wing-half Ray Barlow. Barlow was one of the unlucky ones to feature in that infamous 1950 World Cup defeat to the USA. The stigma stuck and he rarely represented his country again. Albion also had an international centre-forward, Ronnie Allen "who was a great help to me," and in 1954-55 was the First Division's leading scorer. In 1953, they signed the promising young striker Derek Kevan from Bradford. The competition for forward places got more intense. Allen was a shoo-in every week, with the other place in attack often resting between Carter and Kevan. Kevan eventually scored 157 goals in 262 matches for Albion, as well as another 8 goals in 13 outings for England. At the 1958 World Cup in Sweden Kevan was controversially chosen ahead of Bobby Charlton for each of the group games and the play-off against Russia.

Along with Howe, Wilf Carter was a travelling reserve for their 1954 FA Cup Final side. There were no substitutes at that time, but clubs took a 12th man to every game, with additional cover for a big occasion. Indeed, in the 1953-54 season, Albion came close to being the first side in the 20th century to achieve the League and Cup 'double'. After a poor run right at the end, they finished second in the First Division, four points behind the

The *Sunday Independent* of 2 June 1957 used this early picture of Wilf Carter when reporting the news of his signing.
Photo courtesy of the Sunday Independent

Wolves. They then went to Wembley and beat Preston 3-2 in the FA Cup Final. If Carter was only on the fringes of a team that good, it was not a reflection of any lack of quality on his part.

Wilf would not have left West Brom by choice. He makes no secret that he had little time for the manager Vic Buckingham, who towards the end of Wilf's time at the Hawthorns was trying to school him as a left back. Indeed, in his last season there he had a run of 10 League and Cup games at full back and Albion wanted him to stay and play there. But he didn't feel that was for him – he simply lived to see that ball hit the back of the net and nothing else in the game gave him such pleasure. He wanted to be in someone's forward line, either at inside forward or in the centre forward role. Indeed, he signed off from the Hawthorns by scoring five for the A' team in a Midland Combination fixture against Lockheeds (Leamington).

At Home Park Carter made an instant impact, hitting 26 league goals in 44 games, starting with a brace against Aldershot on Saturday, 31 August 1957 in the third game of the season. His first Argyle hat-trick came in a 5-2 FA Cup victory over Dorchester Town. The following Saturday, he repeated the feat with another three against Coventry City in a Third Division (South) game. As the New Year dawned, in front of 38,129 he scored against First Division Newcastle United in the third round of the FA Cup. The disappointing aspect was that goals from the Magpies' Eastham (2), White (3) and Mitchell rather

Future England keeper Ron Springett dives at Carter's feet in a 1957-58 fixture at QPR. Note that the home side played in white shirts and not their traditional hoops.
Photo from the Colin Parsons collection

Carter slots home yet another penalty. He hit the target with 24 out of 27 attempts, with two of his failures coming in a single game against Bournemouth and Boscombe Athletic on 27 September 1958.
Photograph courtesy of the Sunday Independent

spoiled the party for the home supporters. His third hat-trick of the season came in a 3-1 home win against Queens Park Rangers. It was the start of a 19 match run which brought him 20 goals. In goal for QPR was Ron Springett. Not too long afterwards, after joining Sheffield Wednesday, Springett had a brief spell as England goalkeeper. As well as his 32 goals, Carter had impressed with his all round hard work. That season's total goal tally for the team was 67 in 46 matches. Neil Langman, who left for Colchester quite early in the season, was next top scorer with nine.

As he made his name, Wilf Carter became a marked man, literally. His legs still bear the scars today. It must be remembered that the tackle from behind, with the ball often only a minor distraction, was 30 years from being outlawed. Sending offs were rare indeed, with the offence generally something that would now attract a charge of GBH. The 1958-59 season has been covered extensively elsewhere in this book. In summary, Wilf contributed another 22 League goals and three more in the FA Cup. It meant that after two seasons he had contributed 57 League and Cup goals, a good return by anyone's standards. During October 1958 he notched his first (and only) hat-trick on an away ground, in a 4-1 victory at Mansfield.

With Jimmy Gauld weighing in with 21, the 1958-59 pairing looked to be one of the best partnerships the club had ever had. But all was not well beneath the seemingly united surface. As the promotion challenge faltered, in a *Western Evening Herald* column on 4 April 1959, Argyle columnist *Pilgrim* broke the news that at various times during the season, both Wilf Carter and Jimmy Gauld had felt their futures lay elsewhere. He wrote that Carter had been involved in a showdown meeting with the manager, because he felt he was not getting the service he wanted. Gauld had been outstanding for most of the season, but was struggling by Easter. He had deservedly taken a lot of the limelight. But *Pilgrim* revealed that Gauld had felt that his style was not suiting the team, but that he could not change at this stage of his career.

This was shocking news to many supporters, who felt they had by far the best two attacking inside forwards in the lower Divisions. Perhaps Carter, who had started to fall below the phenomenal standards he set in his first season, felt there wasn't room for both of them. Fortunately, they went on to win the League and, temporarily, all was well. Gauld, however, moved on the following summer. He never stayed anywhere for long. Wilf Carter was about to team up with George Kirby, a former team mate of Gauld's at Everton. What an entertaining partnership that turned out to be!

If some thought that Wilf Carter had found his level in the third tier of English football, he was to prove them wrong. Argyle struggled at the wrong end of the table in both 1959-60 and 1960-61. It is the mark of a very good player to score regularly when the team is battling at the wrong end of the table. He continued to do so after promotion, bagging 22 in the first season up, and followed that with a haul of 24. Four seasons gone and he had passed the 100 mark.

On Boxing Day 1960, Argyle journeyed to the Valley and lost 6-4. The

Wilf terrorised defences throughout his time at Home Park. On this occasion Bristol Rovers have to be alert.

reverse fixture was at Home Park the next day. The players returned from London, but came only as far as Totnes. They spent the night there, in Chairman Ron Blindell's Seymour Hotel. Over dinner that night, Blindell spent much of the time trying to persuade joint managers Neil Dougall and George Taylor that Carter should be dropped. The Chairman thought the player had lost his edge, and was no longer worth his place. Taylor, in particular, was having none of it. An injury to George Kirby made it slightly easier to outface the Chairman. However, Taylor maintained in his 1966 memoirs, published in the *Western Independent*, that Carter would have played anyway.

Wilf Carter was already a special favourite. If he wanted to make himself even more of a hero, then he found the perfect way on 27 December 1960. No one who was there will ever forget it. 23,335 saw Wilf find the net on five occasions in a 6-4 victory, the complete reversal of the day before. He remains the first and only man to score five in a match for Plymouth Argyle. Carter's haul included a 33 minute hat-trick, a header just before half time and a penalty in the second half. It was the stuff of dreams. Supporters who had seen both games were said to be giddy. Others left the ground wondering if they could believe what they had just seen. It was a sensational day in what proved to be an ordinary season.

Carter set other records which still stand. His 16 career goals against Charlton Athletic (15 for Argyle and one for West Bromwich) is still a record. Apart from the five goal haul, in season 1959-60 there had been another 6-4 game between the two teams, with Carter getting a hat-trick. In November 1962 he repeated the dose in a 6-1 home success. It is now 46 years since he scored his last goal against them. Despite the galaxy of stars who have since played against Charlton, no one has yet been able to score more times against the south London club.

Carter and Kirby played up front together on nearly 90 occasions. Wilf is of the opinion that George's robust style sometimes cost the team goals. "Don't get me wrong," he said, "George was a smashing bloke and a good friend. But very often his aggressive style led to free-kicks against us when we could have scored". Perhaps Wilf was right to say in 1959, 'Give me my head and I'll get you more goals'. He played in an era when there were no lone centre-forwards, no five in midfield; these formations were still a few years away. One can only contemplate how good he might have been in that role?

In the entire history of the club, only the great Sammy Black has scored more goals than Wilf Carter. Carter's 148 from 274 appearances narrowly beats Tommy Tynan's 144 in 308 outings. Carter hit another 20 in 28 Football Combination games. The elegant Maurice Tadman, a hero in the early 50s, managed 113 in 215 games (including four in each of two consecutive games in October 1950). These three remain the *only* Argyle men to have beaten the 100 goal mark since the War. Wilf Carter is still Argyle's record scorer in the FA Cup, where he plundered ten goals in 11 ties. Of all the players who have played more than 100 games for Plymouth Argyle, only one scored at a higher ratio per game than Carter. The great Raymond Bowden, who went on to Arsenal, scored 86 in 152 games, a ratio of 0.56 per game. Carter' scored at a rate of 0.53. He extends much of the credit for his goal tally to the wingers he played with. He rated Peter Anderson and Harry Penk really highly – "on their day they were as good as I played with anywhere". When asked who was the best player in his time at Home Park, he is reluctant to answer. During his first two seasons he believes it was a team ethic that brought them success. But when pressed, he nominates Johnny Williams as "the one who stood out", quickly adding that "Peter Anderson could have played at a higher level too".

Another abiding memory Wilf has is of the way Jimmy Gauld used to scream out as he fell in the penalty area. Carter had a good record from the spot, his 24 penalties coming from 27 attempts. Many of those came from Jimmy Gauld's theatrical, vocal dives in the box. In addition to his five against Charlton, Wilf scored seven hat-tricks in his time at Home Park.When asked about Jack Rowley it is clear he was full of admiration for the manager. "He was a really nice bloke, a mate of mine really. "I used to stay back some afternoons just to learn from him. "Well, Jack asked and it wasn't advisable to refuse!" He adds, "Although Jack spent little time on the training pitch, on a match day his assessment of the opposition was spot on. "He was good at seeing their weaknesses".

As well as playing for Rowley, Wilf also served under Neil Dougall and George Taylor's joint regime, then under Dougall on his own before Ellis

Stuttard and then Andy Beattie came in. Under the latter he had a nine game run at left-back. He scored 19 League goals, in only 34 outings, in the Stuttard side which recovered from a poor start to finish fifth in the Second Division in 1961-62. He had an uneasy couple of weeks when Vic Buckingham was appointed, but fortunately for Wilf the former West Bromwich boss had a change of heart, resigning almost as soon as he got the job. One regret Wilf has is that he did not get to work with Malcolm Allison. He genuinely feels that Allison's penchant for revolutionary tactics would have suited him. Carter was released at the end of the season prior to Allison's arrival.

The newspapers of the day show that Wilf Carter was the subject of transfer talk on a number of occasions. Perhaps the most famous approach was after Denis Law was sold by Huddersfield to Manchester City. Eddie Boot, Town's manager, saw Carter as exactly the kind of replacement he needed. As he did with another offer from Scunthorpe, and a later one from Norwich, Carter refused on the grounds that he did not want to move his young family so far north or east. Bristol City too showed a strong interest in him and again the club were prepared to cash in on their most prized asset. He laughs when he recalls that on every occasion someone came in for him, despite his outstanding goal record, the club always wanted to sell. If he played today, what would he be worth?

Released by Argyle at the end of the 1963-64 season, Wilf moved along the A38 to join Exeter City. The club was newly promoted to the Third Division, the first honour of any kind in their entire history. In football terms the move did not work as well as either side would have liked. The goals simply never came. Although Wilf says that he enjoyed himself with the Grecians, he acknowledges it could have gone better for him on the field. 1964-65 started well enough, but the early promise shown by the team did not persist. He lost his place midway through the season and scored only four times in 26 outings. 1965-66 was worse, both for the player and the club. In 22 appearances he grabbed just two goals. At the end of a disappointing season Exeter were relegated and cleared their decks, with Carter one of many released.

Just seven years after shooting Argyle to promotion, Wilf was to play outside the Football League. To those of us who had been in awe of his talent at Home Park, it seemed inconceivable. Nothing is forever, but it seemed such a waste. In the summer of 1966 he completed a move to Southern League Bath City, where he stayed for five seasons, playing more often in the back four or in midfield, admitting that he no longer had the speed of his younger days.   His only foray into management came at the end of season 1970-71 when Ian McNiell resigned from the manager's job at Salisbury City. The *Salisbury Journal* (Harley Lawer's first paper) reported that Carter had been the committee's third choice. Did they know who they were talking about? In our world Wilf Carter would be third choice for nothing. With only nine registered players, Wilf predicted "no miracles", a prophetic statement. After narrowly avoiding relegation in his first season the next started well, but halfway through a cut in wages for the entire squad undermined him. Never one to back off when he was in the right, Wilf let the Chairman and the Committee have his views of their actions and on 6 February 1973 he was dismissed. He turned his back on football, returning only to watch the occasional game. It is now more than 40 years since the Carters settled in Bath. They now live in a neat house, close to the large Ministry of Defence site in Combe Down. Margaret worked there for 25 years, and Wilf was for many years a security guard at various Ministry of Defence sites around the city. Prior to that he worked in the engineering sector and had a spell as a hospital porter.

Despite his success at Home Park, easily the best years of his soccer career, a sign on the outside of his house gives a major clue to where his football heart still remains. It reads "The Hawthorns" and has nothing to do with the shrubs that run beside the drive. At 75 years old this man is still a "Baggie" through and through. When charged with the fact that this could cause indignation to any Argyle supporter who sees it he simply chuckled! Clearly you can take the man out of West Bromwich, but taking West Bromwich out of the man has proved impossible.

At 75, Wilf Carter is friendly and approachable, with the warmest of handshakes. He looked slightly embarrassed when told of the esteem in which he is still held by Argyle fans. He is far too modest to comment and smiles, simply recalling that "Yes, they were good days, but I had some good lads around me".

Left and centre, Wilf Carter in 2002, back in one of his favourite haunts, Plymouth Hoe. He came down for Peter Anderson's 70th birthday celebrations. On the right he can be seen speaking to Peter at the function.
Pictures lent by Cleeve Carter

TELEGRAMS
ARGYLE
PLYMOUTH

Plymouth Argyle Football Co., Ltd.

Home Park

SECRETARY · XXXXX

P. J. Galvin.

PLYMOUTH

TELEPHONE
51076

RJRB/AB

4th June 1964

Dear Wilf,

    I am writing to thank you for the very good and loyal service you have given to the Club during the many years you have been with us, and I feel that Exeter are being very fortunate in obtaining your services and extend to you my very best wishes for a successful and happy time at Exeter. You will remember that you were my first signing after coming into the Chair at Plymouth, and naturally it is with very mixed feelings that I see you leaving us.

             Kindest regards,
             Yours sincerely,

             R. J. R. BLINDELL

Wilf Carter, Esq.,
1 Langhill Road,
Peverell,
Plymouth.

A sad day for many supporters and for the Carter family too. They would much preferred to have stayed. We certainly got our £2,500 worth! During our interview for *Thanks For The Memory* Wilf Carter always referred to Ron Blindell as 'Mr.' He told me that whilst he did not have too many dealings with the Chairman, when he did he found him very fair.
Letter lent by Cleeve Carter

WINNERS: The Young Wales XI which beat Young England 2—1 at Wrexham included five reserve players. (Left to right): HOPKINS (Tottenham), BAKER C. (Cardiff), JONES K. (Cardiff), EDWARDS T. (Charlton), EDWARDS M. (Bolton), BAKER G. (Plymouth). (Front row): STEPHENS (Hull), ORRITT (Birmingham), CHARLES M. (Swansea), LEEK (Northampton), JONES C. (Tottenham).

LOSERS: The England line-up was (left to right): SETTERS (W. B. Albion), HOWE (W. B. Albion), SMITH (Birmingham), HODGKINSON (Sheffield Utd.), HARRIS (Wolves), ILEY (Tottenham). (Front row): RILEY (Leicester), HAYES (Manchester City), CLOUGH (Middlesbrough), GREAVES (Chelsea), A'COURT (Liverpool).

23 April 1958 - one of the best days of George Baker's (top, far right) life, when he helped a Wales under 23 side to victory over a strong Young England team at Wrexham. The England side had Brian Clough and Jimmy Greaves in attack. This is the only occasion that Wales has beaten England at under 23 or under 21 level.

The match was played on St George's Day, so history was turned on its head. 11 men with dragons on their shirts slew St George!

Photograph from George Baker's scrapbook

CHAPTER TEN

GEORGE BAKER

In 1952 George Baker asked his boss at the Rest Assured factory in Pontygwaith, South Wales, for some time off work. He had only been there for two weeks when he was given the opportunity of a month's trial at Home Park. He never returned. It was a big move for a young lad, moving from a close-knit mining community to a big city. He acknowledges the friendly welcome at the club, especially from the Welsh contingent already on the staff. Bill Shortt, Malcolm Davies and Dennis John rallied round and made him forget any feeling of homesickness. His first contract earned him £5 a week, nearly three times his wage at the mattress factory.

George, who hails from Maerdy, was an only child, born on 6 April 1936. His father James was a miner and mum Alice a housewife. They were poor but content. His formative years spanned the war, and he particularly remembers the benefits of Double Double Summertime, which allowed him and his friends to play football until late in the long evenings. DDS was an initiative introduced in the war, mainly to give farmers more hours of daylight. The clocks went forward two hours as early as mid February. His early football was played on any flat patch that could be found on the nearby mountain. Later he fell under the influence of Agnes John and her husband Phineas, who ran the Maerdy Royals. It was clear that George was better than most of the lads around him, a fact recognised by Tredegar Schoolboys and then by local scout Owain Roberts.

In 1954 he was called up for National Service and was allocated to the Royal Armoured Corps. He was sent to Oswestry for basic training and then got the best posting he could have wished for, Seaton Barracks at Crownhill. But the dream lasted only a few hours. As he stood on Oswestry Station he was soon aware of some Redcaps calling for Gunner Baker. He was told to report back to barracks; an RAC Company in Sheerness, on the Isle of Sheppey, needed a decent footballer. After several months there he had a real scare, a posting notice which would see him destined for Germany for 12 months. A quick phone call to the Plymouth manager Jack Rowley soon put paid to that. His posting was rescinded and he made his way to Carlisle. It was not the ideal place for a Plymouth Argyle player to spend his weekdays, but it would be easier than getting back from Germany.

Eventually he found himself posted to the Amphibious Warfare School, located between Bideford and Barnstaple. That was much better, although on the 50s road infrastructure it would be four hours by bus to Plymouth. For away games he would go by rail to Taunton, and then either get picked up by the team bus or join them on a train. The Army were helpful by putting him on permanent gate duties, thereby leaving his weekends free.

George has an excellent memory. He recalls signing a fresh contract once he was called up. "You was not allowed to have two bosses. The Queen was your boss and that was it. We signed a token contract at £1 a week, but with it being classed as unearned income we lost 19/6 (97p) in bloody tax". He went on to explain that if he was selected to play for any of the club's teams he got £3/10/- for that week plus expenses, in addition to the massive 25/- (£1.25) a week Army pay. Not only did National Service interfere with a playing career, it didn't seem help the Bank balance either.

Thomas George Baker was a far better player than 78 first team games and 16 goals would suggest. He played another 73 Football Combination League games, scoring on 19 occasions. Before becoming a regular in the reserves he was schooled in the traditional 50s way, first playing in the Plymouth and District, Devon Wednesday and South Western League teams. These competitions were of a very high standard. There were some hard and uncompromising players around then, keen to show the young Argyle lads what football was about. It was not uncommon on a Wednesday afternoon to see people four deep around Cottage Field and Unity Park watching Devon Wednesday fixtures. One significant factor was that in those days the majority of shops closed on Wednesday afternoons. The Plymouth and District side, which also played at Cottage Field, attracted even more crowds as people stopped on their way to Saturday fixtures at Home Park. In the early 50s 6,000 at reserves matches was not uncommon. One of his opponents in an early Devon Wednesday fixture was Johnny Williams who, along with his father, played for Co-op Welfare.

George was 18 when he made his League debut in October 1954. It came in a 2-1 home defeat against Nottingham Forest. George Robertson was at centre-half and Peter Anderson occupied the outside-left berth. That was his only first team outing that season. He waited another year for his next first team action, in a 1-0 home reverse against Swansea. This time he stayed in for a nine game run. It wasn't easy for a young man trying to make his way in the game. The team was in free-fall. They were relegated at the end of that 1955-56 campaign, which was followed by the worst season thus far in the club's history. It was in February 1957 that George started a run of eight games. At this time he was still seen as a winger, playing mostly on the right but occasionally he was selected on the left.

The 1957-58 season saw a major improvement in the team's fortunes and Baker was given the best Christmas present he could have wished for. He was handed the number nine shirt for the Christmas Day encounter at Newport County. Back in his native South Wales, he marked his return to the side with his first goal for the club. That he did it in front of family and friends who had travelled down from the Rhonnda Valley made it even more special. He remained in the side for the final 22 games and hit nine goals, as well as playing in a third round FA Cup tie at home to First Division Newcastle. Significantly, the Anderson, Carter, Baker, Gauld, Penk combination had now come together for the first time; this was the basis of the forward line that would fire the team to promotion the next season. He was used in a deep-lying centre-forward role, as teams

George Baker scores the opening goal in the 2-1 victory at Chesterfield on 1 November 1958. Wilf Carter got a vital late winner very late on.

George Baker (centre front) after his move to Shrewsbury Town in 1960. To his right (as we look) is player manager Arthur Rowley. It cannot be too often that a player has been part of a transfer deal between two brothers.
Both photographs from George Baker's scrapbook

began to move away from the traditional spearhead centre-forward.

1957-58 signalled an upturn in his fortunes, culminating in international honours. In April 1958 his consistent displays for Argyle saw him selected to play for the Welsh Under 23 team against England at Wrexham. In those days the Welsh FA had no jurisdiction over players engaged with English clubs. With Argyle still not out of the Division Three (South) promotion hunt, the club would not release him from a midweek evening game. Straight after the match, that never-to-be-forgotten controversial home defeat against Southend, he left the ground to catch the midnight sleeper. He finally met up with his international colleagues in Rhyl at lunchtime the next day. He trained with his colleagues on the beach that afternoon. The next day it was off to the Racecourse Ground for the match.

23 April 1958 was momentous night for Welsh football, with 13,522 roaring Wales to a 2-1 victory. The England team included the prolific Brian Clough and Jimmy Greaves up front, with Don Howe at right back and Liverpool winger Alan A'Court. It remains the only occasion that Wales has beaten England at Under 23 (and Under 21) level. History was turned on its head with the Welsh Dragon slaying St. George! Within a few weeks Howe (four games) and A'Court (three) both played for England in the 1958 World Cup Finals, the latter deputising for the injured Finney. Neither Clough nor Greaves was selected for the tournament.

Six months later, on 10 December, George earned a second cap against Young Scotland at Tynecastle, helping the Welsh side to a 1-0 victory. In the opposition was the Hearts player Alex Young, who went on to have a glittering career at Everton, where he was affectionately known as 'the Golden Vision'. George's displays for the Under 23s ensured his inclusion in Wales's nominated 40 for the World Cup Finals in Sweden. He then survived the cut to the last 22, but there his luck deserted him. The Welsh selectors decided that Wales had little chance of doing well in the competition. They elected to leave four players on stand-by in Wales, which very conveniently left room on the plane for the wives of four of the Welsh FA members.

Between his two international engagements George reported back to Plymouth for pre-season training. Their close run effort in the previous season meant that Plymouth Argyle would be amongst the favourites for promotion from the newly formed Third Division. His childhood sweetheart Moira had moved to Plymouth to be closer to him. They first met through a Youth Club and when he played for Maerdy. No other girl in the Valley dared give George his half-time orange! Moira lodged with Argyle trainer George Taylor and his wife, the start of a friendship with George's daughter Margaret that has endured these 50 years. Moira loved the Taylor family, though during the hard and relentless work that trainer George put the players through, George Baker's view of her landlord was probably less benevolent.

Moira found work in the Co-op's haberdashery department, and on 22 November 1958 they were married at the Plymouth Registry Office, which was then not far above the railway station. It was a very Welsh day.

George at Home Park on 27 September 2008. As honest and hardworking a player as any who have worn the green and black.
Photo by the author

Rhymney born Argyle colleague John L Williams was best man while Argyle had a fixture that day against Wrexham. The reception was held at Dingles's Dartmoor Restaurant. In addition to the *Western Evening Herald* and the *Western Independent*, their wedding photo also appeared in the next day's *News of the World*.

George played in the first seven games of the promotion season, before a knee injury saw Barrie Meyer replace him. After missing six games he returned for the hard fought home win over Swindon Town, and hit a good spell of form. In late October and early November he scored in three consecutive games. On 4 January 1959 *Pilgrim* expressed concern that national newspapers were carrying stories that Cardiff City were showing a strong interest in taking Baker to Ninian Park. Jack Rowley made it clear that there had been no enquiry from the Welsh club and that it was immaterial anyway – "we are not looking to sell any of our players".

George stayed in the side for a run of 20 League and Cup games but the team was beginning to struggle. His knee was never completely right. Furthermore, his unsung role saw him playing in the worst area of the pitch. The constant rain in the late summer, autumn and winter of 1958 meant the pitches were often heavy, especially down the centre. The crowd began to get on his case and after a 1-0 home defeat against Norwich City he was left out. Jack Rowley was moved to say that George was now a better player away from Home Park. It would seem from reading the reports of the day that the crowd struggled to understand George's deep-lying centre-forward role.

This was a transitory time in football and most supporters expected their number nine to be in the opposition's area scoring goals. In fact, Baker's role was more akin to that of the old fashioned playmaking inside-forward and was a direct copy of the tactic first used by the crack Hungarian team of the early and middle 50s. Subsequently Don Revie, then at Manchester City, introduced the role to the English game and in doing so transformed that club's fortunes. It was known as the 'Revie plan' and it was the undoing of Alex Govan's Birmingham City side in the 1956 FA Cup Final.

After the Norwich defeat Baker missed the next two games, but returned for the 8-3 victory over Mansfield Town. He stayed in the side for another five games before a damaged ankle brought his season to a premature end with just three games to go. He had been injured at Wrexham the previous week but played in a battling 1-0 home victory over Southampton. It was a step too far and he had to remain on the sidelines as his team-mates went on to secure promotion and then the championship. He had scored seven goals in 36 League and Cup outings. But the real story is in how frequently one saw *Spectator* write "from a pass by Baker".

In July 1959 we saw one of the strangest stories ever concerning a Plymouth Argyle player. The local papers carried reports of rumours sweeping the town that Argyle centre-forward George Baker had been killed in a car crash on his way back from Wales the previous Sunday. Despite denials the rumours persisted. Eventually, a strong statement from manager Jack Rowley put a stop to them. The manager was quoted as saying, "I don't know where this rubbish has come from but it is not true." The 'born again' Baker started the 1959-60 season in the side, scoring in a 4-0 hammering of Scunthorpe in the second match. After a 2-0 defeat in the return game he lost his place through injury. He was recalled in the October for a goalless draw at home to Sunderland, a game that would turn out to be his last in an Argyle first team. He stayed at Home Park for the rest of the season before moving to Shrewsbury, in June 1960, for around £6,000. If it was Jack Rowley that had started his League career, it would be Jack's brother Arthur who would extend it. He played 52 times and scored five goals in his two season stay at Gay Meadow. He had a chronic knee injury but continued to play regularly. These were exciting times in Shropshire. Arthur Rowley was closing in on Dixie Dean's record of 379 League goals. Rowley was by then not the most mobile of players and wanted a reliable 'fetcher and carrier'. Baker was seen as the man for the job. On 26 April 1961 Arthur equalled the record with a penalty against Walsall, in a 2-1 home defeat. Such was the interest in the goals record, it was almost an aside that Walsall were promoted that night. A record crowd of 18,917 squeezed into Gay Meadow.

Rowley then hit the 380 mark with a powerful header in a game at

Bradford. The Press almost missed it. George Baker recalled that at Park Avenue the journalists would nip across the road for their half-time cuppa. "Arthur's record-breaking goal was right at the start of the second half and they told us afterwards that they only just got back in time." Arthur went on to score another 54 career goals, finishing with 434 in 619 League appearances. He always acknowledged the role George played in helping him create the record. George was also part of the Shrewsbury side that got to the League Cup semi-final in 1961, losing to Rotherham (then a Second Division side) over two legs. In the Quarter Final they beat a strong Everton side containing the man who George reckons was the best player he was ever on a field with, fellow Welshman Roy Vernon. In front of 15,399 Shrewsbury triumphed 2-1. Everton's scorer that night was Alex Young. Having been in the Scottish under 23 side when George and his Welsh colleagues won at Tynecastle, Young must have been sick of the sight of the man from Maerdy.

By the end of the 1963 season his knee was no longer up to the rigours of the full-time game. He found work in Wellington, Shropshire in a factory making Massey Ferguson parts and also helped a local team. In 1964 the family moved back to Wales and George signed for Barry Town, who got him a job in the docks. By 1966 he was finding the daily journey to Barry too tiresome. He found a job in Ferndale, with the Pyrene fire extinguisher company and was player-coach for Ferndale in the Rhondda League. He was paid £1/15 shillings a week for his player-coach role - £1.75p.

His final job was with the National Coal Board, who made him redundant in 1995. He was by then 61. He now lives in Tylorstown, very close to the house where Moira was brought up and just down the road from Maerdy. They have a daughter Lyn, who is married to Pete, and grandchildren Kelly and Jenna. They all live close by. George is on the Committee of a local Social Club and is chairman of an Old Age Pensioners Association. Looking back over his time in football he rates Stanley Matthews as the best player he has seen in his lifetime, while Stan Williams of Chelsea gets his vote as the most difficult opponent. Of those he played regularly with at Home Park, he believes Wilf Carter was the best all round footballer.

He enjoyed his time at Home Park, particularly the 1958-59 campaign. But there were other career high spots too. The Under 23 victory over England was as wonderful as it was unexpected, and he was on the field the day Arthur Rowley broke Dixie Deans' record. Despite missing out on a trip to Sweden in 1958, he was still recognised as one of he best 22 players in Wales, in an era when Wales had a very, very strong side. Not a bad effort for a boy who learned to play with a scuffed ball halfway up the side of a mountain.

George's recollection of events has been a great help to *Thanks For The Memory*. It was George who first mentioned the Boardroom split; he recalled Corporal Veale VC being around the club and many other important details. He is a most interesting man to talk to and we have become really good friends. And Moira's profiteroles? They are to die for!

A FEW HOURS before playing against Wrexham yesterday, Geor Baker, Plymouth Argyle's centre-forward, was married to Miss Mo Bromley, of Tylorstown, Glamorgan. George is also from Wales. home is at Maerdy, Glamorgan.

Welsh under 23 international George Baker and fiancée Moira were married on Saturday 22 November 1958 at the Plymouth Register Office.
In the afternoon George played in a 2-2 draw against Wrexham, the Welsh side making their first visit to Home Park.

Courtesy of the News of the World 23 November 1958

George and Moira Baker on the night of their Golden Wedding—22 November 2008
Photo by the author

22 November 2008 was also a Saturday and, by coincidence, again the opposition at Home Park were Welsh.
This time Argyle beat Cardiff City 2-1 in a match televised by Sky TV.

A SUPPORTER'S STORY
Colin Bolton

During the 1958-59 football season Prime Minister Harold MacMillan made a famous speech, where he told the British people "You've never had it so good." Having already been fostered with several different families and been in orphanages in Whitleigh and at Astor Hall, Colin would have found no resonance with MacMillan's words. If he had been listening then it would probably have been while he was fitting new cardboard inside his leaking shoes, as unloved as any boy could be.

A visit to Home Park was a release from the unrelenting misery of his routine life, a ray of green light that shone into his dark existence. His father did take him occasionally, but only after he collected Colin from whatever temporary (and generally unsatisfactory) living arrangements he had made for his son.

For 90 minutes he was released from the bleakness. He recalls a different atmosphere in the crowd. The quips from supporters and a sharp reminder "there's a woman here" if anyone swore. If an Argyle player was late in the tackle the call would go out "Come on ref, he got there quick as he could." Colin described his times at Home Park, and down at the Brickfields watching his heroes train, as "the happiness that balanced out the life I had to endure elsewhere."

Colin was clearly a great admirer of the 1958-59 side:-.

Barnsley the goalkeeper, cat like who would grace any goalmouth. Johnny Williams, strong player with the hardest of shots—had a garage up Efford. I worked with his brother Barrie who unfortunately died in an accident. Reg Wyatt a tall, lanky centre half in the Jack Charlton mould. And then of course there was Wilfred Carter and Jimmy Gauld, without doubt the best pairing of my lifetime. They were better than Rafferty and Mariner (I saw both pairings) and I believe Carter was a better finisher than Tommy Tynan. It's a pity Jimmy got caught up in that scandal a few years later.

The wingers were Penk and Anderson. For some years, Peter had a flower shop near Efford cemetery. Alex Govan came from Portsmouth after the season started. Then of course there was Neil Dougall who could really hit a free kick. I remember George Baker too, a real grafter who always put in an honest shift; I think he played for Wales under 23s. Wally Bellett and Len Casey came in at the end, signed together from Chelsea.

A special memory is the amazing game with Mansfield when Argyle ran amok, winning 8-3. And a fantastic solo goal from Jimmy, right at the end against Swindon. The most emotional game I ever attended was the season before, when referee Pullin robbed us of promotion in a game against Southend. I will never forget Wilf Carter trying to overcome the overwhelming odds created by Pullin's baffling decisions.

It is good to report that from his twenties onwards Colin's luck changed for the better. He has been married to Maureen for over 30 years and is extremely content with life.

Jimmy Gauld was one of the quickest players ever seen at Home Park. Growing up he was a schoolboy sprinting champion and his turn of speed was too much for most defences. The headline below followed the goal he scored in the picture above left, one of two he got on the day.
Pictures courtesy Sunday Independent/Colin Parsons

GAULD AND WYLLIE THE MATCH WINNERS

Only Jimmy Could Have Got Those Goals!

Cutting from the Sunday Independent

CHAPTER ELEVEN

JIMMY GAULD

To most Argyle supporters who watched the 1958-59 promotion campaign, Jimmy Gauld was one the stars of the team. Everyone marvelled at the way he ran at tremendous speed, somehow keeping the ball under control whether it was by foot, knee or backside. We loved the manner in which he ran straight at opponents, often resulting in penalties which were then calmly put away by his inside forward partner Wilf Carter. For good measure, Gauld also treated us to some unbelievable goals. Without doubt, he was one of the greatest ever entertainers to set foot on the Home Park turf. He will never be forgotten by those who saw him play. Folklore still has it that Jimmy could be tripped in the centre circle, and then stumble all the way into the penalty area to win a spot-kick.

Long term supporter Colin Parsons, who was 12 when Jimmy Gauld dazzled us all during the 1958-59 season, describes his adulation of the player as 'a love affair.' He makes a more serious point when he says, "Despite modern fitness levels, I don't think I have ever seen anyone quicker in an Argyle shirt".

Although he was adored by supporters, one gets a different story from most of his contemporaries at Argyle. Their success in winning the Third Division title was based on a team ethic, but many of his playing colleagues felt Jimmy's main consideration was himself. Enquiries amongst past colleagues at all his other football clubs failed to produce anyone who could truly say they knew him. From my point of view, as a 10 year old autograph hunter I always found him to be very polite and often jovial. Jimmy would always sign everything he was asked to.

Sadly, within six years of helping Argyle to the Third Division title he had swapped a football jersey for prison fatigues. As the acknowledged ringleader of a major football bribery scandal, on 26 January 1965 he was jailed for four years. At the height of his bent operations, the scams he was engineering were said to be netting anything from £500 to £1,000 a week, an absolute fortune in those days. Some reports said that he was fixing the results of up to 12 games each week, though I could only find evidence of him interfering with a maximum of five matches from a single day's fixtures. In the main the bets seemed to involve three games in a particular fixture list. Whatever the numbers, the scam helped ruin the careers of two men who had been destined to be part of the 1966 World Cup squad. Peter Swan and Tony Kay were the biggest names involved but many other players became tangled in Gauld's web. Whilst it does not take away the pleasure he gave thousands of Argyle fans, for some his image was forever tarnished.

Gauld was born in Aberdeen on 9 May 1929. (Although some websites list his year of birth as 1931 I have gone for the 1929 version, simply because he was of an age with Alex Govan when they were selected for

Scotland Youth for a match in Wales.) After being spotted playing for Hall-Russells, a local shipyard team, he spent three seasons as a part-timer at Aberdeen. After being released he spent time first with Huntley and then Elgin City in the Highland League. In the summer of 1954 he moved to Irish club Waterford. He scored 30 goals in the 1954-55 League of Ireland season, still the second highest individual total of all time and the biggest post-war aggregate. He represented the League of Ireland twice, first against the Football League in September 1954 and then versus the Irish League on St Patrick's Day in the following March.

It was inevitable that his performances in Ireland would attract scouts from across the Irish Sea. In May 1955 he moved to Charlton Athletic, for a fee of £4,000. The London club had just sold Eddie Firmani to Italian club Sampdoria, for what was then a breathtaking £35,000. Gauld was seen as a useful replacement but Firmani was a hard act to follow. A South African with an Italian name, he went on to win 3 Italian caps and is the only player ever to have scored 100 goals in both the Football League highest division *and* its Italian counterpart. Charlton's club historian Colin Cameron recalls that although Gauld was unable to rival Firmani for skill, his incredible bursts of speed down the middle, and his clinical finishing, made him unforgettable.

Gauld featured regularly for Athletic, and in a 17 month stay he made 49 League and Cup outings, scoring a respectable 22 goals. He started well, scoring in a 2-2 draw in the opening fixture at home to newly promoted Luton Town. He dominated the match report of another early season fixture, a 3-2 victory at Spurs, but observed afterwards how fast the football was compared to Ireland. He scored the first, then hounded Tottenham defender Harry Clarke into putting through his own goal before laying on the winner for Stuart Leary. But his finest game for Athletic was said to be on 27 December 1955 at the Valley, when in the 27th minute he opened the scoring in a 3-0 victory over a Manchester United side which went on to win the League. The United team that day contained all of the famous Busby Babes. His final outing in a Charlton shirt was on 13 October 1956 in a 3-1 home defeat to Arsenal.

During a rare interview with the *Sunday Independent* Gauld paid a glowing tribute to the Charlton management team of Jimmy Trotter and Jimmy Seed, crediting them with being the first to try and harness his tremendous sprinting ability within a football framework. Gauld spoke in the interview of being more than a stone heavier at Charlton than he was when he joined Argyle. Trotter and Seed first got him thoroughly fit and then taught him close control of the ball, and the importance of keeping his body over the ball. In that same interview, conducted in October 1958, he also spoke of when he was a renowned sprinter in Scotland. Gauld told *Spectator,* "As a schoolboy I could turn in 10.3 seconds for the 100 yards." Indeed, when the interview took place his record for a Scottish schoolboys' championship still stood. Then at 17 he took part in a professional meeting, earning prize money of £30 for winning the 100 yards, the 440 yards and the Long Jump. It was a good return - but he was still an amateur. *Spectator* learned from Gauld that some weeks later he was lining up for an amateur sprint race. A protest was lodged that he was a professional. Gauld revealed, "I shall never forget how I felt walking across that Aberdeen stadium – out of the amateur game." But for all his good attributes at Charlton and the improvement in his game, in October 1956 he was transferred to Everton for a fee of £10,500. His debut for the Toffeemen could not have been more challenging, away to all conquering Manchester United. He was joining a struggling Everton side but they surprised everyone with a 5-2 victory, with two of the goals coming from future Argyle hero George Kirby. Everton's triumph ended United's run of 31 home matches without defeat, a run which had begun in March 1955 - following a defeat by.... Everton. Amongst Jimmy's goals for Everton was one against previous club Charlton in a 5-0 home win.

There was a pattern to his career, inasmuch that Jimmy never stayed anywhere for too long. After 23 games and seven goals at Everton, within a year he eventually agreed to a move to Plymouth. Kirby had been Rowley's initial target but while watching Kirby he spotted Gauld. The player's father had tried hard to dissuade him from moving down two Leagues, at the same time reminding him how far Plymouth was from his Aberdeen roots. He also warned his son that the Third Division was a virtual wilderness for professional footballers. Despite being 28 years old, in those days a father's words were still a consideration. After spending a few days in Plymouth he politely turned down the club's initial offer. Speaking to a reporter as he boarded the train back to Merseyside, he made it clear that he had liked everything he had seen and heard at Home Park. He said that he had liked the people and the city, but added that he owed a great debt of gratitude to his parents.

Two weeks later he had a change of heart and signed on 25 October 1957, shortly before he made his debut in a 3-0 defeat at Crystal Palace. In the end it was nothing to do with his father having a change of heart – it was that Argyle had allowed him to keep a sales representative's job he had held since his days at Charlton. A week after his Selhurst Park debut he made his first appearance at Home Park on the first Saturday of November 1957, scoring the only goal in a victory over Torquay. The game was watched by 23,765 and it brought together seven of the players who would be the nucleus of the 1958-59 promotion campaign. He took a real battering in a 1-0 win at Newport on Christmas Day 1957, scoring in a 2-0 win. In the return match the next day Newport again saw him as the danger man and tried to stop him at all costs. Finally he had enough and was sent off by one armed Fulham based referee Alf Bond. He was out of the side from the middle of February and did not return until 12 April 1958 in a goalless draw at Dean Court. In all he played 20 League and Cup games that season, but his return of only 6 goals was something of a disappointment. On occasions there were signs that he had unmatchable speed and skill; he just needed to deliver more goals. And he did. Just before the start of the 1958-59 season, on 10August 1958, Jimmy married Mademoiselle Lisetts L'Avedon, a French teacher at Devonport High School for girls. The couple met when Lisetts lodged with trainer George Taylor's family. Taylor's daughter Margaret can recall the time they met.

Jimmy Gauld marries Mlle Lisetts L'Avedon of Monte de Marson, Landes in France at the Plymouth Register Office. She was a French mistress at Devonport High School for Girls. In addition to Jimmy (second left) is Best Man Harry Brown, the former Argyle goalkeeper and Mrs George Taylor and her daughter Margaret. Before they married Mlle L'Avedon had lodged with the Taylor family at their Endsleigh Park Road home.

Photo courtesy of the Sunday Independent

This picture, from the 1959 FA Cup defeat at the hands of Cardiff City, could have been from almost any game Argyle played. If anyone as much as touched Jimmy Gauld in and around the penalty area he would go to ground. Often it was because of the sheer speed he ran at and opponents could not avoid him.

But even the most inept referee would see that the Cardiff man got the ball this time!

From George Baker's scrapbook

"Lissets was a really lovely lady and Jimmy was a real charmer. "With all that happened, goodness knows what kind of time she had with him." The *Western Independent* carried a picture of the happy day and, three weeks later, reported that the couple received a gift from a group of London supporters, shortly before the first home game with Tranmere on 30 August 1958.

The report noted that the presentation was made by Corporal Tom Veale VC, a Vice-President of the Plymouth Argyle Supporters' Club. Jimmy and his bride moved into a club house on 25 November 1958. Perhaps due to the settling effect of his marriage, the 1958-59 promotion season saw Jimmy Gauld fully justify the fee paid for his services. He had a season to remember, with 45 League appearances which saw him score 21 times. He made an additional four appearances in the FA Cup and scored once. Apart from one or two off days, he thrilled crowds and bemused opponents wherever he went. As Colin Parsons told me "He was so consistent I find it hard to disentangle individual performances. He was brilliant at Coventry in the FA Cup, then there was the home match against Swindon (see below) when he scored in the final minute. And who could forget his brilliant display against QPR in a 3-2 win on Boxing Day. In front of 30,000 he got two that day, both from passes by Alex Govan—and he had his shorts ripped off!"

On countless occasions both *Spectator* and *Pilgrim* described surging runs and goals from the obliquest of angles. One of his very best efforts was missed by many of the Home Park faithful. Of the 26,051 watching that October 1958 match against Swindon Town, it was estimated by journalists that at least a third had given up as the match entered the 90th minute, deadlocked at 2-2. On a heavy pitch Gauld, already with one goal to his name, somehow summoned the energy to run at the visitors' defence from the half-way line. As he beat the final defender and shot at goal, the ball was parried by Sam Burton in the Swindon goal. Gauld managed to stab the rebound home. In the *Sunday Independent Spectator* marvelled at Gauld's physical conditioning and never-say-die attitude.

He clearly enjoyed playing against Swindon. In the return match on the final day of February 1959 he scored his only Argyle hat-trick in a 4-3 win, the start of a spell of seven goals in four matches. Once again, as he had done at Home Park, one of his goals came from a run from the half way line. But before we leave that game at the County Ground it is interesting to note who was marking Gauld in that game. Football was very stereo-typed in that era, and it would always have been the right half-back who shadowed the opposition's inside left. Swindon's number four that day was one John (aka Jack) Fountain, who later transferred to York City. Within a few months they would be team-mates at Swindon and five years further on they would be still be close together – in the dock at the Nottingham Assizes! By 1962 the same John Fountain had become one of Gauld's henchmen in the fixed-odds racket. Small world, eh? With the County Ground hat-trick following that brace against them in the previous encounter, it was not surprising that Swindon came in for him the following summer. Reports of the day write of Norwich and Southend

A VERY SPECIAL SUPPORTER
Corporal Tom Veale VC

Born in Dartmouth, Tom Veale VC was a frequent visitor to Home Park. After leaving the Army he earned his living as a chauffeur in the London area, mainly working for the head of Bentalls of Kingston and then afterwards for the top man at Procea Foods. He was a Vice President of the Supporters' Club from 1955 until its closure in 1967, but did not become a Vice-President of the Supporters' Association which formed in 1967-68.

He won his Victoria Cross on the Somme on 20 July 1916, while serving as a Private in the 8th Battalion, the Devonshire Regiment. The citation read:-

For most conspicuous bravery (East of Highwood, France). Hearing that a wounded officer was lying out in front, Private Veale went out in search, and found him lying amidst growing corn within fifty yards of the enemy. He dragged the officer to a shell hole, returned for water and took it out. Finding he could not single-handed carry in the officer, he returned for assistance, and took out two volunteers. One of the party was killed when carrying the officer, and heavy fire necessitated leaving the officer in a shell hole. At dusk Private Veale went out again with volunteers to bring in the officer. Whilst doing this an enemy patrol was observed approaching. Private Veale at once went back and procured a Lewis gun, and with the fire of the gun he covered the party, and the officer was finally carried to safety. The courage and determination displayed was of the highest order.

Private Theodore Henry William Veale was presented with his medal by King George V at Buckingham Palace on 5 February 1917. The medal is now on display at the Devon & Dorsetshire Regimental Museum in the Keep, Dorchester.

The officer he saved was Lt Savill, later to become Sir Eric Savill who designed and founded the world famous Savill Gardens in Great Windsor Park. In a service held in Dartmouth on Remembrance Day 2002, his daughter Theodora Grindell, wearing her father's VC, unveiled a Blue Plaque in Victoria Gardens Avenue, Dartmouth. Members of the Savill family attended, presenting some magnolias to be planted near the memorial plaque.

Tom Veale died on 6 November 1980, days short of his 89th birthday. In view of his heroics in 1916, it is interesting to note that he was born on 11 November, but 26 years before that date became known as Armistice Day.

being alerted to his availability too. Clearly there must have rumours circulating that Gauld wanted a move away from Plymouth. In the April of 1959 *Pilgrim* reported that the player was unhappy with the team's style of play, and that he was reluctant to change the way he played. He felt he would have to move on. The Wiltshire club were not the first to try and obtain Jimmy's services. Non-league Gloucester City made an audacious bid to appoint him as their player-manager. Jimmy was clearly interested in their offer. Just a few days away from his 30th birthday, he obviously had a few years left as a player. He saw it as a great opportunity to get into management, with the £1,500 a year package being a further incentive (a pay rise of at least 50%). Apart from the fact that Argyle were reluctant to release him, a deal was unlikely once Gloucester declared they could afford only a nominal fee, adding that even a small fee would have to be spread over a couple of years. Apart from any other reason, the Board saw a duty to the Supporters' Club to get best value for any player they sold. In the 50s and early 60s it was Ron Lucas and his committee who put up most of the transfer money for incoming players. They had recently seen a loss made on the ill-starred Barrie Meyer transfer and would have been irritated by another similar episode.

Swindon watched Gauld for the final time in the 1959-60 Probables v Possibles public practice match. Although Argyle fans were still fervently hoping there would be a last minute change of heart by the player, a few days later Swindon splashed out their record fee at that time, £6,000. The Swindon Board meeting minutes show that Houghton of Southend was their first choice but that their manager (Bert Head) could go after Gauld as an alternative. Head was sanctioned to spend £7,000. Argyle's initial asking price was £7,500 but the published fee ranges from £6,000 to £6,500, depending upon which newspaper one reads.

With players on a percentage of the fee, plus removal and travelling expenses, moving around was a good way for them to increase their income. In view of the way money seemed to pass through Jimmy's hands, perhaps it offers an explanation as to why he moved around so frequently?

Gauld claimed at the time that he did not want to move and that he was disappointed to find that he was available via a newspaper report. Chairman Harry Deans simply referred everyone to the retained list containing Gauld's name, while blaming the player for wanting a move. We shall never know the truth, but many supporters were devastated to see him leave.

Jimmy did not always show his best form at Swindon, though he was their second top scorer behind 'Bronco' Layne with 14 goals in 40 outings. The team finished only 16th in the Third Division of 1959-60. They were one of five sides who finished on 46 points, but their goal average was inferior to the other four teams. That was not helped by a 6-1 defeat away at Port Vale on 30 April 1960, in what was the penultimate match of the season. History shows that it was ironic that Jimmy Gauld got Swindon's goal that day. There was a great deal of conjecture after that match at Vale Park. The Swindon club were well aware that there was a distinct lack of effort from the players and a whispering campaign started. Swindon historian Dick Mattick knew the story well and gave me access to the Swindon Board's minutes from the period. Initially Jimmy was included in the end of season retained list, which was published after a Board meeting on 25 April 1960. Seven days later the Board re-considered their earlier decision. The minutes show that after a report from Bert Head, Gauld and a Walter Bingley would be added to the list to be made available for transfer. Bingley never went to court but was later named in a case involving his new side Halifax. As Mattick told me "In January 1960 the Board had decided, with the manager, that they would pursue a policy of blooding younger talent. But for an amendment to be made to the published retained list was highly suspicious."

Another minute I was shown adds to the theory that there was deep suspicion over the Port Vale result. On 30 April the ten-strong Swindon Board had decided, by a majority vote, to interview the entire team who had represented the club at Port Vale. Mattick does not know why the Board wanted to pursue that route, but thinks it may have been to try and get other members of the side to inform on the suspected match fixers. By 5 May they had changed their minds and had decided to leave any further action to the manager. Mattick surmises that the directors had realised the devastating effect it would have on team morale, as well as undermining Head's authority.

A website summarising Gauld's time at the County Ground indicated that he was identified as the ring leader and shipped out, although two others who came under suspicion were retained. They were David 'Bronco' Layne and Jack Fountain, both of whom were heavily implicated in future match-fixing probes. As it happens, Fountain was transferred to York City later that same summer and before the end of the year Layne moved to Bradford City, in what was a record £6,000 outlay for the Yorkshire club.

The fact is that the Board minutes neither mention match-fixing nor do they make specific mention of Layne or Fountain. Gauld later admitted that he had fixed the Port Vale match, justifying his cheating by saying "We were both in the middle of the table with nothing at stake. I really could not see the harm in it." However, I was told by Colin Parsons that there were also suspicions about a match between Tranmere and Mansfield, played on the same day. Despite Gauld's assertion that the Swindon v Port Vale match was an unimportant mid-table fixture, if the Tranmere match was fixed for them to win it meant that they avoided relegation.

What does emerge from the Swindon Board minutes is that Gauld was not considered indispensable. In December 1960, just three months after he had arrived, the Board received notice of interest from Norwich City for players Richards, Edwards and Gauld. They sanctioned the manager to proceed with the sale of Richards and Edwards but asked that any move for Gauld be held in abeyance. At this time the Board were considering reducing the number of players to save £100 per week, instructing manager Head to get rid of older players first. Days later another Board meeting authorised Head to sell Gauld if the right offer came in.

Despite the internal furore over match-fixing Gauld continued to act as if nothing was wrong. He approached the manager to seek permission to go off to Canada for two months in the summer to undertake some coaching. The Board were informed of this by Head and although they were reluctant to approve the absence, they realised they could not actually stop him going.

On 8 August 1960 the Swindon Board met. Again Gauld was a topic of discussion. They discussed a request from Limerick FC who wanted Gauld to become their player-manager, subject to Swindon agreeing to release him. The Board decided that they would release him from his contract but not from the transfer fee they required. So, despite the general historical view being that Swindon cut their losses with Gauld, this proves that they were not prepared to let him go for nothing.

On 12 September 1960 Jimmy's name appears in the minutes for the final time. Manager Head had reported to the Board that the player had now been sold to Scottish club St Johnstone. The arrangements were £1,000 immediately, another £1,000 after six weeks and a final payment of £1,000 after 12 weeks. He played only four times for the McDiamird Park outfit and after just two months and 12 days joined Mansfield Town, in exchange for £4,000. With St Johnstone having paid only £2,000 of the original fee, one assumes Swindon would have got their final payment while St Johnstone emerged from the deal with their outlay returned.

Whilst Swindon gained some financial recompense for the player, it could be said that by not taking decisive action they did football in general a disservice. They either could not or would not act over the questionable circumstances around the Port Vale match, though Gauld's confession later certainly moves it from questionable to factual.

He made a bright start with the Stags, scoring three in his first four matches, including one in the Boxing Day game where he suffered a badly broken leg against Hartlepools. As Charlton's Colin Cameron observes, "Jimmy Gauld finished as he started in the Football League - by scoring a goal". Jimmy never played League football again, though it is not known whether it was the injury or the Football Association who finally brought his career to an end. Already a suspected match-fixer, the broken leg seemed to be the catalyst for increasing the velocity of his journey into notoriety. It was downward spiral which would lead directly to a cell in Wakefield Prison. In November 1963, banned from the game after an appearance at Rochdale Magistrates, in a last desperate act to give himself one more pay-day, he broke the 'honour amongst thieves' edict by selling his story to the *People* newspaper. It is said that he received more than £7,000, a massive amount of money in that era. Such was the depth of the newspaper's investigation, they did not break the story until Sunday 12 April 1964. It ran for four weeks.

Gauld travelled all over the United Kingdom with the investigating journalists, Peter Campling and Mike Gabben, visiting most of those who had helped him to fix matches. During each visit he would deliberately lead his former associates into talking about previous betting activity, all the while knowing that their conversations were being secretly recorded. The Judge at the Nottingham Assizes (now the Crown Court) made no secret of the fact that he was appalled by Gauld's behaviour.

Although it was mid 1960 when suspicion first fell on Gauld at Swindon Town, it would be three more years before his name was officially aligned to the fixing of football matches. Although he was not before the court his name came up in a case before Doncaster Magistrates Court on 29 July 1963. In the dock were goalkeeper Esmond Million and inside forward Keith Phillips of Bristol Rovers, and former Mansfield Town captain Brian Phillips. Gauld was named when the Prosecutor outlined the background to the charges. The case had been brought after investigations by both the FA and the police and centred on the fixture between Bradford and Bristol Rovers, played on 20 April 1963. Each of the three players was found guilty and fined the maximum £50. Million was described to the court as a bus driver, while both Williams and Phillips were labourers. Clearly, their clubs had not waited for the result of the court case to jettison them. In evidence Phillips named Gauld as the person who had approached him to make contact with players to fix the game. He added that "other Mansfield players were used as contacts for the other games." He told the Court that the Bradford v Bristol Rovers game was one of five included in a single bet, a wager which lost because Coventry City were held to a draw when they had been backed to win. Million's lawyer, Mr Wilberforce Woodbridge told the court "The real culprits are not in court." Williams' solicitor provided match reports which showed that his client had played very well, with the lawyer contending that his client clearly had a change of heart before the kick off.

The match had ended 2-2, just as the bribe demanded. Rovers were at one time two goals to the good but Million, desperate for money, purposely conceded two late goals. Reports of the day indicate that it was the honesty of other Rovers' players that brought this case to the attention of the authorities. Amazingly, the authorities did not go after Gauld and he remained a registered player at Mansfield.

On 23 November 1963 it was Gauld's turn to appear in the dock. He was found guilty at Rochdale Magistrates Court of trying to influence a number of Oldham Athletic players to play badly. He was fined £10 on each of six counts of 'attempting to corrupt professional footballers by offering them bribes to play badly'. It is understood that at the time Gauld approached the Oldham players his former manager at Plymouth, Jack Rowley, was in charge at Boundary Park. Nearly five decades on, it seems amazing that neither the Football Association nor the police made further detailed investigations into what was clearly a major problem. The evidence in the case at Doncaster had clearly indicated that attempts had been made to fix four other games on the 20 April 1963.

Even now, it is not clear just how many matches were the subject of result fixing facilitated by Jimmy Gauld. After his own court appearance at Oldham case he was thrown out of football. It would seem that he immediately looked for a newspaper that would be prepared to buy his story. With the ineptness from the FA, and the police unable to act without an invitation to do so, one can only surmise that the scandal may have gone on and on without the *People's* intervention. The FA seemed to think that by banning Gauld that was it – no more match fixing. It is only because the *People* newspaper took up the case that a fuller picture of the depth of match fixing came to light. It is clear from reading the newspaper cuttings from 1963 and 1964 that Gauld knew the storm that would engulf him once the newspaper broke the story. It shows that the *People's* solicitor Derek Wiles, who prepared the affidavit, warned Gauld of the consequences of his actions, making it clear that the story would lead to criminal proceedings. He urged the former footballer to consult his own lawyer. An indication of the pressure Gauld must have been under was that Wiles' evidence to the Mansfield Magistrates Court, hearing the committal proceedings, included reference to journalist Michael Gabbert pushing Gauld to sign the affidavit. The paper wanted their pound of flesh.

Within a year of his appearance in a Rochdale courthouse, Jimmy was facing committal proceedings in front of Mansfield Magistrates. The prosecution's outlining of their case showed how big the scandal had become. It was to rock football to its roots. In all there were 14 charges of conspiracy to defraud. It involved ten players. Gauld was the only one named in each of the separate charges. The others were Jack Fountain (York City), Richard Beattie (St Mirren but formerly with Portsmouth), Samuel Chapman (Mansfield Town), David 'Bronco' Layne (Sheffield Wednesday), Peter Swan (Sheffield Wednesday), Tony Kay (Everton but formerly Sheffield Wednesday), Brian Phillips (Mansfield Town), Kenneth Thomson (Hartlepools) and Ronald Howells (Walsall, but with Scunthorpe at the time of the offences).

The presence of internationals Swan and Kay ensured that there was huge public interest. Layne presence in the dock was also commanding attention. After getting 28 goals in 41 games for Swindon he hit another 44 in 65 for Bradford City. At the time of his arrest he had scored more than 50 times in just over 80 appearances for Sheffield Wednesday and was looking like international material. Dick Beattie had been Celtic's goalkeeper before coming south to play for Portsmouth and Peterborough. At the time he was implicated by Gauld he was back in Scotland with St Mirren. Chapman had been at Portsmouth before returning to Mansfield. He was one of the few who was able to make a decent living in the game afterwards, eventually managing Wolves for a season. The rest were no more than journeymen and football turned its back on all of them. The case ended on 26 January 1965. Gauld was jailed for four years and was ordered to pay £5,000 costs. Arthur James QC for the prosecution informed the Judge that "the total costs of the case to this evening are assessed at £6,500".

Phillips and Fountain each got 15 months with 15 guineas costs (£15.75p) while Beattie got a nine month stretch. Thomson, Howells and Chapman faced six month sentences while Layne, Swan and Kay each went down for four months. Swan, Kay and Howells were also ordered to pay £100 costs.

In his summing up the judge did not spare Gauld. Amongst other things Mr Justice Lawton told the former Argyle man, "You are responsible for the ruin of footballers of the distinction of Swan and Kay and you have ruined the life of an intelligent man like Thomson". He went on, "I have reminded myself time and again during this trial that I am not sitting here

TWO FOOTBALLERS FOR TRIAL: OTHERS ON PLOT CHARGE

Two footballers were committed for trial by the magistrates at Mansfield, Nottinghamshire, yesterday in connexion with the allegations in the football bets case.

James Gauld, aged 33, of Berry Hill Road, Mansfield, and John Fountain, a 32, of Dragon Road, Leeds, were committed on bail to Nottinghamshire Assizes on four charges of conspiracy. Both pleaded Not Guilty and reserved defence.

Gauld and Fountain were then in the dock by two other players, Beattie, of Ralston Avenue, Glasgow, and Samuel Chapman, of thorpe Road, Cosham, Portsmouth

All four were charged with to ensure that York City lost port County and Portsmouth Peterborough United on April

Gauld and Beattie face him of ensuring that Peterboro Queen's Park Rangers on 1962 and that St. Mirren le on April 30, 1963.

Gauld, Beattie, and Chap charged with ensuring that to Peterborough on Gauld and Cha ensuring that Mai lington on April 1

THE GO

Mr. H. Skinner, fo that the charges were of agreements where on their own team to winnings as a result.

In 1962 Chapma Portsmouth, was tr Town. At Portsr Beattie, who so was in "fix" a ma In the fir left Portsm to play, but Mr. Skinne Chapman an Gauld, h man and lose again match. money on All the was put dead, whe time book

Gauld l in winning Beattie re of the ris the match By Sept on, Beatt While he met Gau arranged Queen's

By the end of the season, he said, Beattie had again been transfer had gone to St. Mirren. Gauld and got in touch by telephone and arrang St. Mirren should lose against Dunde that occasion Gauld sent money to Sc for Beattie to put on the match.

Detective-inspector P. McLeod, cky police, said that on September nt to St. Mirren's ground, wh he told him that he I me from Det Nottin

"CAPTAIN SAID MATCH WAS FIXED"

ALLEGATION MADE BY PLAYER

During a football match which resulted in a 4—0 win for Stockport County, the captain of the Hartlepool United team told an opposing player to avoid harassing the goalkeeper so much, as the game had been "fixed"— a former Hartlepool footballer told the Magistrates at Mansfield, Nottinghamshire, yesterday.

Andrew Fraser, of Galadale Crescent, Newton Grange, Midlothian, said that his former captain, Kenneth Gordon Thomson, of Whitby Road, Nunthorpe, Middlesbrough, one of three men committed for day for trial at Nottinghamshire Assizes on conspiracy summonses, had offered him £20 to play badly.

The other two men, also accused of conspiring to defeat bets from them were James Gauld of Berry Hill Road, Mansfield, and John Fountain, near Clipstone Road, of Berry Hill Road, near Mansfield, Forest Town, said that after agreeing to play badly I was

is Hibs, I would not do than £300 or £400.
Detective-superintendent of Nottinghamshire Polic Chapman at his home. C alleged that he Gauld, C others used to meet in th Mansfield to discuss matc man replied: "No comm
He said he asked if C bet on a fixed odds co replied: "Only 10s. or £1 alleged one soup on a b Oldham and Hartlepool and they had won £1,300 I'd like to think so.
nother where Beatt tendent

BRIBES OFFERED BY EX-FOOTBALLER

James Gauld, the former Mansfield own football, was found Guilty at chdale Magistrates' Court, Lanca re, yesterday of offering bribes to ballers to play badly. He was fined al of £60.
ld, aged 35, of Berry Hill Road, eld, Nottinghamshire, was alleged pproached the Oldst

REPORTER DENIES HE 'USED' FOOTBALLER

ALLEGED CONFESSIONS OF "FIXING"

FROM OUR CORRESPONDENT

NOTTINGHAM, JAN. 14

Sunday newspaper reporter denied ttinghamshire Assizes today that used a former Mansfield Town ller. James Gauld, as a "cats and agent provocateur to obtain confessions of football

the third day of the trial of 10 present professional footballers of conspiring to defraud book "fixing" a number of matches. 35, called the "master mind has admitted 14 counts. ond trial which opened today, and former Scunthorpe United ld Howells, aged 29, pleaded conspiring with Gauld and aud bookmakers by "throw unthorpe v. Derby County 1963. mination the reporter, Mr. told the jury that after a e run by his paper in 1963 ere dealt with summarily and Gauld at Roch

TRIAL BY NEWSPAPER ALLEGED

FROM OUR CORRESPONDENT

NOTTINGHAM, JAN.

former Scunthorpe Unit Ronald Howells, were tinghamshire Assi asked to substi was in fact and fo Jam

TWO MORE FOOTBALLERS COMMITTED FOR TRIAL

Two more footballers were committed for trial today by Mansfield Magistrates' to Nottingham Assizes in connexion with the football bets conspiracy allegations.

They were Richard Beattie, of Ralston Avenue, Crookston, Glasgow, and Samuel man, of Mabelthorpe Road, Cosham, of Berry Hill Road, Mans trial last week

FURTHER CASE

Detective-inspector J. Whitehead, cross examined by Mr. Edward Hooton, that the allegations against Phillips, were contained in a period of about March and April of last chilips, out adrift

GAOL SENTENCES ON TEN FOOTBALLERS

GAULD GIVEN FOUR YEARS AND TOLD TO PAY £5,000

Ten professional and former professional footballers, found Guilty of conspiracy to defraud by "fixing" matches, were all sentenced to terms of imprisonment by Mr. Justice Lawton at Nottinghamshire Assizes yesterday.

James Gauld, the former Mansfield Town inside forward, who had been described as the central figure in the events, was sentenced to four years and was ordered to pay £5,000 costs.

Two others got 15 months, one nine months, three others six months, and the other three four months.

COSTS OF £6,500

The others sentenced were:—

John Fountain, aged 31, of Dragon Road, Leeds, former captain of York City (15 months and ordered to pay 50 guineas costs);

Brian John Phillips, aged 32, of Clipstone Road, West Forest Town, near Mansfield, Nottinghamshire, former captain of Mansfield Town (15 months);

Richard Scott Beattie, aged 27, of Rolston Avenue, Crookston, Glasgow, St. Mirren, former Scottish international goalkeeper (nine months);

Kenneth Thomson, aged 34, of Samaria Gardens, Middlesbrough, Hartlepools United centre half (six months);

Ronald Howells, aged 29, of Bee Lane, Fordhouses, Wolverhampton, Walsall half back (six months and £100 costs);

Samuel Edward Campbell Chapman, aged 26, of Mabelthorpe Road, Cosham, Portsmouth, former Mansfield Town captain (six months);

David Richard Layne, aged 25, of Middlewood Road, Sheffield, Sheffield Wednesday centre forward (four months);

Anthony Herbert Kay, aged 27, of Kendal Drive, Magull, Liverpool, Everton and former Sheffield Wednesday player (four months, and £100 costs);

Peter Swan, aged 28, of Butler Road, Sheffield, Sheffield Wednesday centre half (four months and £100 costs).

Mr. Arthur James, Q.C., for the prosecution, told the Judge that the total costs of the prosecution "to this evening" were £6,500.

Sentencing Gauld, Mr. Justice Lawton said to him: "Your crime has been great. It is my duty to pass a sentence on you to make it clear to all evil-minded people in all branches of sport that this type of activity is a crime and a serious one.

"Over a long period and from one end of this kingdom to another you have befouled professional football and corrupted your friends and acquaintances. You have done it in order to put money into your own pocket. You are responsible for the ruin of footballers of the distinction of Kay and Swan and you have ruined the life of an intelligent man like Thomson.

"This is not the end. I have to look at the public consequences of your behaviour. I have got to think of the young footballers who came into football in the years when you were operating your criminal enterprises and the example you set and those associated with you gave these young men."

He added that he had not forgotten the tens of thousands of ordinary citizens who paid to watch a match and saw only a dishonest charade.

The Judge went on: "I have reminded myself time and again during this trial that I am not sitting here as a committee of the Football Association condemning people for breaking the rules and to condemn those who behaved in the way you behaved when you sold the reputations of your friends to The People newspaper."

"UNPLEASANT DUTY"

Sentencing the English international players Swan, capped 19 times, and Kay, centre forward, the judge said: "You present me with the most unpleasant part of my duty. I accept you were involved on one isolated occasion and I accept it was really by chance you got involved— the chance of Layne going to Mansfield to watch a football match on a day of

"On the other hand Kay and Swan as internationals should have been able to protect themselves against any blandishments held out. The greater your distinction in football the greater your fall must be".

None of the 10 is now connected with football. Gauld at the time of the offences was with Swindon Town and Mansfield Town and is unemployed. Fountain was a joiner. Beattie an unemployed welder, and Phillips a glazier. Layne runs a cafe. He was on Sheffield Wednesday's pay roll until the trial. Chapman was a light attendant and Thomson a student teacher at St. Bede's College, Durham. Howells was with Scunthorpe at the time of the offences and was a clerk in his father's newsagent's shop. Kay was with Sheffield Wednesday at the time of the offences. He was on the payroll of Everton until the trial. Swan was on the Sheffield Wednesday payroll until the trial.

FINDINGS FOR F.A. COMMISSION

An official of the Football Association, on hearing the sentences, said: "An F.A. commission began to investigate this matter, but it was suspended pending the court case.

"The procedure now will be that the Football League will obtain court records of the findings and these will be reported to the members of the commission for their decision on the next step as far as they are concerned."

Mr. J. Richards, President of the Football League, said at his home at Barnsley, Yorkshire: "This is a very sad day for football. I hope that all connected with the game, whatever position they are in, will see that there is no repetition of this sort of thing."

Sir Stanley Rous, a former secretary of the Football Association, said: "The worst feature of the whole case is that it involved international players of some renown and one can only hope that the strong action that has been taken will act as a deterrent to others.

"From an F.I.F.A. point of view it is a matter of some satisfaction that national associations are being so strict with this kind of misconduct."

Mr. Eric Taylor, the Sheffield Wednesday general manager, said: "We are making no approach to the Football Association regarding cancellation of the players' registrations. We are waiting for the F.A. to tell us what to do."

was with Swindon Town and Mansfield

had rejected a sugges-
Howells, Mr. Michael
his paper was the
t caddish of news-
tice Lawton said:
dish or not, rather a
seem to like it, don't

RAP
[ot
rp lly describes you.
r catspaw Gauld in

completely untrue.
I put that the tape
hould v a trap.
Scun- agree it was a
le, and in which only a
nthorpe
in them e would accept
re away agent provo-
Retford ibbert said that
ut on the s had to lead
the match which would
went on. ween Gauld
sy of Mans idetta against
ad cold fee
getting on ie recording
ry, secondly ween Gauld
e second olverhamp
anited to come o the jury
ice also re-
auld and Chap ion that a
ople involved in the re-
tribute a sum tte the jury.
atened to expose ludge ex-
at Derby and the in their
of lost, so the bet morrow.

Gauld and Chan-
idavits acknowl-
onspiracy
interviewed by th
knowledge of it, but
met him outside o
Wolverhampton and
as recorded on a tape

adjourned until next
last of the 14 cases to

that a tape recording
conversation between
in a car in Bee Lane.

Jimmy Gauld creates headlines for all the wrong reasons. The nation was gripped by the trial which saw two international footballers jailed.

All cuttings from the Times

Engulfed by scandal, Gauld is pictured leaving the leaving the Nottingham Assizes.

Colin Parsons collection

as a committee of the Football Association, condemning people for breaking the rules and to condemn those who behaved in the way you did when you sold the reputations of your friends to *the People* newspaper." Gauld was running most of his operations from the Little John public house, in Ravenshead near Mansfield. Reginald Parry the landlord would lay the single, double and treble accumulators, spread across several bookmakers. It was the bets in December 1962 that aroused national suspicion. After seeing comment in the newspapers that bookmakers were questioning some of the results, Parry asked Gauld if there was anything 'screwy' about them. Gauld assured him there was not. By the Tuesday Parry received a cheque for £922 from one bookmaker. He also received a cheque for £100 from a company who had refused to accept the bet. Pointers of Norwich at first refused to pay out 'pending enquiries.' They eventually paid £380. A company called Oxenham paid out £550, while another firm called Guinness paid out £550 after Parry's solicitor had intervened. With the average weekly wage no more than £8 or £9 it can be seen that this was big, big money. And this was just one weekend's work!

Parry's only role was to place the bets and then clear the winnings cheques through his account before passing cash to Gauld. Parry was never prosecuted, with all the evidence indicating that for a long time he believed Gauld was fortunate rather than dishonest. In Peter Swan's book *Setting the Record Straight* he writes about Gauld using the pseudonym Parry when he put bets on. It would have been more accurate to say he used Parry.

Reading through the reports of the Assize Court proceedings, the charges covered a period from April 1960, when Gauld was at Swindon, and April 1963. But all of the matches specified during the case related to matches played in the 1961-62 and 1962-63 seasons. Are we really to believe that Gauld and his co-defendants were not actively engaged in match fixing during 1960-61? The highest profile game seems to have been the Ipswich v Sheffield Wednesday match which was played on 1 December 1962. It was mainly lower league matches which were the subject of Gauld's influence.

Jimmy Gauld admitted to making a total of £3,375 out of betting on the outcome of football matches. Judging by the account above of just one week's haul being received by the licensee of the Little John, that figure could well be on the low side. Argyle's John L Williams remembers sitting on the Torquay team bus outside Hartlepool's ground. The team were ready to leave but Gulls' manager Eric Webber was still in post-match conversation with his opposite number. John told me, "As Mr Webber got back on the coach he made straight for me. What you have to remember Hartlepool had been at the centre of a number of games believed to have been fixed. Mr Webber told me that the Hartlepool manager had just been told that the police reckoned that Jimmy had £12,000 in the bank when he was arrested. That was a lot of money for them days, a lot of money."

All the indications are that almost from the time he went to Mansfield he was fixing football matches on a weekly basis, increasingly so after he broke his leg. Indeed, prior to that time the Swindon historian Dick Marritt heard stories that Gauld missed no opportunity to promote his match-fixing activity when at the County Ground. Marritt told me "There was a testimonial at Swindon, one night towards the end of the 59-60 season. Several internationals were down to play and one was staying in the Railway Hotel. I remember my dad saying at the time that this particular player was approached during his stay, to see if he would be interested in taking bribes to throw matches. When Gauld put his idea to the player he immediately booked out and did not play in the match." Who knows the truth?

In 1997 the scandal was the subject of a BBC drama. Starring Steve Coogan and George Sewell as the investigative journalists Gabbet and Campling, the play had Christopher Fulford playing Gauld. He portrayed him as a sullen, bitter man, disillusioned by the game he blamed for bringing him down.

Researching the background to the match fixing scandal was not a pleasant experience. Each page seemed to further dismantle the reputation of a man who had given immense pleasure to tens of thousands of Argyle fans. The only smile came when I read the account of a case in the Court of Criminal Appeal 'Regina v Gauld.' *The Times* of 3 July 1965 carried a report of an appeal by James Gauld, at present detained in HM Prison, Wakefield, against an order made by Mr Justice Lawton on 26 January 1965. Mr KM Willock, appearing for Gauld, pointed out to the Lord Chief Justice that as his client had pleaded guilty to all of the offences, the rest of the trial and the costs incurred therein only concerned the trials of Gauld's co-accused. Justice Lawton's order for Gauld to pay £5,000 costs was rescinded and was substituted for one calling for £380. Although the Lord Chief Justice understood Mr Justice Lawton's aim to recover much of the monies Gauld made from the *People* and from betting, in terms of the 1952 Criminal Cases Act he ruled that he would have to allow the appeal.

None of Jimmy's Home Park colleagues know precisely what happened to him after the bribery trials. Some told me they had heard that after he was released from prison he went to live in France, others that he returned to Ireland but no one really knew. Rumours abounded that he and Mrs Gauld went their separate ways but no one really knows. It seems unlikely that they were apart at the time of the court appearances.

Towards the end of the Nottingham Assizes case, Gauld's solicitor made mention of the family. "Apart from the convictions at Rochdale, and these proceedings, my client is a man of good character with a good home life. He is devoted to his wife and children." He went on, "My client has had two weeks in custody in Lincoln prison and to him a cell was a terrifying punishment, for however long he had to spend there".

In trying to piece together his life before and after his time at Argyle I spoke to several former players at Charlton, Everton and Swindon, but it seems he was not a man to stay in touch. 'Bronco' Layne certainly tried to make contact with Gauld but his calls were never returned. The bribery business probably exacerbated his wish to stay anonymous. One thing is certain. None of Jimmy Gauld's team mates at Plymouth were aware of any match fixing during his time at Home Park. This project has led to me forming a genuine friendship with several of the players from that era. I am confident that had it been going on I would have been told, even it was off the record. Indeed, I frequently asked the question and on every occasion offered to make the answer unattributed. It was still the same response – it simply never happened.

Jimmy passed away in St Mary's Hospital, Westminster on 9 December 2004, aged 75. He had been working in London as a property security guard or caretaker, perhaps in the Marylebone area. But nobody *really* knows. Although many people I spoke to were quite ambivalent about the match-fixing, the fact that he then sold out those who had assisted him would seem to be the basis of the loathing he endured afterwards. It is unlikely that he ever got a Christmas card from either Swan or Kay. His key role in the *People's* entrapment of those who trusted him was, to most fair-minded people, abhorrent. It was one of the first "kick and tell" stories to be run by a Sunday tabloid, and one of the most damaging ever in terms of football's reputation.

Jimmy Gauld was a wonderful talent who brightened many a match day at Home Park. Success has always had a way of promoting tolerance of shortfalls in personality. Jimmy was a case in point. One of his Home Park contemporaries, who preferred to comment off the record, summed it up thus. "Maybe you could not help but admire him as a player but as a man he was more difficult to like. "As for the ladies, that was quite another thing again. They all found him to be an absolute charmer."

How good could Jimmy Gauld have been? If he could have past a betting shop with the same alacrity he went by a defender, who knows what he could have achieved in the game? But so many people blessed with great ability on a football field seem to be flawed when away from that arena. Regrettably, our 1958-59 hero was one such player.

In an article for the Swindon Town programme of 23 October 1999, club historian Dick Mattick summed it up perfectly. *"I prefer to remember the shock of blond hair above a sweat-stained shirt weaving through the opposition defence, and the man who was willing to give a youngster and autograph with a cheery smile and a friendly word. Sometimes it is as well that we do not know the future."*

Alex Govan finishes in style in a 5-2 win over Sheffield United at Home Park on 6 September 1952. The attendance was 31,456.

During 1956-57 Alex scored 3 hat-tricks in 10 days. Here he beats PNE keeper Fred Else on his way to the second of those hat-tricks. On the day he outshone Preston and England star Tom Finney.
Both photographs are from Alex Govan's scrapbook

CHAPTER TWELVE

ALEX GOVAN

It is easy to tell when Alex Govan is saying something interesting – his lips are moving! He seems to be able to recall most days of his life, right back to when he first bowled into John Street Infants School in his native Bridgeton, Glasgow.

He had precious little time for matters academic. From his earliest days he was more interested in kicking a football, intuitively knowing that he seemed a little bit better than those around him. The tenement life in Bridgeton made for a close community, and with no television or spare money for regular nights out, there were often a lot of people watching kids playing street football. "There were old fellows leaning against the wall, smoking their pipes, while lots of other folk watched from the windows on the upper levels of the building," he told me as we chatted at his Manadon home. Some amongst those watching knew that Govan's was already a special talent, a wee boy with an inbuilt confidence and a outstanding left foot.

After progressing from John Street Infants to the Elementary school there, entry to the Secondary level was based on academic ability. He had already made up his mind that his schooling would have to continue away from John Street. Towards the end of his time at the Elementary he took part in a football match against the Secondary school side. Alex takes up the story. "The sports master at the older boys school was a wonderful man called Dandy McLean. He told me after the match that I would be going to the Secondary". For once, Govan's inbuilt confidence deserted him and he told McLean that he was pretty sure he would not make the grade. "You will son", the teacher replied, "if nothing else, you will be an important part of the football team".

McLean's judgement was sound. At 11 years of age he was chosen to play for Glasgow Schools at under 15 level, in a game against Lanarkshire Schoolboys at Hampden Park. Although the result is lost in the mists of time, he recalls being totally unfazed about playing. But kit was a problem. Alex did not have a pair of boots to wear. With money very tight his father took him off to 'the Barras', a market place which still exists to this day. Despite the occasion the boy would have to make do with second-hand boots. They searched the place but could not find a pair small enough. Alex chuckles as he tells me, "My dad decided that there was only one thing for it – a pair that was a bit too big and two pairs of socks. The boots were so big I could nearly turn around in them!" He imagines the same scenario today. "If nothing else peer pressure would demand the best boots available, as well as clothes to wear to the match. Parents would be unlikely to see much change from £200".

To emphasise the poverty that existed back then, Alex recalled other visits to the Barras where his dad would go to the 'glasses stall'. "Folk would sell or pawn their specs or those of dead relatives. "People would then come along and keep trying various pairs till they found some that suited their eyesight."

He was the third of five children. He had an older brother and sister and two younger sisters. His father, also Alexander, was a former miner from Prestwick in Ayrshire. He had moved to Glasgow to make a better life for the family and found work as an undertaker. He first settled in the Gorbals, before moving with his firm to their Bridgeton premises.

During the war the Clydebank industrial corridor was a regular target for *Luftwaffe* air raids. Alex junior can recall his mother and father talking each morning when his father came home from work. At 12 years old he was plenty old enough to understand their conversations. From what he told me it is clear that his father saw and dealt with some awful things, events far too horrible to be described in a book of this nature.

He left school at 14. It had not been a tremendous success and he had no qualifications. Although quite scared at the time, Alex now looks back at one school report time with some amusement. His father was of a generation that recognised that a good education was a route away from poverty. He would scrutinise each term's report in great detail. "I was really worried about this particular report. I had tried, albeit unsuccessfully, to forge his signature but it hadn't worked. Anyway the rest went in one at a time; they were all pretty good at school. Father had looked at their reports and issued instructions that they must stay in to further study this subject or that subject."

"As I went in I knew I was in for a hard time. They all stood outside the door smirking, waiting for the crash as my dad would read that I had got three zeroes for cheating – copying other people's work. "He sat in the chair reading it, sighing as he went. Then he just looked at me and said, 'buggered if I know what we are going to do with you son!'"

After school Alex worked for a short time for on a barrow, making deliveries for a chemist. Weeks later he was given a job as petrol boy in a garage at his father's firm. It ended with his father sacking him on the spot for falling asleep in the forecourt cubby hole. Alex laughs as he tells me about a petrol coupon racket he had going. "There was an old boy who used to come in from my brother's firm. He was a bit short-sighted and I used to give him four gallons but write six in the book. He just signed where I pointed, and we could then sell the coupons on to folk who were short of them".

From there he quickly moved on to a small firm, CP Lang Printers. "Through the garage I knew a man from Langs. They made paper bags for bakers and they supplied greaseproof to butchers. I found him in the snooker hall and he told me he was looking for a van boy. I stayed with them until the time I left to come to Plymouth".

Although post-war Argyle had a good scouting system in Scotland, it is likely that he first came to their attention when he played for Scotland Youth against the Welsh. The match, played at Swansea, was his first trip out of Scotland. Future Argyle star Jimmy Gauld was a travelling reserve for the game. The problem for Argyle would be that both Dundee and

Queens Park were also showing strong interest in the player.

Manager Jack Tresarden was determined that the club would capture the young Scotsman, but a problem would be distance. Although Glasgow and Plymouth remain the same distance apart as they were then, the post-war transport infrastructure must have made it seem much farther than we would consider it to be today. That first trip to Plymouth ended with the boy returning to Glasgow due to homesickness. "It was just too far from home and everything I knew." The club then sent scout Alec Hardy up to Scotland to invite him back, this time including his father in the offer of a free journey and free accommodation. Alex explained "Not unlike many Scots of his generation, my father was partial to a drop of whiskey. "We were down there for a week. Director Bob Heath looked after dad in the Grand Hotel and ensured the room was always sufficiently stocked. "Needless to say, by the end of the week dad was telling me what a good club this was to play for, what a nice place Plymouth was, how good the ground was and how pleasant all the people were and so on!" But once more he returned without signing, but during that second visit, the club had suggested a good reason for him to sign for them. Director Dudley Coles was the head of a large building company. With Plymouth recovering from the blitz, it was explained to young Alex that they could employ him as an apprentice carpenter, which would lead to him being excused from conscription. Coles told Alex that with the amount of construction going on in Plymouth the military authorities would look kindly upon anyone engaged in building work.

Alec Hardy was once more on young Govan's tail, tracking him down while he was having a trial at Scottish Junior Club Kilsyth Rangers. Hardy told Alex afterwards, "Look son, you are wasting your time here. You are far too good for this lot". The boy finally gave in, with the offer of keeping him away from conscription being a key factor. At the third time of asking he was an Argyle player, signing his first contract with the club on 24 August 1946. "If my memory serves me right Tommy Docherty signed for Celtic on the same day. "We had played against each other in schools matches."

It was something of a 'ghost' apprenticeship. Alex would have to clock in on site each morning – he was part of the team building the Ham Estate – but could then go off to Home Park for training. He rarely got back much before clocking out time! "Unfortunately, it was only half a story they told me. "They forgot to say that although I could disappear off to Home Park from the site whenever the club wanted me there, no one told me that to complete the apprenticeship I should also have gone to night school. "Looking back, I didn't make many door frames but I made a hell of a lot of tea."

Although Dudley Coles Limited did not prevent his enlistment, one of his colleagues there did play a key part in the rest of Alex's life. In 1946 one of the foremen on the firm, Phil, took Alex along to a dance at the Sutton Trust Hall in St Budeaux. He introduced Alex to a young lady called Sylvia Jolly. Six years later they married and have lived happily ever after. His call up papers arrived in 1947 and he joined the Royal Air Force, and serving just over 18 months. Once conscripted, it was just like everything else in his life – he took it in his stride and made the best of it. While in the Air Force he played plenty of football, representing the full RAF team in games against the Army, the Royal Navy, an England Select XI and the Oxford University side. Like a lot of other players National Service was an interruption to his progress. With Argyle in the Second Division he needed to be in full time training and to be there to catch the manager's eye. He did play regularly for the reserves during his military service. In his two spells with the club he played 128 Football Combination League games and weighed in with 47 goals. The bulk of these appearances were in his first period at Home Park. It was traditional for young players in the immediate post-war period to serve long periods learning their trade in the 'stiffs'.

Once he had signed the young Scot was impatient and wanted to be in the first team. He scored on his Football Combination debut at the start of 1946-47, in a 2-0 victory over Bournemouth. The reserves would draw 12,000 to 14,000 back then. Alex is convinced that many of them were there to keep up with the result from wherever the first team was playing. "With no TV, radio and all that, they used to announce the goals from the first team game over the tannoy at the reserve matches. It was a real attraction to people. It was probably the only way they could get to know the progress of the first team game." Despite the large crowds the reserves attracted, the boy wanted to test his skills in the Football League. He challenged Tresarden to give him a game and, surprisingly, the manager gave in. "I told him that I hadn't come 500 mile to play in the reserves. "I was surprised when he put me in against Coventry though, because you didn't really speak to the manager in those days."

Taking the place of future manager Ellis Stuttard, his debut came on 5 October 1946, in a 2-2 draw at home to Coventry City. He remembers going close with a couple of headers but only had one more outing that season, in a 3-2 defeat at Bradford PA. "The manager told me after my debut that he was pleased with my performance, adding that whilst I wouldn't play next week, or the week after that even, I would play when he thought I was completely ready. He asked me to trust his judgement and, as a very young man, I could not have asked for fairer than that from a man who had been an international before the war and a good player with West Ham." (Tresarden played in the West Ham side for the famous 'White Horse' FA Cup Final of 1923, as did former Argyle player David Jack.)

A combination of Govan's military service, the side's eternal struggle close to the foot of the Second Division and Jimmy Rae's succession to the manager's chair, meant that in each of the 1947-48 and 1948-49 seasons Alex made only 2 outings. He then made just a single appearance in 1949-50 and was still waiting to score his first goal for the club. These were troubled times for Argyle. They had finished 19th in 46-47, then 17th 20th before being relegated in 49-50. Football was much different then and clubs were reluctant give young players a chance, especially in a struggling side. It was unusual to see too many first team players who were under 21 years old.

Season 1950-51 was where it really started for Alex Govan. He made 35 League appearances in the Third Division (South) and hit the net on ten occasions. He also played in three out of four FA Cup ties, including a 2-1 home defeat to a powerful Wolverhampton Wanderers side that was to win three separate League titles during the 50s. "I think there were 40,000 in the ground, with two deep around the running track." In the League, Argyle finished fourth. Importantly, the side was quite settled and would form the nucleus of the great 1952-53 side who achieved Argyle's highest ever finish.

Alex explained to me what it was like back then. "It is amazing what we achieved in the circumstances. You have to remember that after the war Home Park was between being a bomb-site and a building site. Our training kit was second-hand submarine jerseys that someone scrounged off the Navy. The names if the Navy boys who wore them in the submarines were still on the labels!" (See page 147.) It is for that reason that Govan nominates Jack Tresarden as the best manager he has known. "Jack definitely laid the foundations for that team. "He was left to start from scratch after the war with next to no players, no ground to speak of and no facilities. "It is amazing we held on to a Second Division place for so long after the war."But things were on the up, both for the club and for Govan. Few people were surprised when in 1951-52 Plymouth secured the single promotion slot from the Southern section of the Third Division, on the way becoming that last Argyle side to have scored more than 100 goals in a single campaign. Govan played another 35 times, scoring on 9 occasions. Despite their success in the league, their FA Cup lasted no further than a first round trip to the Den.

Through the years the slogan 'good enough for the Third but not good enough for the Second' has been applied to many Plymouth teams. This side were no different – nobody expected great things in the first season back in the second tier. How wrong they were! Argyle roared into fourth place, the nearest they have ever come to reaching the First Division. Govan played in 33 of the 42 League matches, netting ten goals. Recalling the excitement that season brought he told me "Although the Birmingham side of the middle 50s was the best I played in, I have no doubts that this was the finest team Plymouth Argyle has ever had. The only disappointment was the FA Cup. We had beaten Coventry and I then got the winner against Barnsley in the next round. They had a young Irish lad in their team that day who nobody had ever heard of. Danny Blanchflower was his name! Then in the fifth round we had the luck of the draw, with a home tie against Gateshead from the Third (North). I'm afraid we were all guilty of counting our win bonus beforehand, but in front of a big crowd (29,736) we went down 1-0".

It is clear that Govan had great respect for the legendary Jack Chisolm. "In those days the captaincy was a very important role, both on and off the field. There was no manager in the dugout shouting – the captain was there for that. 'Chissie' was a great man, on and off the field. He was brilliant socially. He would tell us that he had arranged, say, a dart match against the Cherry Tree. You would be told to be there at 7.30 sharp and

The pictures above show Govan in his Birmingham City days. For a couple of seasons he was one of the most feared forwards in the land. He also helped Birmingham City to the 1956 FA Cup Final.
From Alex Govan's scrapbook

Alex Govan returned to Argyle in 1958 after an unhappy spell at Fratton Park. Here he shows off his replica shirt, presented on 27 September 2008 when some of the 1958-59 players returned to Home Park. They were being honoured on the 50th anniversary of their success.

Photo by the author

there was no way you would not attend. I remember him telling us one night that the landlord had agreed to stand us all a pint and a sandwich. He then said to us that if the landlord offered a second free pint we were to accept, even if we didn't want it. "Chissie told us that he would drink it!" Just after the 51-52 title win he called us together to say that the landlord of the Harvest Home had shown his appreciation. He gave me £2 for each of you so that means that I owe you £2. By the time I left for Birmingham at the end of the next season he still owed me £2. But who cares, he was a wonderful man for the club and the town."

Govan's season finished four matches from the end, in a 2-2 draw at home to Notts County on Easter Monday 1953. It turned out to be his last game for the Greens prior to a surprise summer move to Birmingham City. Alex and his young wife Sylvia were on holiday in Scotland, visiting Govan's parents in Bridgeton. They received a telegram from Home Park, with Jimmy Rae asking Alex to reply with the nearest telephone number he could be called at. (Communications were a little more difficult 56 years ago!) When they spoke Rae explained that the club was trying to sell him to Birmingham City. He added that he did not want the player to go, but Govan was instructed to meet Blues' manager Bob Brocklebank that evening at Glasgow's Central Hotel.

Despite the couple being wined and dined by the City boss, Alex was not the least bit interested in moving to the Midlands, or to any other location. With his wife being a Plymouth girl he could not envisage the transfer taking place. Govan initially turned down the move, but there was a second day of negotiations. Brocklebank had returned to the Govan household to ask for another meeting. This time, during a second dinner meeting, the Blues' boss told the player to go for a walk and then concentrated on persuading Govan's wife on the advantages of re-locating to the Midlands. "Whatever he said worked," said Alex. "By the time I returned the forms were ready to sign. My wife had been persuaded by the offer of a brand new house in the leafy Sheldon district – one of the Birmingham Board was a big developer. We were in a flat in Lisson Grove in Mutley at the time, so the thought of a brand new, modern house was something worth considering. After a few wee negotiations about the rent I became a Birmingham City player". Although clubs could not pay more than the maximum wage, it was possible to offer perks that did not breach the rules. "I told Brocklebank that if the rent was reduced from £3 a week to 30 bob (£1.50 today) I would sign. And don't forget, the rent included all my gas and electric".

Govan moved in exchange for £6,500, money that would turn out to be essential to Argyle's survival. It was inevitable that with Argyle having finished 4th in a competitive Second Division (a point and two places above Birmingham incidentally), other clubs would be alerted. Alex told me that although the move came a surprise, he was often told by Neil Dougall that the St Andrews club were keen on him. "Neil had met his future wife Monica when he was at Birmingham. "He used to go back there and see her at weekends. "Every week he would come back and tell me that Birmingham wanted me to go there."

It turned out to be a wonderful move for Alex Govan and within a few months his wing partner at Plymouth, Gordon Astall, joined him in the second city. Despite his initial reluctance to leave Plymouth Alex can now appreciate it was the best time of his professional career, by some distance. Things started well for him with a goal in his debut, a 2-0 win against Hull City. In his first season (1953-54) they finished 7th. The next season saw them promoted as champions, with the team amassing 92 goals in 42 outings. Each member of the regular forward line (Astall, Kinsey, Brown, Murphy and Govan) got to double figures, with Alex finishing second top scorer to Murphy. He remembers them going to Doncaster on the last day in need of a win. He scored the final goal in a 5-1 victory. He reflects, "I am proud that it was me who had last word in such a successful season". He made two winning visits to Home Park in Birmingham's colours, scoring with his *right* foot in the first encounter, a 3-0 win for the visitors. Jimmy Rae was waiting for him in the tunnel, chiding him that he never ever used his right foot during his years at Home Park.

But there is one particular day of that campaign which stands far above the rest - 11 December 1954. City were at home to Liverpool, who were mid-table after coming down the previous season. In a Press interview some years later Alex described the events of that day. "Before the game we would have taken just a 1-0 win. "Although we had beat Port Vale 7-2 the week before Liverpool had a few decent players. Billy Liddell was a Scottish international and they had a flying young left winger called Alan A'Court. Then there was Geoff Twentyman who went on to play a key role when Bill Shankly went there a few years later. But once we scored our first they folded like a pack of cards. After 16 minutes we were three up, but Liddell pulled one back three minutes later. That just seem to inspire us and my old Plymouth team-mate Gordon Astall made it 4-1 for half time. Four minutes later Astall got his second and it was soon 6-1. I scored the seventh in the 77th minute, after full back Jeff Hall and Astall had hit the bar. We then scored again in the 85th and 86th minutes to run out 9-1 winners. Strangely, I am hard pressed to remember any of the Birmingham goals, yet to this day I can shut my eyes and see Billy Liddell's".

Just as in his earlier experience at Plymouth, the promoted team took encouragement from their promotion campaign and finished 6th in their first season back in the top-flight. It remains the highest Birmingham City has ever finished in the Football League. In addition they reached the 1956 FA Cup Final, losing 3-1 to Manchester City, the previous year's beaten finalists. It was the game made famous by the fact that City goalkeeper Bert Trautmann, that year's Footballer of the Year, played with a broken neck for the final 20 minutes. City had Don Revie, who later managed Leeds and England, playing in a (then) unusual deep-lying centre forward role and he ran the game. In the Birmingham side that day was future Argyle skipper John Newman, called in when Roy Warhurst dropped out through injury. Birmingham had been credited with being the first team to reach Wembley without playing at home, and they did not need a single replay. Alex remembers thinking what a blow it was to

lose Warhurst. "From memory we were about 4/9 on favourites. "We never considered we would lose but that is football for you. "Despite the result, it was a wonderful day and I was proud to be the only Scot in the side.
"No disrespect to anyone else, but if Warhurst had played I am certain we would have won the game."

Alex Govan talks fondly of Warhurst and he also had a lot of time for another ex Plymouth player there, Len Boyd. "I was always glad I played in front of that Birmingham defence. I would have hated to play against them." He chuckles as he recalls how they could get stuck in with the best of them. "I often had to tell Warhurst to be careful and remind him that I was on his side. He was a hard man. There were plenty of tough individuals around then – people like Scoular of Newcastle and Docherty at Preston. But none of them mixed it with Roy. Len Boyd was a hard man too and Boydy could really see a pass. His passing was exceptional."

In addition to finding the defeat hard to take he had another deep, much more personal regret about the 1956 FA Cup Final. "My brother died of TB the year before. He was only 34 and would have loved to have seen his brother playing in a match like that. I still find that sad to think about now".

No story about the 1956 FA Cup Final and Alex Govan could be complete without reference to the club song that he is credited with introducing. No one quite knows in which part of the 1956 Cup run that the Harry Lauder song "Keep Right On To The End Of The Road" became the team's anthem. One version of events says that it was when Birmingham were at Arsenal for the quarter-final tie. At manager Arthur Turner's behest, Alex led the players sing-song on the coach with Harry Lauder's paean to persistence . Fans waiting outside the bus for autographs heard the players and took up singing it. Govan is also credited with saying during a Press interview prior to the Sunderland semi-final that it was his favourite song. "Whatever way it happened, when we scored our third goal at Hillsborough that day, every Blues fan was singing it. It was my proudest moment in football—bar none." And what is more, that song has endured as the club's favoured anthem these 52 years. It will be one of the greatest ever epitaphs to any player who has played the game.

Their season was not over after the FA Cup Final. Birmingham City had been invited to an annual exhibition match which was always played during the Edinburgh Festival. Hibs and Hearts would pick a combined XI against English First Division opposition. "I was the only Scot in the Birmingham side so I was really pleased to play in that one." He also played for the Football Combination select XI against the Holland national side. "Although it representing the Combination it had nothing to do with reserve players. Birmingham were in the Combination League so their players were eligible. The manager was George Hardwick and the great Spurs player Tommy Harmer played too. Holland were not the power they are now and we beat them 4-1".

Season 1956-57 saw the former Plymouth man hailed as one of the best players in the First Division. Don't forget, this was in an era when players of the calibre of Stanley Matthews and Tom Finney among many others graced the top tier. Although City finished only 12ᵗʰ in the League, Govan amassed 24 goals, finishing with one more goal than the great Tom Finney. In the end he finished ninth in the leading scorers with household names John Charles (Leeds) 36, Jackie Mudie (Blackpool) 32 and Nat Lofthouse (Bolton) 28 amongst those who finished above him.

During the season he scored no fewer than four First Division hat tricks, three of them early in the season in a period spanning only 10 days. On Wednesday 29 August 1957 he netted three at Fratton Park in a 4-3 success. "The Russian Navy were on a visit to Pompey at the time. The club must have give them tickets because there were a lot of them there, all dressed in red tee shirts. Our change kit was red so they shouted for us." After a 2-0 reverse at Burnley City the following Saturday, City were at home to Newcastle on Wednesday 5 September. He grabbed another three and then repeated the feat by hitting three more on the following Saturday at home to Preston (3-0), the latter in front of 44,500. The match was billed as a battle between the left wingers—Finney and Govan. In the event Finney played at centre-forward.

Alex remembers being interviewed for television by a young David Coleman, then with ITV at the fledgling ABC station in the Midlands. "I did an interview after the Newcastle game on the Wednesday. David Coleman told me that he would ask me on again after the Preston game if I got another hat-trick. I was feeling that confident I asked him what time and where, on live TV! It was good money too, ten guineas (£10.50 and worth half a week's wages). In them days we pooled all that kind of thing and shared it out amongst the lads at the end of the season".

His fourth League hat-trick of that season came against Leeds United in a 3-2 win, a game which was the last John Charles played in England before his £65,000 move to Italy. And Alex provides a marvellous story about that match. "Years and years later a fan came up to me and said that he had a pound note signed by John Charles after he scored in his last game in England against Birmingham. He produced it from his wallet. I told him that I too played in that match and got three goals – let me sign it too and it will be worth a lot more!" Govan's only regret is that players were not presented with the match ball in those days. "The trainer grabbed it and it was dubbined up and used again the next week."

That season saw them have another good FA Cup run, losing 2-0 in the semis to the great pre Munich Manchester United side. He confirms a widely held view in saying, "they were a class side, that is for sure. They were so strong and skilful all over the pitch." On the way to the semi finals he hit his fifth hat-trick in a 5-2 success against Southend United.

He has one more memory of that season. "In a match against Tottenham I came up against Danny Blanchflower again. "He was no longer the unknown boy I had played against when Plymouth beat Barnsley in the FA Cup. Anyway, I went into a challenge with him and caught him. I went over to see how he was. He looked up at me and said 'I thought you were a better player than that.' I felt really bad about that – I was never a malicious player." In the remaining part of 1957-58 Alex Govan played nine times for Portsmouth, scoring twice. On his debut he scored the only goal, against old rivals Aston Villa. It was soon after his transfer from St Andrews and he returned to Birmingham on the same train as the Villa lads. "They were fine with me but their captain Johnny Dixon reminded me that I had never previously scored for Birmingham against the Villa."

Not surprisingly, he remains a household name at City and is a frequent visitor to their St Andrews ground. He is immensely popular with the Birmingham support. At the top of his game he was undoubtedly the finest winger never to play for Scotland. Although Alex Govan is not a man for regrets or post-mortems into what may have been, he remains disappointed that he missed out on international honours. He was chosen only once, for a friendly against Austria. Unfortunately the match was to be played just three days prior to the English FA Cup Final (a minor consideration for the Scottish FA!) and Birmingham, understandably, would not release him. He was never invited to play for his country again.

He never quite recaptured his exceptional form and on transfer deadline day in March 1958 he was transferred to Portsmouth. Players had little say in those days and if a club wanted to move them on they would be gone. Although he still worked as hard as any man who ever played, the electric speed had waned. Birmingham had signed Harry Hooper from Wolves and eventually the club felt able to move Govan on. But no one could take away his record there, which in addition to the Second Division title and the FA Cup Final appearance, included a 2-1 home victory over Inter-Milan where he scored both goals. He also got to play at the Nou Camp against Barcelona in the same competition.

The move did not seem to work for either party and he was only at Fratton Park for six months. Whereas Birmingham had been on the up and up, Portsmouth were in severe decline. When he signed, no one was to know that it would become their penultimate season in the First Division. In 1948-49 and 1949-50 they had won consecutive championships; at the end of the 1958-59 they were relegated and started a journey which eventually see them descend to the Fourth Division.

During the summer of 1958, Govan, on holiday in Plymouth, had a chance meeting with Jack Rowley on a golf course. They knew each other from Rowley's playing days. Alex was surprised when Jack told him that manager Eddie Lever had been replaced at Portsmouth by Freddie Cox, who had moved along the coast after a successful spell at Bournemouth. Jack warned Govan "You won't like him. If you ever have to leave make sure you tell me." Rowley's words were prophetic. Alex returned for pre-season and everything was very different at Fratton Park. In a recent interview (January 2008) Alex told the Portsmouth *Sports Mail* "Mr Cox was one of the first tacticians and you had to play his way or you were out. Up until then there had not been a lot in the way of tactics or systems used to get the best out of players – it was thought you could either play or you couldn't." Govan played just twice more for the Hampshire outfit. First Cardiff and then Brentford came in for him but he turned both down. "After I refused the Brentford offer Cox was livid and threatened that I would end on the dole. "I told him to lift the phone and speak to Jack Rowley. In September 1958 I signed for Plymouth for the second time."

Govan's scathing indictment of Cox was endorsed by their relegation at the end of the season he left. After November 1958 they did not win a League game for the remainder of that season. During the month Govan left the club Cox also sold off Ray Crawford, who went on to earn great fame under Alf Ramsey at Ipswich, and Johnny Gordon who became a star at Birmingham. In March 1959 Derek Dougan left Fratton Park for Blackburn, pausing only to deliver a withering verdict of Cox's prowess as a manager.

Apart from the hiatus at Fratton Park, it is clear that Alex had a wonderful time for during his five years and three months away from Plymouth. Although Anderson and Penk had started the season as first choice wingers, and the team were undefeated, Govan quickly got his first game, due to an injury to Peter Anderson. He was given the captaincy for the night of his return to his first Football League club, in a 3-0 victory over Bury. He had a series of niggling injuries but appeared another 19 times in the League side and scored six times. He also played in the 3-0 home defeat by Cardiff City in the FA Cup. Towards the end of January he was just running into good form when he was injured again. Argyle lost both the home games he missed and he was recalled, and scored, in the famous 8-3 victory over Mansfield. From a personal viewpoint, I will never forget the marvellous headed goal he got against Brentford on Easter Monday. Although he was not the biggest of men, he reckons to have scored about a third of his career goals with his head. At the end of the season he had played sufficient games to earn a Third Division Championship medal. It complemented his 1950-51 Third (South) medal in his first spell at Home Park and the Second Division winner's medal with Birmingham in 1954-55. Then, of course, there was the small matter of his 1956 FA Cup runners-up medal.

He turned 30 in the summer of 1959 and many thought his vast experience would help the side on their return to the Second Division. It did not work out that way. He played in the opening game of the season, then missed the next three before returning for a 6-2 defeat at Middlesbrough. Left out again he was then recalled immediately after the team suffered a 5-0 home defeat to Derby County. He scored on his return in a 1-1 draw at Rotherham and was given a run of eight games. The side won only once, a 6-4 home win over Charlton (the season before the game where Carter got 5!), in which he scored what was to be his final goal for the club.

Alex was given a player-manager's role in the South Western League team, but in February 1960 for the return match at the Valley, an increasingly desperate Jack Rowley recalled both Govan and young winger Johnny Penny. They came in at the expense of Anderson and Penk. Wrexham were keen to take Govan to the Racecourse Ground but he had no intention of moving away from his adopted city for a second time. He turned his back on the professional game and became the landlord of the Hyde Park Hotel on Mutley Plain. Although he and Sylvia remained there for nearly eight years, Alex is adamant that running a pub was not really for him. Later they had a grocer's shop, but with the advance of the large supermarkets, they saw the writing on the wall and sold out. After leaving Argyle Alex Govan managed Truro City before taking charge of Plymouth City's youth team, a side that won every trophy open to them.

Despite the vast amounts of money on offer today, Alex Govan does not envy the modern player. "The way I looked at it was this – just after I started in the game I was a young man on £8 a week, renting a place off a man who only earned £4 a week in the Dockyard. We had no right to complain about the level of wages back then." Wages apart, he simply doesn't see the great camaraderie in the modern game, something that Alex saw as an important part of his life back then. "We were all on roughly the same money. It must surely affect team spirit if the boy on the seat over there is on twice the money you are. If you had earned more money than them, some of those boys I played with would not have passed the ball to you. I just don't see how it can work to have different wages in the same dressing room, with the manager often on less than the players. How does he get respect?"

Alex Govan is marvellous company and time spent with him goes very quickly. He can laugh against himself too. "When you think of it, life is strange. Apart from wanting to get away from Freddie Cox, I got the move back to Plymouth in 1958 because I thought it was best for the family. We would all be together here. Now my son Ian is into property and lives in Spain, my other son Tom (who at one time was also on the Home Park payroll) is a sports master at a school in Harwich and daughter Angela is also a teacher. She lives in bloody Stroud! So much for my master plan! We spend half of our lives travelling to see them."

Alex and Sylvie spend time in Prestwick each year, the birthplace of his long-suffering father. Despite the annoyance of his middle son's lack of effort at school, I think Alex Govan senior would have come to be exceedingly proud of what his son achieved.

Assistant Trainer Bill Harper pictured in one of the submariners' jerseys that Alex describes on page 139. This is what passed for training kit when Alex Govan was making his way in the game in the early 50s.
Bill Harper was a great servant to Plymouth Argyle, first as a goalkeeper, then trainer and finally as groundsman, including the 1958-59 season.

Courtesy Plymouth Argyle

A SUPPORTER'S STORY
Nigel Springthorpe (and the late Bob Morrish)

After an unbeaten opening run of matches, my good friend Bob Morrish and I planned to watch Argyle continue the roll with a win at Colchester. We couldn't afford the train fare, decided against a hitch-hike and settled for the 120 odd mile round trip 'cycle ride. Bob Morrish left London for Colchester very early in the morning. He was no cyclist and borrowed a very basic bike, without gears. I never expected him to pedal the 60 odd miles each way. We had discussed the possibility of doing the trip together - on separate bikes, of course - but talking about it is different to actually doing it. In the event, I was ruled out because of a soccer injury. I had joked about the possibility of it being a smooth, level ride through the East End and then a mere breeze through the notoriously flat Essex countryside. On reflection, my words were obviously taken too seriously. Once it became clear Bob was going ahead with the journey, I recall us looking at the map the night before. His route was the A13 through the East End before joining the A12.

His aim was to take regular stops, with a sandwich and a drink at Chelmsford. Bob left before I was up, so I was unable to see him off on his historic adventure. I didn't see him until the following morning when he was flat out in bed. He wasn't interested in talking about the game, which was understandable, but he did say that he had climbed back on his bike immediately after the game.

He didn't stay overnight in Colchester because of lack of funds, which had been the deciding factor in his pedalling both ways. I also recall feeling guilty about having made light of the mileage involved. However, with the passage of time, I like to think I was forgiven. Eventually, we began to laugh about it. He never told me how long the whole trip had taken and decided it was a statistic best left to my imagination.

Worst of all it was Argyle's first defeat of the season after an undefeated opening run of eight games; and over 10,000 were there to see them go down 2-0, including my saddle-sore mate!

Later in the season I struck luckier when I went down to see the FA Cup first round replay at Gillingham, played on a clear but bitterly cold Wednesday afternoon. Argyle won 4-1, with a hat trick from Barrie Meyer and a spectacular goal from Jimmy Gauld. He was running so fast as he tucked the ball away that he ran headlong into the advertising hoardings around the ground.

Gauld featured again when I went to the Good Friday match at Brentford. Argyle lost 3-0, never mastering the greasy surface or getting on top of Brentford's forwards Towers and Frances. As ever Gauld was tightly marked but slipped free towards the end. The goalkeeper came sliding out, but Gauld nipped around him but clearly stepped on the man's hand. Most of the 29,000 in the ground erupted. By the time the ref knew what was happening innocent looking Jimmy was back chatting to his mates.

CHAPTER THIRTEEN

PETER ANDERSON

Peter Anderson is without doubt one of the best ever Plymouth born players to have made it as a first team regular at Home Park. And he certainly started at the very top. Taking the place of Alex Govan, he made his debut at the end of the momentous 1952-53 season, in the most successful post-war side ever. He scored in his second game, a 1-1 draw at Doncaster and again in a 3-2 home win over Swansea Town. He went on to rack up 259 first team appearances and scored on 46 occasions. He also made 135 Football Combination League appearances and netted 8 goals.

Peter was born in North Prospect on 11 September 1932 and was one of eight children. His first memories of playing football stem from impromptu games at Laurel Bowl. But his talent really began to develop when the family moved to North Down Crescent. Once there he would spend 'every waking hour' at the nearby sloping football ground. He attended Ford Secondary Modern and acknowledges the help and advice of the sportsmaster there, Fred Uglow.

His talent was clear to see. At 14 he was playing in the Devon Wednesday League. Normally, in a men against boys contest men will prevail. Not in his case. Despite his small stature, Peter's obvious skill helped him avoid the many physical challenges that were an accepted part of football in the 40s and 50s. He went on to play for Oak Villa (and not Astor Institute!). He laughed as he told me, "I have never known where that connection with Astor Institute came from. I used to read it in the away programmes and the Argyle handbook and wonder where they got that idea. "I can say categorically I never went near the place."

Whilst at Oak Villa he became the youngest player ever to be selected for the Devon County senior side. Villa played their home games at Weston Mill, on a pitch where Camels Head Fire Station now stands. Peter recalls that they changed in Cantell and Endacott's premises nearby. Football ran in the family. Brother Vic played for Launceston and Plymouth United and was, at one time, Devon's most capped player. Another brother Roy was also a good amateur, but collapsed and died during a match in Newton Abbott with the family on the sidelines. Peter feels that the war stopped both brothers advancing further in the game.

By 1949 Peter had played for Plymouth Schoolboys and he signed for Argyle as an amateur. "You had to be careful," he told me. "Argyle would sign you as an amateur and would keep you at that status for as long as they could. It was cheap for them to fill the reserves and third team with players who were costing them just a few bob in expenses".

Fortunately for Peter, Blackburn Rovers showed an interest in him and he was invited up to Lancashire for a fortnight's trial. The Ewood Park outfit offered him professional terms but he did not fancy moving to the north. Argyle heeded the warning that they may lose a talented young player and he accepted their offer of part-time professional terms. After that debut in season 1952-53 he was picked another four times in the 1953-54 campaign. He was chosen for the opening two fixtures, but after a 3-0 reverse at Forest he was only chosen twice more. From the heady days of 4th the team had slipped to 19th at the end of the next season.

In September 1954 he was recalled to the side and featured in a 1-1 home draw with West Ham United. He held his place until injury curtailed his season two games from the end. He scored eight goals in 32 outings, including three in consecutive games in October and November. On 19 February 1955 he scored the winner at Craven Cottage, Argyle's first away win of the season and player-manager Jack Rowley's first game in charge. Although that should have made a lasting impression on the new manager, as we will see later, Peter's feeling is that Rowley was not always 100% fair to him.

Peter started 1955-56 as first choice at outside right. But in the sixth game of the season, a few days before his 23rd birthday, disaster struck. In a home fixture against Stoke City on 5 September, in front of 21,000, he suffered a broken leg and missed the rest of that season. There are those in the ground that day who said that the crack of his bone could be heard all around Home Park. Although Argyle had made a poor start, from a personal viewpoint Peter had played very well. On the opening day at Hillsborough he had scored twice in a 5-2 defeat, and he followed this with goals at Doncaster (1-3) and at Hull City (1-1). It would seem that he had a real liking for Yorkshire!

In the early 50s a broken leg could be career threatening, but by the end of August 1956 he was recalled for a home fixture against Reading. He probably wished he hadn't been for the side went down 6-0. He retained his place for the subsequent defeats at QPR (0-3) and Newport County (1-4). He was replaced by Charlie Twissell for three games before being recalled for a 3-0 defeat at Norwich City. 1956-57 was, at that time, Argyle's worst ever start to a Football League campaign and Anderson did not feature again until a November home game against Brighton. On 1 December 1956 he scored his first of the season in a 3-0 win at Gillingham, with the team now inching away from the spectre of applying for reelection. It remained an in and out season for Peter – he made 23 appearances - but at least he was back playing again and feeling no ill effects.

Peter Anderson never lost the feeling that during Jack Rowley's tenure in the manager's chair, he would often be the scapegoat for a defeat. There were a couple of occasions when the team lost heavily and Peter noticed that his omission would be the only change.

In the summer of 1957 Rowley signed Harry Penk from Portsmouth. Although Penk had not been a first team regular at Fratton Park, he arrived with a reputation for being able to operate on either flank. There would now be three main contenders for the wing berths in Penk, Anderson and Olympic international Charlie Twissell. Anderson and Penk got the nod for the opening fixture at Shrewsbury, a disappointing 2-0 defeat. Peter was then injured in a 4-2 home win against Aldershot and did not play again for six games. He was recalled in late September for a solitary goal victory at the Dell and from then on missed only the final game of the season. He and Harry Penk proved to be an excellent pairing. A feature of their game was that they would quietly and quickly switch wings, either to give the opposing full back a different problem or to see if they would have better luck against a different opponent. They were great friends then and still keep in regular touch today.

For those of us who aspire to being a professional footballer, it would seem a glamorous life. Peter Anderson, although pleased to have achieved what he did in the game, seeks to differ. "You have an awful lot of time on your hands. It is simply not possible to train all the time and even though the money, compared to the working man, was pretty good, the great deal of leisure time at your disposal tended to become expensive".

Peter Anderson skips pass the challenge of Dennis Hunt in the FA Cup replay at Priestfield Road. Argyle won 4-1 with goals from Meyer (3) and Gauld. Anderson has an excellent game on the wing.
From the Colin Parsons collection

When asked about the most difficult opponents he encountered he splits them into two camps – the clever and the uncompromising. "Without a doubt Don Howe and Alf Ramsey were the best I came up against. They were very clever, appearing to let you play. But you quickly realised that it was on their terms. They were just waiting for the perfect moment to make a challenge. It did not surprise me that both stayed in the game and reached the highest level". Anderson nominates Jimmy Langley as the absolute opposite. "He was a hard, rugged bloke. You knew you were in for a difficult afternoon when facing him."

There was also another in the Langley mould, much closer to home. He laughed as he told me about the weekly practice matches. "We used to play a weekly practice game, often with the first team attack against the first team defence. "This would often put me in direct opposition to Pat Jones. Old Pat didn't differentiate between practice matches and real ones. He only knew one way to play. He was in your face the whole time – if you got past him he was there again snapping at your heels. Whatever the level, in Pat's world every game was a contest to be won. He was a hard man was Pat, but a lovely bloke who gave Argyle fantastic service."

When asked about the best player in his time at Home Park, like many others he chooses Wilf Carter – "he was a really good all round player". But Peter prefers to talk of the men rather than their ability, and nominates Reg Wyatt, John 'Cardiff' Williams and Harry Penk as the best mates he ever had at Argyle. It is very clear he misses his old friend Reg. Even their birthdays were close and they played together in the 1947 Plymouth Schoolboys side. Peter still stays in regular touch with Reg's widow Margaret. He and John 'Cardiff' see each other at least twice a year, and Peter is often a guest at the Williams' Merthyr home. When it comes to playing memories, he remembers two great FA Cup ties in 1962. In the third round Argyle were drawn at home to West Ham. Peter recalls that despite the presence, amongst others, of Bobby Moore and future Argyle boss Ken Brown, the Greens walloped them 3-0. "We were going well in the league and we played some fantastic one-touch attacking football." In the next round they drew the biggest attraction of them all at that time – Tottenham Hotspur. They were reigning League Champions and FA Cup holders. In front of 40, 040 Spurs prevailed 5-1, with Anderson getting the consolation goal for the home side. "I know we lost but it was still a proud moment. I think it was a Jimmy McAnearney shot which came off the post and I just had to poke it past Bill Brown. I still think we were better that day than the score would suggest, but they were a good side. The build up to it was fantastic, probably the most exciting week in my time in the game".

Like most of his generation he was compelled to serve two years in the military. His was conscripted into the Royal Air Force, winning the RAF Cup with his Innesworth side. The final was at RAF Cosford and Charlton's Eddie Firmani was in the opposition team.

When I asked Peter who was the most talented player of his lifetime, his answer was quick and absolute — "Without doubt it was Denis Law. I'm pretty sure I played against him as a youngster when he was at Huddersfield. You could see even then that he was an exceptional talent".

Peter Anderson is not a man for regret or recrimination. But he does get the impression that that are a lot of people who think Argyle weren't formed till the 70s or 80s. "I know that is how my old mate Reg felt." He acknowledges the role the Argyle Legends are now playing and thoroughly enjoyed the 1958-59 reunion on 27 September 2008. Eight of the old team were guests of the club for the Nottingham Forest fixture and then enjoyed a celebration dinner at the Astor Hotel that night.

27 September 2008

After spending the afternoon at Home Park Peter Anderson (right) and John L Williams get together before Dinner at the Astor Hotel, both wearing their prized Argyle Legends' ties. The evening was arranged and paid for by the Argyle Legends to celebrate the 50th anniversary of their 1958-59 title success.

Their friendship has endured for all of the 50 years since they first met. Both remarked on the pitch, and throughout the evening, how much they missed "dear old Reg Wyatt."

Photo by the author

But the reunion with former playing colleagues that was extra special was at Staddon Heights Golf Club in September 2002, on the occasion of his 70th birthday. The light of his life, daughter Alison, covertly invited as many former Argyle colleagues as she could find. With her dad completely oblivious to any of the arrangements, she picked him up to take him for a quiet dinner at Newton Ferrers. He takes up the story. "Alison and my son in law picked me up from home. "On the way the car seemed to develop a mechanical fault, so they took a detour via Plymstock and the Staddon Heights Golf Club. It was decided that we would nip in there for a drink. We had the bar to ourselves, not another soul in there. Then the screens were drawn back and there they all were, all my old team mates and many friends from outside football. Alison had arranged it all and kept it a complete secret – it was a wonderful night."

Staddon Heights golf club is a place dear to Peter Anderson's heart. The 70th birthday memories apart, he still plays the course twice a week. He still plays off 11 and denies that he is 'a bandit'. Indeed he thinks he could now do with a couple of more strokes! Alison apart, golf is his passion. And of course his two grandsons aged 22 and 18.

After making just 5 appearances in the 1962-63 season Ellis Stuttard agreed to let him move to Torquay United. Dave Corbett, a former protégé of Stuttard's at Swindon was the first choice on the right. During the summer of 1962 Stuttard recruited Everton winger Micky Lill for £12,500 and Anderson seemed to be third choice. His final five games were all deputising for the other two when they were injured. In what turned out to be his last two home games, against Walsall and Derby, he signed off with a goal in each of the two wins. At 30 years old it would seem that Stuttard let a very talented player go too early, arguably one of a very few mistakes Ellis ever made. But with Lill having cost a fairly substantial fee (then), perhaps Stuttard felt obliged to play him when he was fit. As it happens Micky Lill never really settled and he was transferred to Portsmouth before the end of his only season at Home Park. Peter Anderson went on to play 77 times for the Plainmoor club and scored 18 goals, including one in his opening game for them. For some of his time there he was re-united with his best mates from Argyle—Reg Wyatt and John L Williams. He left Torquay at the end of the 1964-65 season.

In 1966, eleven years after he first broke his leg against Stoke City, Peter suffered the same fate again. By this time he was playing part-time for Bideford. It happened in a local derby against Barnstaple. "Playing then was more for the fun of it than the money" was Anderson's slant on it. It was a real nuisance because we had the flower business next to Efford Cemetery and we were expecting Alison. It couldn't have come at a worse time and I certainly never contemplated playing again." Not too long afterwards Argyle sent a side to Bideford to play a testimonial for their former winger.

Peter Anderson feels very strongly about the wages today's players earns. "I find it quite ridiculous when I see what some of these people are paid." He admits he watches very little televised football. If he does he finds himself channel hopping. When asked about the improvements he sees in today's game, he feels that the biggest advance has been in addressing the dietary needs of footballers.

After 19 years in the flower business, in 1980 Peter opted to go into the dockyard, working in the Naval Stores logistics area. Good wingers must be attracted to the Naval Supply organisation—when I first went to work at Bull Point ammunition depot one of my storekeeper colleagues was the greatest Argyle player of them all—Sammy Black. Peter served the Royal Naval Supply and Transport Service for 17 years. "I retired wishing I had gone in years before. I thoroughly enjoyed my time there".

Home is in a quiet Plymouth cul-de-sac, where he is thoroughly at ease with himself as he waits for the next round of golf. He is glad of his good health and pleased that he has not become a burden to anyone. I thoroughly enjoyed our time together and he is about the most relaxed man I have ever met.

Listening to the interview tape again when I got home, I picked up on what he said about Pat Jones— "a lovely bloke who gave Argyle fantastic service". He is far too modest to admit it, but that is a description that also fits Peter Anderson and his time at Home Park.

CHAPTER FOURTEEN

ERIC DOUGHTY

The end of the 1957-58 saw the retirement of a genuine Plymouth Argyle stalwart. Left back Pat Jones decided to hang up his boots after 441 outings. He had come in for the final three matches of the 1946-47season and then did not miss another League game for the next six campaigns. Apart from a spell out because of a serious groin injury, he had been an automatic selection for 11 seasons. It was a fantastic record and for manager Jack Rowley it could have been a major blow.

But Pat Jones was the past and Jack had to be concerned with the now. He had identified Arsenal's Eric Doughty as a replacement. Although Doughty had not managed a first team appearance at Highbury he was a regular in a strong Arsenal reserve side. It is clear from the letters between Arsenal and the player and one Rowley wrote to Doughty (see next two pages), that the Argyle manager had never seen him play. These two letters are marvellous examples of the difference between then and now. Then there was no pernicious agent to recommend a player, no DVD or video of the target for the manager to study. There was a fixed wage structure so agreeing terms did not take too long. It was all very basic; Arsenal named their price and Jack Rowley trusted someone else's judgement.

With Argyle having agreed a fee of £1,000 with the Highbury club, the next move was down to the player. With his former Arsenal colleague Archie McCauley in charge at Norwich City, they too were alerted to Doughty's availability. During his National Service in the RAF, 2523183 Aircraftsman Class 1 Eric Doughty had spent time at Innesworth, Tangmere, Corsham and Martlesham Heath in Norfolk. He had really enjoyed his time in East Anglia, so a move to Carrow Road was appealing. He admits that he has often reflected that, had he chosen to go there, he may he have avoided the injury at Hull. Furthermore, he may have been part of the fantastic Norwich City run to the FA Cup semi-finals that season, a feat that captured the imagination of every football supporter in the land.

Neither Eric nor his wife Doreen had liked London. The city was still coming to terms with mass immigration and the frequent thick smog often made life unpleasant. Eric had first been in rooms in Southgate with Peter

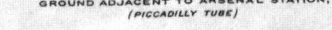

ARSENAL FOOTBALL CLUB LTD.

GROUND ADJACENT TO ARSENAL STATION,
(PICCADILLY TUBE)

TELEGRAPHIC ADDRESS:
GUNNERETIC, FINSPARK, LONDON.
TELEPHONE: CANONBURY 3312.

W. R. WALL.
SECRETARY

ARSENAL STADIUM,
LONDON, N.5.

WRW/JS   June 12th, 1958

Eric Doughty, Esq.,
50, Frederick Avenue,
Peasedown,
Nr. Bath, Somerset.

Dear Eric,

        When you telephoned the other day I believe I
told you that Plymouth Argyle had made enquiries
about you.

        I had a telephone call from Mr. Jack Rowley
(their Manager) this morning asking for permission to
get in touch with you. I know they had a Board
Meeting at the end of last week and so it seems as
if they intend to pursue the matter, and I thought
I would let you know in advance so that if you hear
from him you will know what to expect.

        I hope all goes well and that you get fixed up.
They know the fee and you can take it that if the
fee is paid we shall give you your £600 benefit
without any more ado.

        Kind regards,

                        Yours sincerely,

                        W R Wall

                        Secretary.

Transfer negotiations 1950s style. These two letters perfectly illustrate
the extraordinary difference between transfer negotiations then and now.
It is quite clear from the letter on the right hand page that Jack Rowley
had never seen Eric Doughty play. Clearly he trusted someone's judgement.

TELEGRAMS
ARGYLE
PLYMOUTH

Plymouth Argyle Football Co., Ltd.

MANAGER · J. F. ROWLEY
SECRETARY · A. H. COLE
PHONE (PRIVATE) PLYMOUTH 61425

Home Park

PLYMOUTH

TELEPHONE
61176
61177

June 12th. 1958

Mr. E. Doughty;
50 Frederick Avenue
Peasedown
Nr. Bath. Som.

Dear Sir:

    I have received permission from the Arsenal F.C.
to approach you on behalf of my Club: so could you please
let me know if you are willing to join them providing we come
to terms with your Club re your transfer fee.

    I am told you are married: age 26: height 5'10" and
your best position is L.B. a position which is at present
vacant in our league side.   The house situation is quite
good as at the time of writing we have four vacant.

    Thanking you in anticipation

        Yours sincerely

        <u>Manager.</u>

Both letters courtesy of Eric Doughty

Gore and his lifelong mate, Bristolian Con Sullivan. "Mrs Gudgeon was the landlady, one of many on Arsenal's list of pleasant people to rent from." Once married in 1952, the couple took rooms in Muswell Hill. London was, metaphorically speaking, a world away from their Somerset upbringing. In 1956, when Doreen fell pregnant, she had a number of blackouts. Eric was concerned about her welfare during the times when he would be away playing football, so it was decided that it would be for the best if she returned to her family in Radstock. He then moved into digs with Welsh international Dave Bowen, who went on to be manager of Northampton Town, his first club in England. By the time Eric was made surplus to requirements at Arsenal, daughter Linda was two. Doreen was quite clear about it; she wanted to stay in the Westcountry. They quickly agreed that a move to Devon would best suit their circumstances. Eric contacted Jack Rowley and in their trusty Ford Anglia they travelled down to Plymouth in late June 1958. Terms were soon agreed and Rowley's traditional tour of the city, including a look at their allocated club house in Langhill Road, quickly sealed the move. Doreen told me, "My immediate feeling was that I wanted to live there forever. When we moved down the neighbours were outside to greet us, offering to assist wherever they could. It could not have been more different than our experiences in London."

Pre-season went well and Doughty impressed with his skilful approach. He played in both the Public Practice matches and at 5 feet 10 inches and weighing close to 12 stones he was built to cope with the rigours of the Third Division. Although in his six years at Arsenal he had not made it to the first team, it was clear that training every day with household names had rubbed off on him. He looked a good capture, comfortable on the ball and particularly strong in the air.

Eric Doughty is blessed with an excellent memory and began by telling me how at first he found it difficult to believe the difference in facilities. "At Arsenal medical science was quite advanced and they trained at a large ground in Hendon, except for any FA Cup week when the whole group decamped to Eastbourne. There were large and well-equipped treatment rooms at the Arsenal stadium, fitted with ultra-sound equipment. There was a canteen and lunch was supplied for no cost, so they were already connecting physical condition with diet." He continued, "As you took the field at Highbury there was an oxygen cylinder and mask at the dressing room door. We were instructed to take a deep gulp of the gas, the idea being for us to be able to mount early and sustained pressure on the opposition". He went on to tell me about frequent visits from eminent London surgeons and professors of medicine, and how the players would be told precisely how their bodies functioned and how they could improve their physical performance. "I once had to go to Harley Street during pre-season," he told me. "When the season finished we were told to put on weight, so that we could take it off when we returned to training. I could not seem gain weight so was given a thorough examination to find out why. Nothing was left to chance at Highbury as they sought to gain every ounce of advantage medical science could offer".

"I soon found that Arsenal, in terms of facilities, was a world apart from Home Park". He related what a marvellous place the Arsenal Stadium was. "I have never to this day seen a carpet like the one in the trophy room there. The pile must have been six foot high! I played on every League ground in London and played with and against some famous names. It was a time when the PFA were pressing for the removal of the maximum wage. Jimmy Hill came to Highbury to address the players and I was impressed. I recall playing against him when he was in Fulham's second string. He could run but had little in the way of skill. Another man who stands out in my memory was Ron Greenwood, who was on the coaching staff. A real visionary he was."

But he didn't care what Arsenal had. He was a Plymouth Argyle player now and, provided he steered clear of injury, he was likely to be the first choice left back for a long time to come. With Doreen and Linda happily ensconced in Peverell, life was as good as it could get for the Doughty crew. They were friendly with the Carter family who were a few doors away and Neil and Monica Dougall were just around the corner. And, just as the Carters had found, the Crispin family were very friendly and welcoming too.

It was with great anticipation that Eric climbed aboard the team bus on Friday 22 August 1958. With the team bound for a mini northern tour for fixtures against Hull City (Saturday) and Rochdale (Monday), Eric's long wait for his first Football League appearance was nearly over. Apart from travelling reserve John 'Cardiff' Williams, Doughty was the only new man in the party. He knew for certain that he would be playing.

After an overnight stay in Doncaster they moved on to Boothferry Park on the Saturday. Eric remembers being excited but not overly nervous. He was finally in the club team that mattered to any professional player, the 'chiefs'. At ten to three he and the rest of his team made their way into the tunnel. It was like any other football afternoon in his life – the smell of liniment, the rattle of leather studs on concrete and that unmistakable buzz of the start of a match, exacerbated on this occasion by it being the opening day of the season.

For 30 minutes all went well. Hull started strongly but they offered little threat to Geoff Barnsley's goal. Eric found that he had more time to recover than in many Arsenal Football Combination fixtures, with the pace of the Third Division not as frenetic as he had imagined. His Arsenal background meant that it had been dinned into him that he must never be more than ten yards from a colleague. He had been taught to get the ball down and concentrate on keeping his side in possession.

As play moved up Argyle's left flank a colleague found himself hemmed in. Doughty instinctively made himself available to receive the ball, but it came at him a bit higher than he would have hoped. With his leg outstretched, he tried to bring it under control. He takes up the story. "A Hull forward came across from my right. I think it was a chap called Bradbury, or it could have been their centre-forward Smith. He was a big bloke, whichever one it was. As he came across me his studs got tangled in mine and my leg was wrenched around nearly 360 degrees. As I hit the ground

I knew it was even worse than bad. I do not blame the Hull player; it was a genuine challenge without any malice. The pain was indescribable".

The only aid trainer George Taylor could offer was the 'magic sponge', kept in an old football bladder full of cold water. That (and smelling salts) was about the height of the trainer's medical equipment in those days. In the lower leagues science was about as far advanced as the days when they used to throw a canary down a coal mine to detect gas!

Eric was taken off the field and treatment continued. With no substitutes in those days Eric, his knee heavily strapped, was instructed to takethe pitch for the second half. George Robertson had been struggling to control the Tigers' left winger Metcalfe so Doughty was told to patrol the right flank and help where he could. *Pilgrim* described how Doughty could barely walk.

After the match, a creditable 1-1 draw, the team moved on to their overnight hotel at Timperley, Cheshire, ready for the Monday fixture against Rochdale. Doughty hobbled to the coach without the aid of crutches. 50 years on it is clear that the countdown to the end of Doughty's football career had started from the moment he had fallen to the Boothferry Park turf. Eric clearly sees the decision to make him play the second half at Hull as the beginning of the end. He understands why it was done – "that was the norm for those days and I was given no choice. It was, if you like, my duty to my team-mates. But it should not have happened." He was not seen by the Hull City doctor afterwards and it was never suggested that he went to Hull Royal Infirmary to let a trained medical eye assess his injury.

After a very uncomfortable night, during which Doughty had to call trainer George Taylor for painkillers (a brave decision!), Jack Rowley arranged for the injured full back to visit the Old Trafford treatment room. Two experienced (but unqualified) Manchester United support staff each had a look at the knee. The United men solemnly agreed that it looked a bad one and the knee, still seriously swollen, was carefully strapped.

Eric remembers the day well. "It was barely six months after the crash at Munich. Johnny Berry was there rehabilitating and one or two others I didn't immediately recognise. I think one may have been Jackie Blanchflower? Matt Busby was also in the room. In fact, the United medical staff suggested that I borrowed Busby's crutches, the ones he used after he left the Munich hospital." Nearly 24 hours after the injury occurred, Eric's first respite from the constant pain was those crutches. He endured two more uncomfortable nights at the Cheshire hotel, before starting the all day bus journey to Plymouth on the morning after the 2-0 success at Rochdale. It was eight in the evening when the coach pulled into Home Park. It was now more than 72 hours since the injury occurred and still no trained medical person had assessed the injury.

He reported to the Home Park treatment room on the Wednesday morning and started two months of rehabilitation. Although it was getting slightly better and much of the pain and swelling had gone, Eric knew it wasn't right. During the course of the interviews for *Thanks for the Memory* several of the other players commented on how hard Eric worked to strengthen his knee. On 17 October 1958, nearly 8 weeks after the injury occurred, Doughty was admitted to hospital for an operation to remove his cartilage. The club paid the £75 cost for private treatment. Even after that he knew it wasn't completely right. Apart from the cartilage injury he had also stretched both the anterior and cruciate ligaments. The surgeon told him during his initial examination that they were badly discoloured. "I haven't done it for years," he told me, "but there was a time when I could slide my knee cap in and out. My recovery wasn't helped when during a practice match an over-zealous tackle popped it out involuntarily." Itis no coincidence that almost all the former players interviewed for *Thanks for the Memory* cited the advances in medical science as the single biggest improvement since their playing days. It would be interesting to compare Doughty's treatment with the rehabilitation programmes undertaken in recent years by Romain Larrieu and Paul Wotton. By chance, Eric and I met up a week after Arsenal's Eduardo was badly injured at Birmingham last season (2007-08). As Eric ruefully remarked, "He would never have had a chance of coming back from that in my day. Now, with all the modern advances, he will almost certainly play again.

Eric Doughty was from a sporting family. His father, a miner in the Somerset coalfields, was a fine player for Radstock Town and also a sprinter of some renown. Eric's two brothers Ted (Bath City) and John (Trowbridge Town) were part-time professionals. Arsenal spotted Eric when he was 18, tracking him in each of his three appearances for the Somerset County side. He was spotted by Gloucester based Arsenal scout Colly Borton, who had good connections with the Radstock area. He was then invited to play in London Midweek League trials against Brentford, Charlton and Leyton Orient.

Eric had been one of the stars of the all conquering Peasdown St John team. That team rather shaped his life for it was while playing for them that he first encountered Doreen "and we just took up with one another". It was also where he came to the attention of the Somerset selectors. He had followed his father into the Somerset coalfields, though sensibly taking a job above ground. At the time Arsenal signed him he as training as an electrical engineer at the Braysdown Colliery. During his six years at Arsenal, where he joined as a left-half, Eric rubbed shoulders with some of the game's all time greats. Even some who didn't quite merit 'great' were extremely fine players. The manager was Tom Whittaker, a man for whom Doughty had the utmost respect. Coaching the reserves, and Doughty's main mentor at Arsenal, was George Male. Male had been a part of the great Herbert Chapman Arsenal side that won three consecutive titles from 1932-33 to 1934-35 and had a part in three other title winning sides. He also played in the 1932 and 1935 Cup Finals and made 19 appearances for England. Male had originally been a left-half too, but was successfully converted by the great Chapman to right back. So when Male suggested to Eric that he may have a future as a full back, who better to take such advice from?

The Arsenal that Eric Doughty joined was a powerful club with a very strong staff, full of past, current and future international players. The star players were Don Roper (297 Arsenal appearances) Jimmy Logie (296), Wally Barnes (267), Leslie Compton (253), Joe Mercer (247), Doug Lishman (226 with 125 goals), Alec Forbes (217). The war had probably cost the older ones 150 to 200 League appearances. Of the younger players on the staff David Herd, who went on to make his name with Manchester United, was there too, making 166 appearances and scoring 97 times. Cliff Holton, another striker, played 199 games and scored 83 goals. That so many people made such a great number of appearances is some indication as to how difficult it was to break into the side.

The great Tommy Lawton was there too, though he was by then no longer at his peak. Eric recalls him as a man who lived life to the full, complete with Jaguar car. The maximum £17 wage was barely sufficient to support Lawton's lifestyle, though it was three times what the working man could earn. "But even if he was past his best, he still had this remarkable ability to hang in the air", was Eric's verdict on the great man.

Amongst the up and coming players were Derek Tapscott, who had recently joined from Cardiff, as well as youngsters John Barnwell and future Argyle player Jimmy Bloomfield. Arthur Milton was also at Highbury during Eric's early days there. He was the last man to have gained full international honours in football and cricket. Indeed, while Eric was rehabilitating from injury at Home Park Milton was in Australia on a losing Ashes tour. In another story about his time at Arsenal, Eric recalled that within weeks of him joining Arsenal the England team came to Highbury to play a full scale practice match. "The forward line was Matthews, Raich Carter, Lawton, Mannion and Finney. Matthews was incredible – in my view he had everything. He was up against our full back Lionel Smith, himself an international. I was just a yard away from the action. It was amazing – Matthews had such quick feet and once he dropped that shoulder he was away. I will never forget it".

So for their £1,000 it is clear that in Eric Doughty Plymouth Argyle had certainly bought someone who had seen some great players at very close hand. Hopefully for Argyle, a legend had been replaced by someone with the skill and endeavour to become another one. That he was good enough to have been invited to sign for a club with such an illustrious group of players, says much for the ability he must have shown when he went to Highbury.

Eric Doughty was as stunned as anyone by the untimely death of Tom Whittaker in October 1956. He was a few months past his 58th birthday. It was widely felt at the time that the strain of running Arsenal had been a contributory factor to his heart attack. Not too long before his death Whittaker had taken Doughty, now 24, to one side, and urged him to keep progressing as he was. He told Eric he was on the very edge of the first team. Once Jack Crayston took over, Doughty was once more marooned on the second rung of the selection ladder.

Though he would not realise it at the time, it could be that in some ways Whittaker's death would become a double blow for Eric Doughty. In 1925 Tom Whittaker was on a tour of Australia with an FA party. During that tour he broke his knee cap. He never played again, and turned to studying physiotherapy. Whittaker was seen to be the power behind the Herbert Chapman throne, for it was he who designed the training and treatment methods at Highbury which led to their consecutive titles. Indeed, because of his own injury, and the lack of treatment available at that time, Whittaker also undertook a specific study into knee injuries. He became so expert that Harley Street surgeons took advice from him when they were called upon to treat knee injuries. Perhaps he was the one man that, had he survived, could have got Eric Doughty playing again.

Eric returned to something approaching full fitness in early 1959, some five months after he had been injured at Hull. He managed a few South Western League games and appeared in a Football Combination game against QPR on 14 February. Though he survived a full pre-season in 1959-60 he knew he would never again be the player he once was. The problem was that the knee would swell after every game, with no one able to stop the fluid forming each time. He remained with Argyle for much of the 1959-60 season but was not going to be retained. Crewe were amongst those interested. But Fred Ford, a long-term Doughty admirer persuaded Eric to join him at Bristol City. Their physio Les Bardsley was convinced he could strengthen and repair Eric's knee. Doughty came to know ever step in the Ashton Gate ground, as went up and down every day trying to strengthen the knee.

Regrettably it did not work. At 28 Eric was out of work and did not play again at any level. In addition to Doreen and Linda, he now had daughter Elaine to think about. She had been born on17 September 1959. When you meet Eric Doughty he immediately comes across as an honourable man. It was not surprising to hear that he refused any offer of financial assistance from the Ashton Gate club. As far as he was concerned Fred Ford had shown faith in him but it had not worked out. "Why should they have paid me; they gave me a chance when few others would have? I didn't think it was fair that they should pay up my contract." Just over two years before Eric and Doreen had been contemplating spending the rest of their lives in Plymouth, including after Eric' career had run its expected course. One accidental collision on a soccer field and the dream was gone.

It was not long before Eric found a job with F and J Clark, the famous Somerset shoe people. Over the years he rose to a Senior Foreman post, working for them for 34 years, mainly at the Rushill site. His time at Clarks coincided with the greatest expansion the company ever saw. Fortune was in his favour for once, for it was not long after he retired that the company began to really struggle against cheaper foreign competitors.

He was due some good luck. Before the injury at Hull he had already had the disappointment of Tom Whittaker's untimely death, just as he had got within touching distance of a first team game. When new manager Jack Crayston kept getting reports of Eric's consistent displays, he came to a reserve game to see for himself. One Wednesday evening, after 89 impeccable minutes Eric misjudged a last minute header. It allowed the opposition to equalise – and, of course, it had to be Tottenham. Crayston turned to Len Wills instead, who went on to make 195 first team appearances. He was that close to being the Arsenal left back.

As well as misfortune in his football life, he and Doreen have had some ill fortune away from the game too. Like their Golden Wedding celebration that had to be cancelled. On the day before it was due, her brother-in-law died. Her sister had already lost a previous husband, killed in a car crash. There was no way they could proceed. They do not dwell on some of their misfortune but they do sometimes think that they may have been granted more good luck than they have had.

Although Eric played only the one first team game for Argyle he still takes an interest in the club. He became a regular visitor to Home Park when Doreen's sister Sylvia's husband used to play for Argyle – the great Tony Book. Even now, although he doesn't come to watch, he still has a connection with the club, albeit a slightly tenuous one. Doreen's brother's grandson is Ashley Barnes, a promising young striker who in this Golden Anniversary season recently broke into the first team at Home Park.

As we wound down our interview, the talk of Tony Book led us on to former Argyle manager Malcolm Allison. "I found Malcolm to be a very likeable man, and a generous one too. Sadly Malcolm is now in the grip of Alzheimer's and is being cared for in a nursing home. Tony still goes to see him but he doesn't know much about what is going on around him".

My final question of Eric was a hypothetical one. In view of the players he had played with and seen during his time at Arsenal, I asked him if he thought, from what he had seen, that Johnny Williams could have played at the very highest level of the game. His response was unequivocal. "I don't think he would have simply made it in the First Division; I think he would have taken it by storm and been a real star". It is an opinion that accords precisely with what many fans of a certain age have thought for years.

On the journey back to Hampshire from Eric's home at Peasdown, I listened to the tape of our interview. It immediately struck me that Eric's loss to the game was greater than I first envisaged. It struck me that this was a man who would have made an extremely shrewd manager or coach. He had been schooled in the right way at Arsenal, and his cameo at Hull gave a clear indication that he was he was a very good footballer. Of course, no one will ever know, but it was something I felt very strongly. He was able to recite almost word for word everything George Male told him. He had a clear understanding of how the game should be played and, as previously mentioned, he had rubbed shoulders with some of the greatest names the game has ever known. He is also very organised in everything he approaches.

Although Eric retired from Clarks all that did was to give him even more time to devote to the Radstock Working Mens' Club, where he is the secretary and treasurer. In 1981, when he could see that legislation was leading to greater scrutiny, he took (and passed) accountancy exams. Now 76, with the letters CAD after his name, he also serves as a specialist skills director for the Norton Radstock Regeneration Company, with special responsibility for social housing. Retired? It is the same as 'lucky', Eric Doughty couldn't spell the word!

CHAPTER FIFTEEN

HARRY PENK

Harry Penk clearly loves sport. At school he played soccer as a winger, rugby league as a scrum half and was an all rounder at cricket. As an adult he became a professional footballer, was an outstanding amateur cricketer and at one time played golf off 11. His early passion was cricket, and his love for the game has never faded. However, once he got to 50 years of age he felt his best cricket days were behind him and he started to play golf more seriously. After playing socially with a group of lads near his New Forest home, with whom he went on golfing breaks to St Mellion and Scotland, he became a member at various clubs in the area. He laughs now when he recalls that gradually all his golfing buddies moved away, some even settling abroad. "Obviously they didn't want to hurt my feelings about my golfing prowess, so they found it easier to move away!" Until a recent short illness he still played the occasional game of golf.

Harry Penk played all his full time professional football on the south coast. First he joined Portsmouth, in the late summer of 1955. In June 1957 he moved to Plymouth Argyle, where he spent three seasons. His final League club was Southampton, where he stayed four years. Penk did not get into professional soccer via the traditional route, in that he wasn't considered good enough to gain any representative honours when playing at school and youth level. Indeed, it was in schoolboy cricket that he showed the greater promise. He played for Wigan Schools for two years, captaining them for the second season. They played all over Lancashire, against towns like Leyland, Chorley, Southport and Preston. In a match against Preston Schools the opposition were all out for 56. To this day Harry remembers the report in the *Lancashire Evening Post*, the first words ever printed about him. "When Penk got to the wicket, Wigan were 6-6. Barely taller than the wickets, he was undefeated at the end as Wigan forced a tie." Those early words epitomised Harry Penk; throughout his sporting career he was small in stature but big enough for a challenge. I am sure that if the local newspaper had not reported his cricketing prowess, it is unlikely that Harry would have told anyone how well he did. He remains an extremely modest and likeable man.

Although not selected for any representative soccer games, the local Council School saw him as a useful outside right. On leaving school he first joined the Orrell St Luke's FC, competing in the Wigan and District Sunday School League. Later his cricket club, Norley Hall, decided to form a soccer team so that the group could continue to meet in the winter. He left Orrell and he turned out for them. It was there that he came to the attention of Wigan Athletic, then a Lancashire Combination League outfit. After joining them in 1953, a series of stirring displays in the reserves saw him win a permanent place in their first team. He was a little worried that he would not make the grade at Springfield Park but the manager told

Harry Penk (centre) and Jim Nightingale (right) chat to manager Jack Rowley shortly after signing in the summer of 1957. Harry went on to have a successful time at Home Park but railwayman Nightingale failed to make the grade. *From Harry Penk's scrapbook*

Harry Penk was never the biggest of men, but here his face clearly shows that he is surprised how much bigger the players are now! He is seen here beside Pilgrim Pete on 27 September 2008, just after being presented with a silver salver, replica shirt and Argyle Legends tie. The gifts were a token of the club's appreciation for his efforts in the 1958-59 promotion season. He considers his time at Plymouth Argyle as the most satisfying of his career. He and his wife Barbara loved their time here. With their open top Morris Minor they would have been the Posh & Becks of the day! *Photo by the author*

him not to be concerned. That manager was a man by the name of Ted Goodier, who a few years later was one of the applicants for the Argyle job when Jack Rowley was appointed. In his first season Wigan won the Lancashire Combination, the Lancashire Combination League Cup, the Liverpool Cup and the Lancashire Junior Cup. By early 1955 Penk was attracting the attention of Football League clubs, with Portsmouth showing the most determination to land his signature. Harry remembers their scout being at Rochdale one winter evening, for a Lancashire Combination game against the Spotland club's second outfit. "There were a couple of inches of snow, and it had frozen. "With the scout being there it increased the crowd to 15!" They then watched him again against Southport reserves, with Portsmouth boss Eddie Lever visiting Haig Avenue to make a personal assessment.

Pompey had been League Champions twice since the war and was considered to be a top club. But Harry Penk remained unimpressed, annoyed at the way the move was being conducted. He had read about it in the papers but, as yet, no one had talked directly to him about it. He told a local journalist that he wasn't sure he wanted to move so far away from his Lancashire home, though he did concede that he had no ties. Despite the fact that Harry was now 20 years old, his father would still have a say in the move too. He wanted his son to complete his painter and sign-writer apprenticeship before he did anything else.

Harry, meanwhile, was secretly hoping one of the Lancashire clubs would come in for him. He had grown up supporting Bolton Wanderers and Preston North End; Burnley and Blackburn were not too far away but, other than Portsmouth, only Stoke and Aston Villa expressed real interest. A year or two before there had been talk of him signing for Blackpool as an amateur. Like Portsmouth they were a top club at that time, with two recent Cup Final outings behind them. But with Stanley Matthews occupying their right flank, it was seen as something of a graveyard for up and coming young right wingers.

After long negotiations between Lever and the Wigan Board the move was finally agreed. Portsmouth would pay Wigan £2,500 with another £500 due after 12 First Division appearances. At the time it was a record fee paid to a club in the Lancashire Combination. But there was a proviso. The deal would become void if Penk was called up for National Service. Because he had elected to complete his apprenticeship, his call-up papers were not activated until he was 20. He was known to have an ear disorder which was likely to preclude him from military service, but he still had to travel to Liverpool to undergo a medical. The doctor was sympathetic with Harry, telling him that his medical condition made him unsuitable for acceptance into the Army. He told him not to be too downhearted and to try again in a couple of months. With a polite, "Aye, thank you, I'll do that," he hurried back to Wigan, knowing all the while that his ear would never improve sufficiently – especially now that the kindly doctor had shown him how to make the symptoms prevail! Portsmouth agreed that Harry would be allowed to return to Wigan each summer, so he could continue to play cricket for Norley Hall.

The move to Portsmouth was completed in September 1955 and by October he was putting together a string of impressive performances in the Football Combination side. Supporters took to him very quickly, and he felt settled in his new surroundings. *Portsmouth Evening News* Pompey reporter *Stroller* first interviewed Harry in the November. He was captivated with the young man from Wigan, giving equal measure to Harry's skill and to his likeable nature. He noted that "it was difficult to make the young man talk about himself." The most he had been able to get out of him was, "Aye, I like it here. Combination football? It's a bit faster than what I was used to". *Stroller* then lamented that all Penk wanted to talk about was "the merits of the pictures showing that week or the latest popular songs".

In the same article Portsmouth manager Eddie Lever added his own praise (the reporter referred to the manager as Mr JE Lever – *how* 1955!), pointing out that "six or seven weeks more full time training will see him become even faster and trickier". He even compared Penk to Johnny Hancocks, the flying Wolves and former England right winger who had been terrorising First Division defences for several years. Lever went on, "Harry can crack a ball with either foot and I have seldom seen a player who can cross a ball so perfectly". Although his Football Combination League debut ended in a 1-0 defeat to Bristol City Reserves, he then starred in a 7-2 win over Swindon's second string. In a 2-0 success over a strong Tottenham reserve side Harry found himself up against Ron Henry, who became one of the stalwarts of the Tottenham double winning side in the 60-61 season. In goal for Spurs was Ron Reynolds, who later was a team mate of Harry's at the Dell. Lever continued to be impressed with the young winger and he made it into the first team for the final six games of his first season at Fratton Park.

His debut came on 31 March 1956, in a 4-0 home win against Charlton Athletic. Future Plymouth team mate Jimmy Gauld played for the London side. Although his promising reserve displays had all been on the right wing, in the first team he played on the left flank. There were two main highlights. The first came in his fourth game, when he found himself facing Don Howe in a 1-1 home draw with West Brom. He rates Howe as the cleverest full back he ever played against, and is not surprised at how good a player and coach he became. The other major memory was a visit to Old Trafford for the penultimate game of the season. United, with the famous Busby Babes carrying all before them, had run away with the 1955-56 title and there was a crowd invasion *before* the match. United won 1-0 but Harry remains grateful to have had the privilege to see those great United players at first hand. Portsmouth finished 12th.

The next season was something of an anti-climax for him. Although his form in the reserves was good he did not gain a regular place in the first team. He played only three games, scoring in two of them. He notched the only goal in a home fixture with Charlton and the following week got one at Roker Park in a 3-3 draw. It is not as if Portsmouth were having a good season; they finished seven places lower than the previous campaign. Much to his disappointment, he was not retained and a £4,000 fee took him along the coast to Plymouth. As was the way then, he rented a room in a house in Burleigh Park Road. A house-mate was George Baker.

Without hesitation Harry Penk nominates his time at Plymouth Argyle as the most enjoyable of his professional career. In his first season he played 44 times and scored on three occasions, helping the side to third place in the last ever Third Division (South) competition. His fiancée, Portsmouth girl Barbara Bates had joined him in Plymouth, taking a job in Dingles. On 12 July 1958, two days prior to pre-season training starting, Harry and Barbara were married at St James Church, Milton, in Portsmouth. Best man was a Pompey player by the name of John Phillips, a local lad who played at half back.

They returned to Plymouth on the following Monday and for £2/15/- (£2.75) rented rooms in Meredith Road, later taking the whole of the upstairs of a house in Peverell Park Road. The rent there was £3/12/6 for the upstairs, plus 7/6 for garage (£4 in all). The owners, George and Freda Passmore lived in the lower half of the house. Barbara was just 18 when they married and looked on the Passmores as surrogate parents. Their relationship even survived Barbara's disastrous attempt at washing the curtains in their flat. "They really shrunk and I was beside myself with worry about how Mrs Passmore would react." She laughs now as she recalls the incident. "They were really good about it though. "But I will never forget my first ever spring clean!"

They became very friendly with full back Bryce Fulton and his wife Diane, who also lived in Peverell. They would often go round for an evening's television – "Bryce had one and we didn't" is how Barbara remembers it. In a marvellous example of how communications have changed, Barbara told me that to keep in touch with her mother she would telephone her each week from a telephone box. At an agreed time, her mother would go to a neighbour, one of few people who in those days had a phone in the house.

1958-59 was a good season for all concerned. The team started well, with just one defeat in the first 19 games. The 20th was at the Dell, and although Argyle went down 5-1 Harry was one of the few to escape criticism. Penk was more provider than scorer, but he scored a number of vital goals in the promotion run, none more important than the only Argyle goal in a draw at Accrington that clinched promotion. Of the nine goals he scored that season, four of them were on northern grounds. A feature of Argyle's play was the way that wingers Penk and Anderson would frequently swap wings. Both told me that is was not something they did on instruction from the manager; "we just seemed to do it when we felt it would help the side." 50 years on they are still friends and stay in regular touch.

The following season was not as successful for Harry. The team struggled in the Second Division and, like several other players, he was in and out of the side. He played in 25 League games and scored only twice. He got another goal in a 3-2 third round FA Cup defeat at the Hawthorns, a game remembered for Jack Rowley's experiment with full back Wally Bellett playing at centre forward.

He was placed on the transfer list at the end of the 1959-60 season and although Northampton and Chester showed interest (see letters overleaf), he chose to move along the coast to Southampton. The Saints had just been promoted as champions of the Third Division. Clearly Ted Bates had not forgotten the fine display in Argyle's heavy defeat at the Dell the previous season. Although the stars of his promotion side were wingers Terry Paine and John Sydenham, the latter was about to be called up for National Service. Bates knew that Penk would prove an able deputy for either winger. On 10 September 1960 he made his Saints debut in a 1-1 draw at Ayresome Park. In March 1963 he lined up at the Dell against Argyle, in a 1-1 draw, and his final Football League appearance for Southampton was on 26 October 1963, in a home fixture against Leeds United. In all he made 52 appearances for the Hampshire side and scored on six occasions. Although he enjoyed his time at Plymouth more it is clear that Harry had the greatest respect for the Saints' legendary manager Ted Bates. "He was the first manager I had who took the time to explain things to you, to help your game" is how Penk remembers the great man.

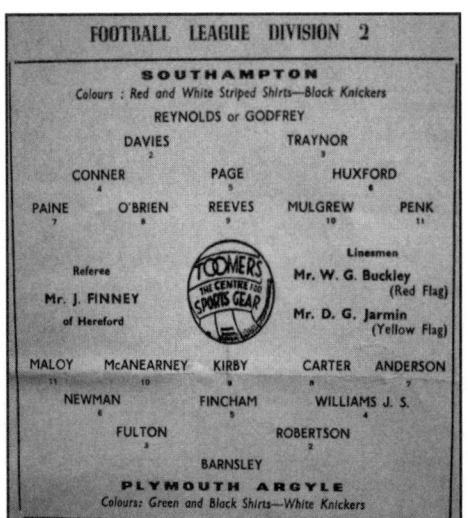

Harry Penk finds it difficult to say whether he was a better on the right or left wing. Apart from his natural modesty, it is clear from several interviews during his career that he genuinely didn't know. At Wigan he played mainly on the right. At Fratton Park he was a right winger for the reserves yet played all his first team games on the left. In an interview with *Spectator* shortly after he arrived at Home Park he was non-committal. "I can put in corners equally well with left and right foot. When I play on the left I can move better, whereas on the right I do tend to cut inside more."

After parting company with Southampton in the summer of 1964 he then moved along the A36 to Salisbury as a part-timer, while at the same time getting a job at Husband's shipyard at Marchwood as a painter and sign-writer. He was to work for them for 28 years, before falling victim to a downturn in work at the yard. Thereafter he worked for a few years running his own painting and decorating business. He and Barbara recall that they were much better off financially once he went part-time. As well as his time at Salisbury he had four seasons at Basingstoke before spells at local sides Cowes and then, as a favour to a friend, New Milton. By that time the money was not a consideration – this was still a man who loved his sport.

Harry Penk had some special times in the FA Cup from early in his career. In his first season at Springfield Park, Wigan, then a non league outfit, took the powerful Newcastle United to a replay. He watched the replay, in awe of some of the great names in the opposition. The next year Wigan went down 3-2 at Barnsley after leading 2-1, with Penk scoring one of the Wigan goals. Barnsley were a strong side at Oakwell and this was the first time any team had scored more than once against them at home. He did not play an FA Cup tie for Portsmouth but in January 1958 he got a first hand look at those Newcastle stars he saw at Springfield Park. As a member of the Argyle side beaten 6-1 at Home Park, success against the Magpies eluded his team again. He was more fortunate on the following Monday when he took his driving test. "The examiner was quite formal from the start of the test. When we pulled over and he told me I had been successful. After that he was much more interested in what I thought of the match."

There was more FA Cup magic when in January 1961 Southampton were drawn at home to Ipswich Town, in the a third round tie. Ipswich, under manager Alf Ramsey, were on their way to the Second Division title and were a very strong side. Future Argyle skipper Andy Nelson was at centre half for Ipswich on a day they would prefer to forget. Saints were slow to start but bizarrely, after scoring five goals in 22 minutes, led 6-0 at the interval. Penk scored the fifth. As often happens the goal bonanza dried up in the second half, Southampton running out 7-1 winners. That same Ipswich team not only won that season's Second Division title, but with almost the same line-up took the following season's Football League Championship. Harry Penk got great credit from both Terry Paine and his manager Ted Bates that day. Paine wrote in his recent biography that Harry worked for the team in a way that first choice John Sydenham did not. Manager Ted Bates used Penk's acknowledged football brain and willingness to track back to counter Ramsey's 'wingless wonders'.

Soon after dropping out of the League, Penk's FA Cup adventures continued. During his season with Salisbury they qualified for the first round proper of the FA Cup and were drawn away to a Peterborough side which included Derek Dougan. Salisbury were eventually outclassed and lost 5-1, but Harry had the pleasure of supplying the cross for team-mate Joe Stocks to score the Salisbury goal.

Once playing football was no longer an option he had no interest in coaching. He could now devote his leisure time to what is perhaps his first sporting love, the game of cricket, plus an occasional round of golf. Speaking to his former cricket captain, it sounds as if he wasn't very far off the standard to make a living from the game. I have seen several score cards from games he played for both Portsmouth FC and Plymouth Argyle against decent teams. He was never out and always got a wicket or two.

Barbara and Harry Penk now live in an idyllic New Forest village, close to their family in Marchwood. They have two sons, a daughter and four grandchildren. It was daughter Lynn who was the catalyst for *Thanks For The Memory* - my chance meeting with her in Romsey was the first step in what became a 16 month journey back in time. Researching and writing the book has been a very enjoyable experience; meeting Harry and Barbara Penk has been much more than that.

Proprietors:
C. W. CROOKES
C. K. CROOKES

R.A.C. Approved

FURNISHED CARAVANS
TO LET

CARAVAN SITES

**CHALLABOROUGH BAY
HOLIDAY CAMP**

BIGBURY - ON - SEA
—— South Devon ——

Telephone:
Bigbury-on-Sea 334

CARAVAN CLUB SITE

ALL ELECTRIC
FURNISHED BUNGALOWS
TO LET

CALOR GAS DEALER

May 26th

Dear Harry,

I have a friend connected with Northampton F.C. and he would very much like you to go there, but cant afford the fee Argyle are asking for you.

If you are interested would you write to the Players Union, requesting a reduction of transfer fee, also if you like you could ring David Bowen Northampton 31553 any morning.

Please keep this to yourself, and I would like to know how you get on.

Yours Sincerely, CW Crooke

Two letters from 1960. The one above is written by director Cliff Crookes, but at a time when he was not on the Board. Crookes was genuinely well liked by all the Plymouth Argyle players. He was generous with cheap or free accommodation at his Challaborough holiday complex and, as this letter shows, he had he players' welfare at heart. His "please keep this to yourself" request is quite understandable!

CHESTER FOOTBALL CLUB, LIMITED

Members of the Football Association, Ltd., The Football League Ltd., Div. IV.,
Cheshire County Football Association, Cheshire County Football League, West Cheshire League
and Chester & District League.

President: T. SARL-WILLIAMS, Esq.

Chairman of Directors :-
S. ARGYLE, Esq.

Secretary :- W. P. Peters
Telephone - Ground 21048

Manager :- Stanley C. Pearson

Registered Office :-
"THE STADIUM,"
SEALAND ROAD,
CHESTER.

June 14.

Dear Harry,

You dont know me, but I am interested in good players, and I note that you have not been retained by Plymouth. I know you have appealed against the fee, and I would like you, in the event of your fee being reduced, to let me know. I would like you to come here very much, I realise that you probably want to go to a better club, sorry, not better, but in higher company! I say not better, because, this is the happiest little club I know, and, as regards the team, I have some really good youngsters coming up, and I think that with the addition of one or two experienced players, we could easily get promotion this season. You would enjoy it here, and, if you wanted to, you could live at Wigan, and travel through daily. Anyway, Harry, I am interested, and I would appreciate it very much if you would let me know the outcome of your appeal.

Yours Sincerely,
Stan Pearson.

Another delightful example of the genteel way transfers were conducted in the late 50s and early 60s. Harry Penk was clearly in demand! He eventually decided to go to promoted Southampton, where he helped the Hampshire club establish themselves in the old Second Division. Argyle teammate Tommy Barrett had already moved to Chester. Note the name of the Chester Chairman. *Both letters lent by Harry Penk*

PENK IS FAST BECOMING AN IDLE OF CROWDS

BECAUSE he is such a quiet and modest young fellow, it is difficult to encourage Harry Penk to talk much about himself.

Spelling wasn't the strong point of this *Portsmouth Evening News* sub editor in 1955! Harry made a real impact on the supporters at Portsmouth. Just as at Plymouth, many felt that he was released too early.

The great Jimmy Dickinson leads Pompey's cricket team out for a 1955 friendly against United Services, Portsmouth. Harry Penk is extreme right.
Photo courtesy Portsmouth Evening News/Harry Penk

The photograph on the left sees Harry Penk with two great Hampshire CCC stars, South African Barry Richards and (centre) feared West Indian fast bowler Andy Roberts.

Hursley Park Cricket Club was a huge part of Harry Penk's post-football life. Their captain Chris Westbrook describes Harry as an obdurate batsman who sold his wicket very dearly. He could bowl fast and slow, was a fine close fielder as well as being a decent wicket-keeper too.

When asked Harry could not decide whether he would have preferred to play in an FA Cup Final or in one of the One Day Cricket Finals. The year after he retired from Hursley Park they reached the village knock out final at Lords.

A Charity Cricket game in Wigan sees Harry Penk (2nd right in front row) sharing the stage with Rugby League legend Billy Boston (3rd from left in the back row).

Far left, Barnsley keeps Argyle in the game with a flying save at Gillingham in the 1958 FA Cup replay. *Courtesy Colin Parsons collection*

Left, Barnsley is pictured at the start of the 1958-59 season. He was a very amusing man, with all of his colleagues nominating him as the 'joker in the pack.' *Courtesy Mike Curno's collection*

21 year old Geoff Barnsley and his wife Amy chat to manager Jack Rowley (left) after their first visit to Plymouth in July 1957.

Photo courtesy of the *Sunday Independent*

CHAPTER SIXTEEN

GEOFF BARNSLEY

A day or two after Wilf Carter signed for Argyle, young goalkeeper Geoff Barnsley, a former colleague at West Bromwich Albion also decided to leave the Black Country and sample life on the south western peninsula. It was clear he was destined to have a long time in reserve football if he stayed with the midlands outfit. He had one first team outing for West Brom, in a 3-1 defeat against Preston North End. He played against Tom Finney, thought by many to be the greatest forward England has ever produced.

Barnsley fitted the criteria Rowley and Blindell had agreed. He had been attached to a First Division club and was deemed good enough to play at that level. If he stayed, such was the consistency of John Sanders it was clearly going to be a case of 'dead man's shoes'. Just as with Wilf Carter, the club could sign Barnsley knowing he had already fulfilled his commitment to National Service. He served in the Royal Artillery for two years from April 1954. After undergoing Basic Training at Oswestry he was then posted to Woolwich Arsenal, where he was part of a 25 pounder gun team. He was conscripted on the Thursday, but travelled home on the Friday to join the West Bromwich Albion party travelling to Wembley for the 1954 FA Cup Final.

His liaison with Plymouth Argyle could not have started in a posher place. He recalls that Argyle officials were at the Café Royal in London, attending the 1957 Football League AGM. Barnsley and his wife Amy were invited to go and meet Jack Rowley and Secretary Bert Cole to discuss terms and the availability of club housing. Chairman Ron Blindell was also there. On Monday May 1957 he reported to Home Park and signed "before they changed their mind." He was recruited as deputy to Harry Brown, who was destined to retire at the end of the 1957-58 season. Jack Rowley rarely gave players a false expectation, and in the main would explain if they were being signed as a deputy to the current incumbent. To be understudying a player getting towards retirement seemed a better deal for Geoff than simply waiting and hoping.

Leaving the industrial Midlands was something of a wrench, but the Plymouth they arrived in was a bustling place full of new and nearly finished buildings. It was a new experience to be able to see the sea whenever it took their fancy. Once Arthur Humm's School of Motoring had taught Geoff to drive, they were able to get a car and appreciate the local sights. Geoff, Amy and their two children first moved into a temporary house in South View Terrace. It wasn't as good as they would have liked but they then loved their 'proper' house in Beechroft Road. It was a happy time in their life. Talking to them now, one can imagine the Barnsleys' was a fun house where laughter was an important element of life. After a steady start in the reserves, on 16 November 1957 he came in for his debut, in a 6-2 FA Cup first round win against Watford. It was the start of a 23 match run which saw only three defeats. After the Watford game the following Saturday saw him make his Argyle League debut at Carrow Road, Norwich. He played very well in a 1-0 defeat. Significantly the Argyle side that day featured nine members of the side that was the backbone of the 1958-59 promotion season. In the 20 League games he played in that first season he conceded 17 goals, unfortunately four of them coming in a 4-2 away defeat at Exeter City. He kept 11 clean sheets. On 22 February 1958, in a 3-0 home win over Northampton Town, Barnsley set off on a sequence of five games without conceding a goal, three of which were away from Home Park.

There was no way back for Brown until injury terminated Barnsley's run of first team games. He was hurt in the 1-0 home win against Port Vale on Good Friday 1958. Harry Brown returned for the final eight games of the season, starting his recall with three consecutive shut outs. But the supporters had seen enough of young Barnsley to know that Rowley's eye for a player had again served him well. His dead-ball kicking was not as good as Brown's (who had a prodigious kick), but he had showed great agility, courage and his handling was excellent.

With Harry Brown retired and taking over as mine host at the Drake's Drum in Plymstock, Geoff started the 1958-59 season as first choice. At 5'10" and 11 stone 6 lbs he was, for those days, the ideal height and weight for a goalkeeper. He enjoyed a run of 37 League & Cup games, before a real off night in a home defeat against Accrington Stanley cost him his place. It was a dreadful evening, with the heavy rain and slippery ball only adding to his problems. The crowd turned on him, conveniently forgetting his consistent displays over the previous 16 months. 50 years on it seems the only game his wife Amy can remember him playing. She teases him about it now but at the time Geoff was far from amused. He lost his place to Bob Wyllie for five games, but a 3-0 defeat at Brentford on Good Friday saw him recalled at Newport County the following day. He had an excellent match in a dogged 1-0 win. There were just seven games to go after that and Barnsley did not concede more than one goal in any of those games.

But there were many more good days than bad for Geoff Barnsley. In some ways his lack of flamboyance may have been his undoing. He was unspectacular but sound, never more than at Bradford on 13 December 1958, when on a tricky, frozen surface he gave a faultess display. The Saturday before, in a 2nd round FA Cup tie at Coventry he put in a remarkable performance. The latter was all the more admirable in that it came after a 5-1 mauling at Southampton the week before.

He started the 1959-60 season as first choice. Bob Wyllie failed to settle in the area and had moved on. The affable Scotsman John Leiper started as his deputy. It was a difficult season for everyone, Barnsley included. The promotion side of 1958-59 was augmented by the arrivals of George Kirby and Jimmy McAnearney from Sheffield Wednesday and Johnny Newman from Leicester City, each of them pleasant men who did nothing

Newman were tough and uncompromising on the field but they were the most affable of people away from the pitch. Experienced goalkeeper Dave Maclaren was brought in from First Division Leicester City but Geoff Barnsley never saw him as a threat. They were rivals for the jersey but for all of that were firm friends. The side struggled for much of the season following their promotion, culminating in Jack Rowley losing his job in March 1960. But Geoff remained an ever present in the League side and played his part in an excellent League Cup run.

Like many others who plied their trade at Plymouth in the late 50s and early 60s, nowhere else was ever the same for Geoff and his family. It was evident to me, even as a youngster, that the 1958-59 group had a remarkable camaraderie. They clearly enjoyed each other's company and whenever Geoff Barnsley was around there was laughter. He was not retained at the end of the 1960-61 season. Former West Bromwich Albion Manager Vic Buckingham was only at the club long enough to prepare the retained list. He laughs about it now but it was definitely a wrench. "Vic Buckingham, who had sold me to Argyle from the Albion, came to Argyle just about long enough to sell me again". This time it was to Norwich City, who were looking for a replacement for keeper Ken Nethercott. The veteran custodian had been one of the heroes of the amazing 1958-59 Norwich FA Cup success.

After his pleasant time at Plymouth, as soon as he joined the Carrow Road payroll Geoff immediately felt that the FA Cup run had seem to make the Norwich club a cliquey place. Geoff and Amy took over Nethercott's club house. Amongst their neighbours were other Cup heroes, captain Ron Ashman and elegant midfielder Roy McCroahan. After what Geoff saw as a career stalling two years, where he made only eight appearances, he jumped at the chance to join Torquay United. It was an area he and Amy and the kids had come to love – they still holiday there now several times a year. Again the move did not work out and he played only six times for the Plainmoor club. After ten years as a full-time professional, with nearly 150 appearances to his name, the family returned to their Black Country roots. After a season with Dudley Town and two more with Bilston he hung up his gloves. Despite Geoff having played for West Bromwich, Plymouth, Norwich and Torquay, his wife Amy has only truly supported one club – "There is only one team; I've always loved the Wolves" is her clarion call.

During the interview with Geoff Barnsley I tried to explain to him how it felt to be sitting talking to one of my childhood heroes. He told me that he probably understood that feeling more than most. "When I returned to the Midlands Bert Williams, the great Wolves and England goalkeeper, had a sports shop in Bilston. He also ran a goalkeeping school and he asked me to assist him. "Imagine that, eh? I found myself working alongside a man who was my greatest boyhood hero. I understand exactly where you are coming from Steve".

Geoff Barnsley was a popular member of the playing staff. The other players, without exception, named him as the joker of the group. That sense of fun has lasted the 50 years since he last played for Argyle. To this day he finds it difficult to be too serious about anything for too long. At the time the Barnsleys arrived Eric Davis was in the process of moving to Scunthorpe United. The couple were first put in a house in South View Road, before being allocated Eric's former home in Beechcroft Road. They loved it there. Geoff explained to me that a vicar lived next door. "I think he was from that big church at the end of Mutley Plain. Anyway, when we got dropped off from away trips late at night George Robertson would get off at the same place. He could never walk past next door without shouting up 'Goodnight vicar".

Whilst in the Army Geoff played in an unusual match at Falkirk, billed as the British Army versus the Scottish FA. He has no idea why, but the game was covered by live television. He thought perhaps it was an experimental broadcast, as both televised football coverage and floodlights were still in their infancy. He remembers that in the Army side that night were Mel Charles, Albert Quixall, Alan Finney, Frank Blunstone, Trevor Smith and Mel Hopkins, another illustration of how good some of the 1958-59 side were. After football Geoff worked for 26 years with the disabled, assisting on their holidays and with sports. It was then a Residential Home and Day Centre but is now a Treatment and Assessment Centre. He now concentrates on his family and has high hopes for grandson Liam who is a goalkeeper with Wolves under 12s.

Geoff Barnsley taking decisive action at Roots Hall in the vital and hard fought 0-0 draw with Southend United.

The goalkeeper sometimes had his critics but no one could fault his bravery. He took many knocks fighting the Argyle cause, often playing when he should not have.

He was sold on to Norwich City for £2,000.
From the Colin Parsons collection

During his return to Home Park on 27 September 2008 I asked Geoff Barnsley if, for old time's sake, I could get a shot of him standing in the goal. He readily agreed and said he would adopt a typical pose. All through the research for *Thanks For The Memory* there was a common theme from his former team mates — Geoff Barnsley was the joker in the pack. 50 years on it is clear that nothing has changed!

Photo by the author/inset courtesy Harry Penk and Plymouth Argyle

181

Two of John L Williams' prized possessions, his Third Division Champion-ship medal and his Welsh under 18s Cap. The cap is mainly red, with a blue background to the dragon and 1952-53 etched on to the peak in blue.

Photographed by the author

CHAPTER SEVENTEEN

JOHN 'CARDIFF' WILLIAMS

Although his hair is now silver and he sports a moustache, in terms of build, it is surprising how little John Lloyd Williams has altered in half a century. He has hardly gained an ounce in weight and looks the picture of health. He still runs 10 miles a week and in the past few years has competed in two London marathons, the Welsh half marathon and the Great Cardiff Run. He was born on 27 January 1936, in Rhymney, South Wales, a town immortalised by poet Idris Davies in his ballad *The Bells of Rhymney.* It was a powerful piece, set to the melody of 'Oranges and Lemons', about the effects on the area of the 1926 General Strike and the Great Depression. In later years it was set to music by Pete Seeger and, among others, it was recorded by the Byrds. As well as writing poetry, Idris Davies also played the organ in the Church attended by John's mother. She knew him well.

By the time John was born, though the worst of the Depression had passed, many still lived in poverty. With his mum, dad and older sister Margaret, he lived in his maternal grandfather's house in Clarendon Road. He remembers a secure and happy childhood. John has a remarkable memory, easily recalling particular instances from his early years.

He tells how his father, one of 18 children, would work a nine hour shift in the local pit, something he did for 45 years. The seam where he hacked at the coal was no more than 18 inches high. Until the 1948 nationalisation of the coalfields there were no pit-head baths or showers. John remembers his dad sitting in the kitchen in a tin bath filled with hot water, washing the grimy black dust from his body. But he never washed the length of his spine – he thought it would cause a weakness".

War was declared as John was approaching his fourth birthday. The war did not directly impact on Rhymney, but the heavy bombing raids on Cardiff in late 1940 and early 1941 brought it close on occasions. His father took him for a walk, to a place where the main rail line ran across a road. "There were craters everywhere, perhaps 20 or 30," he told me. "Dad explained to me that there must have been a reason why they could not drop them on the target, so they probably went after a train as they left the area to return to Germany. He was good like that, my dad was. He was always explaining things to us." Two incidents stick in John's mind from 1944. He was taken down to a main road nearby, which runs from Gloucester down to Swansea and recalls seeing thousands of US servicemen and their vehicles. He remembers his dad musing that something big was about to happen. David Williams wasn't wrong – D Day was just a few weeks away. A week or so later his dad called him and his sister from their beds and ushered them to a window. "He told us to look up and always remember what we had seen. I can still see it now, thousands of lights in the sky. It was the gliders being towed to France for the War."

As the war ended, John had progressed from Upper Rhymney School to the local secondary school. It was here that his football talent started to be noticed. Able young players tend to score a lot of goals, wherever they play in the team. John Williams was so outstanding that he came to the attention of the Welsh Youth team selectors, no mean feat for a boy who had rarely ventured out of Rhymney. He was not attached to the ground-staff of any professional club, though he had played for Tredegar School-boys.

At just 16 years old he was selected to play against England Youth at Fratton Park. Wales went down 3-1 but John had the consolation of scor-ing their goal. He cannot recall anyone else in the Welsh side who became a professional. In the England side he remembers Jim Iley, who later played for Nottingham Forest and Newcastle, and Geoff Cox. 10 years later he and Geoff would be colleagues at Plainmoor. Typical of his neat and tidy approach to life, John's cap from that day has been maintained in pristine condition.

After his excellent display against England the first professional club to come in for him was Hull City. He had a successful trial and was offered terms, but his mother would not hear of him moving so far from home. Cardiff City (then in the First Division) showed an interest and on his 17th birthday he signed professional terms for £6 per week. To this day, he cannot speak highly enough of Alf Sherwood, a senior professional at Ninian Park. Despite being a first team player and a Welsh international, Alf was nothing but helpful and kind to the young man. John was able to live at home, travelling to Cardiff by train each day on a £1 weekly return ticket, paid for by the club.

Joining Cardiff meant leaving behind the job his uncle had found him in the Rhymney Brewery. He had planned to be a carpenter but that meant delaying National Service until he had completed the apprenticeship. He preferred to get it over with and was called up at 18, joining the Royal Army Service Corps and spending the majority of his time in Bielefeld in Germany. Although he played football while in the Army he did not serve with any other professionals. John regrets never being tasked with any assignments to Berlin, but he did visit Belsen, something he describes as too horrible ever to forget. He also recalls being confined to barracks for two weeks when the Germans were celebrating after formally being given back their freedom. He was demobbed in 1956. As with many young pro-fessional footballers of the day, it was a crucial time for his career to be interrupted, but he took up where he left off and again became a regular in Cardiff's Football Combination side. Both first team wing-halves were internationals and there was another waiting in the reserves. After two years he could see no prospect of progress, so went to see manager Trevor Morris to ask for a transfer. Towards the end of the 1957-58 season Mor-ris told him that Norwich City were interested in signing him.

Norwich were about to play a friendly against Leicester, and their man-ager Archie McCauley was keen for John to play in it. John travelled to Norwich and acquitted himself well, in what was virtually the Canaries' first team. He remembers Johnny Newman being in the opposition that night. Williams liked what he saw of Norwich and the Carrow Road ground. The fee would be £4,000 and McCauley wanted him to sign. He returned to Cardiff and spoke to the manager, saying he wished to be transferred to the East Anglian club. But while he had been away, Plymouth had expressed an interest, so John travelled to Devon and, after speaking to Ron Blindell and Jack Rowley, he left with a transfer form given to him by the Argyle boss. Rowley told him that if he wanted to join the Home Park staff he should just sign it and post it back. Plymouth offered better terms, understanding that John would need to live in 'digs'

Gordon Fincham signs from Leicester watched by Jack Rowley (left),and Secretary AH (Bert) Cole. John L Williams looks to be making sure Fincham is not on more money than him.
Photograph lent by John L Williams

if he signed for them. What John has never understood is that Argyle offered only £3,000, yet Morris was keener for him to go to Devon. He was told that if he signed for Plymouth, Cardiff would pay a £300 benefit but if he went east, that offer would be withdrawn. The benefit payment swung it and Plymouth now had a second John Williams on their books.

With Tom Barrett injured John made his debut against Bury on Thursday 18 September 1958 and kept his place for the next 14 games, before losing out to new signing Len Casey. His spell out of the side included the third round home FA Cup tie against his former club Cardiff. He was devastated at missing that game, a disappointment that remains with him to this day. It was March before he regained his place, in an evening match at Tranmere. Johnny Williams was moved forward to inside right and John 'Cardiff' replaced him at wing half. Argyle lost 2-0 but the side played better than they had for weeks. However, he was left out for the next two games, a 2-0 success at home to Chesterfield and a 3-0 defeat at Brentford on Good Friday.

As the party left Griffin Park, bound for South Wales and an Easter Saturday encounter with Newport, John had an inkling that he could be recalled at Somerton Park. By chance, he found he was playing before the manager actually told him. The landlord of his Plymouth digs came up for the match, John having offered to get him a ticket. The landlord had travelled up with director Cliff Crookes. In those days the manager had to clear the selection with the Board, and thus Crookes knew John would be included.

He is glad he played, for his parents came down from Rhymney to watch, as did one of his old secondary school teachers. John reckoned that his father gained as much pleasure from being introduced to Jack Rowley as he did from watching his son play in the match. He laughs as he tells how his dad was trying to explain the rules of the game to his mother. David Williams told his wife, "The greens, that's our John's team, have to kick the ball into that goal down there, and the yellows, Newport, have to kick it into the one down the other end". "Mother's view was that it may be easier if they both kicked it into the same goal!" The day ended well with Argyle taking a precious two points courtesy of a Wilf Carter penalty. For John, his own day was made when Alf Sherwood, by then plying his trade at Newport, came to the Argyle dressing room and sought him out, telling him, "I am so pleased for you son, that you have made it into someone's first team. Good luck for the future, you deserve it." The following day *Spectator* was fulsome in his praise for the young Welshmen's tireless display. He retained his place for the remaining seven fixtures. He can still remember the wonderful feeling of securing promotion at Accrington, the scenes the next day in the city and at Home Park. Thousands had turned out. Then on the following Wednesday the 1-1 draw with Bradford City nailed the championship and the celebrations kicked off again. At the start of the season Jack Rowley, a man John admired immensely, had advised him that he was being signed as cover for injuries, so to play in more than half of the 46 fixtures represented a successful first season.

Although John remained at Home Park for another three seasons he could never establish himself in the side. With Casey already on the books, he was pushed further down the pecking order when Johnny Newman arrived from Leicester City. He only made ten more appearances in the League, three in the FA Cup and two in the League Cup. In 1959-60 he remembers playing at Anfield, where despite a 4-1 defeat he had an enjoyable day. He also has cause to remember the 0-0 draw against Aston Villa in the League Cup, a match which was unusual for being abandoned after 90 minutes. The referee ruled the ground unfit for extra time to be

John at Home Park on 27 September 2008 after receiving an Argyle Legends tie, a replica shirt and a silver salver commemorating the 1958-59 title winning campaign. A proud man with an awful lot to be proud about.

Photo by the author

played. After the game Gerry Hitchens, the Aston Villa centre-forward and a full England international, came to look for him after the match. They had been at Cardiff together. In his typically modest way, John didn't go looking for Hitchens because he thought he wouldn't remember him.

It was whilst playing for the reserves that John Lloyd Williams made national news, with his photo appearing on every back page. On 9 December 1961 Tottenham reserves were due at Home Park. During the week prior to the game Spurs signed Jimmy Greaves from AC Milan. He could not be registered in time to play in the First Division so he was included in the Football Combination fixture at Plymouth. Williams was Argyle reserves' left half and would be given the task of marking Greaves.

In the event John played very well, watched by more than 12,000 supporters and famous journalists like Clive Toye, Ian Wooldridge and Clement Freud. He drew great praise for his tenacious and dogged display, despite Greaves scoring twice. At one stage, so close did Williams stick to his task, he ended up accidentally getting Greaves's boot in his face. Greaves was the first to his side to check that he was all right. As the players left the field for half-time, Greaves was asked to make the draw. John doubtless stayed with him for that too.

At the end of the 1961-62

Up close and personal! John L Williams during his brave battle to contain Jimmy Greaves.
Courtesy Sunday Independent

season he moved to Plainmoor, where he spent three seasons and played in 42 League games. After Torquay he could have moved along the coast to Weymouth, where his former Torquay boss Eric Webber was in charge. But John's father had suffered a stroke and he wanted to return to Wales. He played as a part-time professional for Merthyr Town in the Southern League and then Ton Pentre in the Welsh League. When at Merthyr they were drawn against Wrexham in the Welsh Cup. Jack Rowley was at that time manager at the Racecourse Ground and took time out to welcome his former charge. "That was typical Jack, like," John told me.

He says that he was never as well off as when he went part-time and got a job. He spent 20 years as a Training Officer at the Hoover plant in Merthyr. John is married to Eileen (nee Roberts), whose dad Reg was once mine host at the Oporto pub, at the top of York Street and then the Cornwall's Gate. They have three grown up children and four grandchildren. Daughter Deborah has lived in California for 14 years. John still works 13 hours a week at the Merthyr Asda and Eileen is a lecturer at a local College.

With another couple of inches in height, and perhaps another stone in weight, John 'Cardiff ' Williams may have achieved more than he did in the game. He was a strong and combative individual but the game was very physical in his day. Some of the other players told me how John would literally push himself to exhaustion in some of the games he played. He deserves to look back on his career with great pride. He has that gold medal from the Third Division title winning campaign and his Welsh Youth cap too. Many have achieved far less in the game. He remains one of the nicest men ever to have donned the green and black. As with several of the 1958-59 group, first team appearances do not always tell the full story. Ellis Stuttard was happy for John to stay at Home Park, because of the fine job he was doing for the reserve side. With his sharp football brain, dedication to fitness and sober lifestyle, Ellis saw him as the perfect example for young professionals coming through the ranks. John preferred to try and find first team football at Torquay.

John Williams outside his Merthyr home. The house name is Welsh for "View Of The Brow."

Photo by the author and inset courtesy of the Sunday Independent

FOOTBALL STARS
★ OF 1959 ★

A SET OF 44
26
JOHN WILLIAMS
(Right-Half)

A pupil of the Junior Mixed and Secondary Modern Schools in his native Rhymney, this skilful half-back played for both. Then, while a Tredegar School player on Saturday mornings, he also played for his Boys' Club in the afternoons. He represented Welsh Boys' Clubs. At 16 he had trials for Hull City. He joined Rhymney Town, signed for Cardiff City, then Plymouth Argyle, where he won a Div. III Championship winner's medal last season. A Plymouth League cricketer, he also played for Glamorgan Colts.

PRESENTED WITH
THE WIZARD
THE STORY PAPER FOR BOYS

JOHN WILLIAMS

A very young Johnny Williams, photographed at about the time he broke into the first team while still a part-time professional. 54 years on he remains grateful to Jack Rowley giving him his first chance and also for then persevering with him.

The picture was used during a 1959 issue of football cards in the *Wizard* comic, but clearly they did not know their JS from their JL! The text on the reverse describes the other John Williams!

Printing techniques were much cruder than they are now—the lop-sided appearance of the reverse of the card is how it was and not the author's error.

From the Colin Parsons collection

CHAPTER EIGHTEEN

JOHNNY WILLIAMS

Although he was born in Bristol, Johnny Williams moved to Plymouth at a very early age. He first went to school at Eggbuckland Primary and then on to Tamar. He learned his football in the city and, to all intents and purposes, is a local. His father Sid was a printer who moved from Bristol to take up a position with the *Western Morning News*. John recalls that his father worked permanent nights. The family lived at 139 Efford Road.

Williams did not make it into the Plymouth Schoolboys side. He was one of those unfortunate kids whose birthday fell at just the wrong time. At the point of age qualification he was only just past 14 and by the next year he was over 15. But his talent won through in the end. His father, himself a decent footballer and cricketer, believed in his son and took him to Home Park for a trial. Johnny was quickly signed as a part-time professional. With Plymouth born Reg Wyatt and Peter Anderson in the side, plus George Robertson and George Baker having come through from the juniors, the nucleus of the 1958-59 promotion side had cost no more than a £10 signing on fee each.

After no more than a handful of games in the Plymouth and District and South Western League sides Johnny Williams quickly broke into the reserves. At that time he was seen as an inside forward, a distinctly different role than that of the wing half position he eventually made his own. Jack Rowley saw his talent very early in his tenure as Argyle boss. Indeed, it was the manager rather than any of the training staff who saw the lad's potential as a wing half back, realising that the player's hard tackling would better serve the team if he played in a less advanced role.

Weeks after he was playing for EEM Department and Co-op Welfare he was just 20 when he made his first team debut on 10 September 1955, in a 1-0 home victory against Blackburn Rovers. He was still a part-time professional, having elected to complete his apprenticeship as an electrician in the Dockyard. He made 22 further Second Division appearances, plus an outing in a third round FA Cup defeat at Brisbane Road. He scored his first League goal in his third appearance, a trademark long distance effort in a 4-1 defeat against Liverpool at Anfield. Unfortunately his debut season ended in relegation. Although a part-timer, Williams was definitely one of Rowley's successes. There were too many other players on the staff who were simply not up to the standards required for the Second Division.

It began to look as if many were not up to life in the Third (South) either. Argyle made a catastrophic start to life in the third tier, and after playing in the first three games the young Williams was taken out of the firing line after a 6-0 home defeat at the hands of Reading. The Langman brothers took the place of Williams and the luckless Welshman Dennis John. Having played in the final two games of the previous campaign,

Dennis was brought back for the drubbing by Reading. He was never given another League outing. Young goalkeeper Peter Dyer also bit the dust and apart from once when Harry Brown was indisposed, he never played again. In what were two of the poorest ever seasons at Home Park it was hard for anyone making their way in the game. But Johnny Williams' future turned out to be much brighter. Rowley purposely used the lad's time out of the side to convert him from inside forward to wing half. After the gap of six games, Rowley recalled Williams at right half. He never looked back and apart from a few games as an inside forward he was to make the number four shirt his own. He played in all of the remaining League games of that 1956-57 season and both FA Cup ties - a 2-0 win at Exeter followed by a 1-0 reverse at Torquay. By March 1957 he had completed 50 first team appearances.

When fit, Johnny Williams remained an automatic choice until 1965. In 1957-58 he missed only two League matches and one of the three FA Cup ties played that season. After missing a home 2-2 draw with Shrewsbury on 21 December 1957 he returned for the away fixture at Newport on Christmas Day. It was to be the start of a remarkable run where he would miss only one game from then until 9 March 1963.   It meant that he played in 201 out of 202 League matches. Even the one he missed was not through injury; he was required to play for the British Army versus the French Army in Paris on Sunday 14 December 1958, forcing him to miss the goalless draw at Bradford the previous day.

Not only was Johnny Williams a remarkable athlete, he was also a man who took great care of his appearance. At the same time that I started to watch Argyle regularly, I was also beginning to take notice of the pop music scene. I remember thinking, even at ten years old, that Johnny Williams looked exactly like the guys in my sister's *Pop* magazine. His decision to complete his Dockyard apprenticeship impacted on his time of entry into the Army for his National Service. It meant that he would be in the Army for most of the 1957-58 season and all of the 1958-59 term. One of the things that originally drew Rowley's attention to Johnny Williams was his phenomenal fitness. *Pilgrim* once reported that Rowley had joked with him that the other part-time players were reluctant to train with Johnny Williams, because he was so much fitter than the rest.

Jack Rowley realised that with Williams enlisting as a PTI in the Royal Army Medical Corps at Aldershot, the lad would be able to maintain a decent standard of fitness. During his National Service he missed only that Bradford game due to Army commitments. Williams told me when we met that this was due to the fact that Jack Rowley was a good friend of his Army boss, a Major Howells.

During the time of National Service no one was exempt, except those who could not reach the standard for physical fitness. This meant that the Army was full of young professional footballers drawn from all four Football League divisions. The British Army XI often looked like a United Kingdom representative side. It was no different in Johnny Williams' time. It is a testament to his ability that despite the standard of players available, he held down a permanent place in the full Army team throughout his two year conscription. It was the clearest sign yet that he could have held his own in the English First Division, a fact endorsed by the interest shown in him by Stan Cullis, the manager of the greatest side Wolverhampton Wanderers ever had. In February 1957 Wolves were on the way to the first of two consecutive League Championships. They were the most powerful side in the land. But Cullis wanted Williams, clearly seeing him as a player capable of holding his own at the very top level. Cullis even travelled to Plymouth to make a personal assessment. But it wasn't the most

Soccer Round-Up

JOHNNY WILLIAMS, WATCHED BY THE WOLVES, SAYS

I would like to play for a First Division club but I thin I should finish my apprenticeship first " said Plymouth Argyle's right-half Johnny Williams follow rhampton Wanderers we which

straightforward of situations. The player was still a part-timer, and after his time in the Dockyard was over he could expect that official looking envelope, inviting him to serve in the Armed Forces for two years.

Whilst most supporters who answered my call for their impressions and memories of the 1958-59 season chose either Wilf Carter or Jimmy Gauld as their favourite player, a large number plumped for Johnny Williams as the most exciting. The players of that era also recognised his ability, though Williams is the first to admit that as an attack minded wing half, he sometimes forgot about his defensive responsibilities.

Some say he should have gone to a First Division club and pitted his wits against the very best. But that overlooks the fact that there was no financial inducement to move. Whether a player was in the top or the bottom tier a club could pay no more than the maximum wage set by the FA. He did later concede that moving to Wolverhampton did not appeal but he would have looked seriously at any offer from a top London club. The interest shown in the player was a huge endorsement of Rowley's early judgement. After Wolves were turned away— "£15,000 would not be enough" was Rowley's take on it—a year later Everton were said to be watching the player closely. It was often said that John did not want to uproot from Plymouth. However, when I put that to Shirley, John's wife of 50 years, she was quick to point out that the players' contracts in those days made it impossible for them to move if the club did not want them to.

While he was at Arsenal Eric Doughty had rubbed shoulders with some of the finest First Division footballers day in day out. He seemed to be the ideal man to ask how Johnny Williams would have done in the First Division. His answer was instant and categoric. "Not only would he have survived at that level; I believe he would have been an absolute star." That is an opinion that would probably be endorsed by anyone who saw Johnny in his hey day.

If further proof were needed then it came in a match in Edinburgh, watched by Matt Busby, still convalescing from Munich. He watched the British Army XI play a Scotland XI at Easter Road and, as we saw in an earlier chapter, the great man very impressed. The Army side that night was Bert Slater (Falkirk and later Liverpool); Alex Parker (Everton), Graham Williams (West Bromwich); Williams, Plenderleith (Hibs), Gordon Milne (Preston and later Liverpool); Alex Scott (Rangers), John Smith (West Ham), Gerry Hitchens (Aston Villa), Peter Dobing (Blackburn Rovers) and George Mulhall (Aberdeen and later Sunderland). Other than Johnny Williams, during the remainder of their careers all of the others played at some international level. Many became full internationals. He is one of the few players to have played against Argyle while still registered for them, when he appeared for the British Army in a testimonial for Secretary Bert Cole (though the proceeds went to Assistant Trainer George Reed's family). And he also scored in a 3-3 draw.

Although he never played in the First Division, Johnny Williams shrewdly planned for the time he could no longer earn a living from the game he graced. In 1965 he and Shirley invested in the Johnny Williams Service Station at Efford, not a stone's throw from the house he was brought up in Efford Road. Later he also had other garages at West Park and Southway, the latter at one time managed by his brother Peter and now run by his son John. He and Shirley—they celebrated their Golden Wedding in March 2008– were a little unlucky with the West Park business. The opening of the Parkway quickly reduced their passing trade but shrewdly they stuck with it. Soon trade returned, with many local people finding it easier to get in and out as traffic levels through West Park reduced. Younger readers may be interested to know that prior to the Parkway being opened, circa 1979, the A38 ran from Marsh Mills via Forder Valley, along through Crownhill and West Park before turning right on to Normandy Way to cross the Tamar Bridge.

In 11 seasons spent almost entirely in the first team—he only ever made 14 Football Combination appearances—he had played 448 games scoring 55 times. He made 411 starts in League games, and made 19 FA Cup appearances and 17 in the League Cup. He also made a single appearance as a substitute. Many of his 55 goals were spectacular. It is difficult to remember another player, and that is in any era at Home Park, who could cause such a buzz of anticipation in the crowd. With the ball at his feet, anywhere from 40 yards from the opposition's goal, their goalkeeper could prepare for action. There may have been the odd tap in but there were some memorable long range efforts. I remember one in the first season after the 58-59 promotion season, in an early 1-1 draw with Sheffield United. Argyle were chasing shadows and were one down. He burst forward from inside his own half and let fly from fully 30 yards. The Blades' goalkeeper was a former England international but had no chance with what *Spectator* described as a rocket. It went in off the cross bar and I remain convinced that when Sheffield United restarted the game the top of the goal was still quivering.

Another that sticks in my mind could have been the best of them all, but it was disallowed as someone strayed offside. It was against West Ham in the FA Cup in 1962, when from all of 35 yards Williams hit the hardest shot I can remember seeing. The Hammers' goalkeeper, Scottish international Lawrie Leslie, was guarding the net at the Devonport End. As he made a despairing dive high to his left the ball was already on its way back out, having cannoned off the inside of the metal stanchion supporting the net. West Ham had by coincidence been Argyle's first round opponents in the League Cup, this time at the Boleyn Ground. Williams gave notice that night that he could shoot from range when he scored Argyle's second in a 3-2 defeat.

Another amazing effort came at Leicester in the League Cup semi-final January 1965. I have only seen it on a grainy piece of black and white film, but it was a spectacular hit. The League Cup was a happy hunting ground for Johnny Williams. In the opening season of the competition, 1960-61, he hit three in eight outings including the winner against Torquay in a second round replay and two in the twice replayed fourth round against Villa. In his 17 appearances in the competition he scored six times.

Johnny Williams was the last of the 1958-59 group of players to leave Home Park. His automatic selection began to falter under Malcolm Allison, who seemed to want a different type of player. Then in 1966, in one of a series of baffling decisions on players, manager Derek Ufton made it clear Williams did not feature in his plans. In exchange for £6,500 Johnny completed a circle by returning to the city of his birth, joining the Eastville payroll. Signed by Bert Tann, he made 69 appearances for Rovers while increasing his goal tally by another 10. It carried him past the 500 League appearances mark. After two seasons Fred Ford became manager there and demanded he move to Bristol. He had only moved on the proviso that he could remain in Plymouth, to see to his burgeoning business interests. Ford decided to release him. After a spell helping Billy Bingham on the coaching side, when the genial Irishman left the club Williams elected to follow him out of the door. He then had a short stint as player-manager at Bodmin Town before appearing as a part-timer with Falmouth Town. He had a major part in bringing great success to Bickland Park.

Johnny Williams autograph was never the easiest to obtain. He would never sign before the game, rushing by with a, "I'll sign them all after the game." That was almost true. You would get your reward but only if you stayed in line. At 10 and 11 years old that seemed a tad irksome, but looking back it was a very good lesson. Of course, Johnny was in the Army at the time so he was probably just passing on some of what he got every week from the Sergeant-Major!

For many years he has lived in a popular Plymouth suburb and has two children, Debbie and John. They in turn have given John and Shirley five grandchildren—Sophie, Ruby, Jamie, Brogan and Elisa. He looks back on his time at Argyle with great affection and did not have a bad word for anyone he played with. We shall never know how he would have fared in the First Division. But he was a far better player than Argyle's overall record in his 11 seasons would indicate. One Third Division winner's medal and a League Cup semi-final was scant reward for one of the most talented individuals ever to grace Home Park.

50 years on and Johnny Williams has a message for the picture editor of the *Sunday People*. This is the right way around for a number four! Johnny Williams was the first to admit that he did not always pay sufficient attention to his defensive duties. However, the picture (above left) shows him helping Geoff Barnsley to clear his lines. It looks as if the picture was set into the paper the wrong way around.

The picture on the right is from the visit by the 1958-59 players in September 2008. Johnny shows the replica shirt presented to him by current Chairman Paul Stapleton.

The picture from the Sunday People was sent in by Dave Soden. The 2008 picture is by the author. The inset is from Sam Bailey's scrapbook.

Another picture from the return to Home Park of some of the surviving members of the 1958-59 promotion side. Here Johnny Williams shows his appreciation of the reception given by the fans of today. Like the rest of his former colleagues, he was greatly moved by the reception they received. They were especially taken by the number of young supporters who stood and gave them a great ovation.

Just before this photograph was taken John spotted the Nottingham Forest substitutes having a half-time kick about. Famed for his powerful long range shooting, he turned to me and said "I"d love to have had a go with a ball like that one." I suspect there are many goalkeepers from 40 and 50 years ago who were very glad that he didn't!

John still looks remarkably fit and is no heavier now than when he played.

Photo by the author

CHAPTER NINETEEN

BARRIE MEYER

Barrie Meyer was amongst the last generation of sportsmen who earned a living both as professional cricketer in the summer and a professional footballer in the winter. In 1958 there were quite a few men who played both games at a professional level. Around the time that he moved to Home Park there were five or six in Meyer's Gloucestershire CCC team who played both games at a high level. By the end of the next decade, it is highly probable that there were none. Chris Balderstone, who like Meyer played both games and became a first-class umpire, could well have been the last – but that is just a guess based on failure at numerous quizzes! Argyle's previous well known cricketer-footballer was George Dews, who was an integral part of the successful sides of the early 50s. At the very time Meyer was putting pen to paper in Bristol, to seal his move to Home Park, his Gloucestershire team mate Arthur Milton was in Australia playing in the Ashes. The caps he earned in that series made him the last man to be capped by England at both cricket and soccer.

Although his career in professional sport had started in football, by the time he joined Plymouth Argyle's payroll Barrie Meyer considered himself to be a professional cricketer who would only play football when there was no cricket. The sole reason that Meyer was made available for transfer was due to the Eastville club's insistence that he choose between playing cricket for Gloucester, or attending pre-season football training. No one doubted his ability as a centre forward or inside forward and he had a good record in front of goal. But Meyer, 'BJ' to his friends, declined the offer to participate in his club's preparations in 1958 and was placed on the open to transfer list.

One weekend late in that August Jack Rowley had been spotted talking to Meyer during a cricket match at Cheltenham. *Spectator* reported that once Rowley had been seen by a national sports journalist "that set the hares running". By the following Monday Bristol City were showing a keen interest, though Rovers had no intention of allowing a decent player to go to their Ashton Gate rivals. Cardiff too were interested in the player's availability. Both moves appealed to Meyer, for he had only recently brought his parents from Bournemouth to a house in Bristol. Even 50 years ago, hindsight offered the same benefit as now. Meyer was being denied a move to two clubs which would have suited his domestic situation, while his club was forcing him to join the most westerly club in the Football League. Perhaps it should have come as no surprise that the relocation was comparatively short-lived. It is also a good example how players from that era could be bought and sold against their will.

Unfortunately for Meyer, Bristol Rovers were keen to sign unsettled Argyle back John Timmins. John and his wife had not settled in Plymouth and Rovers were keen on a player/cash deal which would see Argyle pay Rovers around £3,000 to £4,000 in a transaction with an overall value of

£7,500. With Argyle manager Jack Rowley undergoing much needed nasal surgery, a relic from his playing days, Bert Cole undertook the negotiations with the player. The Argyle secretary was an old friend of his Bristol Rovers counterpart. Both Cole and Mr Gummow were both keen bowlers. The deal went through at 4.30 on Meyer's 26th birthday, 21 August 1958.

On September 1958 he scored twice in his Home Park debut in a 3-0 win over Bury. He then scored against his hometown club in a 3-1 victory before getting two at Doncaster as Argyle fought back from 4-2 down to win 6-4. He scored a hat-trick in a 4-1 FA Cup first round replay against Gillingham, deputising for the injured Carter. His final game in an Argyle shirt was his most ineffective, in a 3-0 third round defeat at the hands of Cardiff City on 18 January 1959. He had been a surprising choice, for the newspapers were reporting that he was unsettled and was training in Bristol. Within a month of that tie he had moved to Newport County. In all he had scored five times in eight league outings and three times in two FA Cup matches. His skill was never in doubt but he hated the travelling. He also remembers that he could not properly shake off a troublesome hamstring injury. Barrie was another who believed that Wilf Carter was the outstanding player of the group.

Meyer learned his football in a park adjacent to a professional football ground. For those who know Bournemouth's ground, it was in the King's Park at the eastern end of the stadium. A local youth club spotted him and he soon made their number ten shirt his own. In the 1948-49 season he was chosen for Hampshire Boys' Clubs and helped himself to six goals as they beat first Berkshire, then Buckinghamshire and a combined Devon and Cornwall side. The final was played on a Saturday morning at Charlton's Valley. Barry then rushed back down to Hampshire to play for his local Youth Club side, only to lose that game as well. After a such a successful season it was not surprising that he was chosen for England Boys' Clubs against the Welsh at Wrexham. He scored in a 3-1 win. He can recall that some of the boys in the England side were attached to professional clubs, but 60 years on understandably struggles to remember their names. In not much more than 40 games he registered 50 goals and attracted the attention of a number of Football League clubs. Fred Hyde, a scout for Bristol Rovers was the first to call, offering Barry the opportunity to play in a trial match the following Saturday.

Thanks to his brother's wedding he had to forego that chance. But the club were having a second trial match, to give final opportunities to some of their existing staff to win a new contract. Barry told me that it was a hard match. "To be honest I did not do as well as I had hoped. But immediately after the game I was called into the manager's office and offered terms. They offered me £10 to sign and then £7 a week during the season and £5 for the summer. I felt I was already well paid at £3 in my job with a little building firm!" Settled in digs in Bristol with some friends of his family, by the early part of 1950 he had impressed manager Bert Tann sufficiently to force his way into the Rovers Football Combination side. Not long after the commencement of the 1950-51 campaign Tann told him that he would be playing in the first team against, of all teams, his home town club Bournemouth and Boscombe Athletic. He scored the second in a 2-0 win but had an early introduction to the ups and downs of football. Having retained his place for the following week's fixture at Exeter he sustained a nasty ankle injury. In early 1951 he was called up for National Service, joining the RASC at Aldershot. After basic training he was posted to Hilsea Barracks in Portsmouth, which enabled him to keep playing for Rovers at weekends. It will be seen from several of the previous chapters that conscription seemed to work against many players of the day, inasmuch that it interfered with the progress of their career. For Meyer, his time in the Army turned out to be life-changing. He was asked to take the gloves for the battalion cricket team and he excelled. Barry was very honest about his time in the Army, telling me that he could hardly have been luckier. I played a lot of cricket at Hilsea and we also had a football team in a local league. I once went about five weeks without ever wearing a uniform".

But by 1953 he was back in Bristol full time. Although the Army had given him a taste for cricket, he had in football terms fallen down the pecking order at Eastville. For much of the 1952-53 season he had to be content with reserve football. But it was a good season for the club as they took the Third Division (South) title. In 53-54 he was in and out of the first team but the following season he sparkled. He made 40 first team appearances and scored 20 times. Although manager Bert Tann seems quite a benevolent man, he found Meyer to be frustratingly inconsistent. Speaking to Barry's biographer he reckoned that had Meyer been more consistent he would have been a top, top player.

The high spot of Barrie Meyer's soccer career came on 9 January 1956. 35,872 squeezed into Eastville to see Rovers entertain Manchester United in a third round FA Cup tie. On a muddy pitch Rovers scored the shock of the round, registering four goals without reply, with Meyer getting one of them. He remembers to this day how magnanimous Matt Busby was in defeat. This was years before the word rotation came into the football dictionary and United's side was Wood; Foulkes, Byrne; Colman, Jones, Edwards; Berry, Doherty, Taylor, Viollet and Pegg. At that time they were one of the finest sides in Europe, if not the world. To say the least, it was a remarkable result. Not much more than two years later Barry was numbed by the news of the Munich Air crash. As much as anything, it was the fact that they were so sporting in a defeat they could never have contemplated. "They were great players but great men too" was how he saw it.

During his time with Bristol Rovers Meyer played against Argyle on six occasions, scoring one in each of the two games in the 1953-54 season. The 3-3 draw at Home Park on 7 November 1953 was the only time in his six encounters against Argyle that he did not finish on the winning side. The return match at Eastville that season saw Argyle go down 3-1. At Easter 1955 they played twice in four days with Rovers winning 3-1 at home and by a single goal at Home Park. In the 1955-56 season, when Argyle were relegated, Meyer helped his club to a 2-1 victory at Eastville and another 1-0 success at Home Park.

In all he played 406 first-class matches for Gloucestershire, scoring more than 5,000 runs in the three day game, averaging 14.19 with a highest score of 63 (which he made three times). In addition he took 709 catches and made 118 stumpings. England wicket-keeper Jim Parks made the point that averages do not tell the full story, indicating that he was always glad to see the back of BJ. Many have said that if Meyer had made more runs he would have challenged for an England place. He was a fine wicket-keeper but played in an era when there were many good stumpers in the game, most of them English. In the one day game, which Barrie confesses was not so much to his liking, he averaged just under seven. He took 47 catches in his 44 games, but due to his county's strong batting line-up he only made it to the wicket on 25 occasions. Although cricket came between Meyer and Bristol Rovers, it was football that gave him his breakthrough at Gloucester. Bobby Etheridge, the regular first eleven glove man preferred to accompany Bristol City on a soccer tour, giving BJ a chance that he literally took with both hands.

During my call to South Africa I asked him who he thought was the finest batsman he had ever kept to. He answered very quickly, naming a man who he had played both with and against, the elegant England Test player Tom Graveney. After falling out with Gloucestershire Graveney went on to star for Worcestershire. He felt that the best bowler he ever kept to was Mike Procter, although he also enjoyed the almost telepathic relationships he developed with Gloucester spinners David Allen and John Mortimore. When I asked him who was the best footballer he had played against, the answer was something of a surprise. "Setting aside the great Manchester United team that came to Eastville, I would have to say Stanley Matthews." I was frantically trying to think where their paths would have crossed on a soccer field. I was pretty sure they had never played in the same division at the same time. Barrie eventually went on to say that it was during a Gloucestershire cricket tour of Bermuda. "We had no fewer than six professional footballers in our ranks and Matthews was coaching out there. "He guested for their national side and against a Gloucestershire CCC soccer team."

Many people never get to witness even one outstanding sporting event in their life, yet alone participate in them. Well, maybe that is because Barrie Meyer had more than his fair share! While he was playing football he had that great FA Cup upset against the Busby Babes. As a cricketer he played in one of the best remembered one day matches there has ever been. In 1971 the nation was gripped by one of the most tense one day finishes there has ever been. It was a Gillette Cup semi-final between Lancashire and Gloucestershire at Old Trafford. The start was delayed by weather before Procter and goalkeeper/cricketer Ron Nicholls each made 50s as Gloucester posted 229-7 off their allocation of 60 overs. With four overs remaining Lancashire needed 27 more to win. With dusk approaching umpires Jepson and Bird (who else in a crisis!) called the captains together. Jackie Bond the Lancashire skipper was batting and he wanted to continue, citing the crowd as the main consideration. Barrie remembers it being the worst light he has ever played in, but soon after Bond elected to continue David Hughes smashed 24 off an over from John Mortimore. So exciting was the cricket, the BBC delayed the 9 o'clock news. Meyer believes it to be the most repeated highlights of any cricket match ever.

When he finished his playing career in football and cricket he went on to establish himself as a top international umpire. Even then, his knack of being involved in memorable sporting events did not leave him. He was one of the umpires standing in that never to be forgotten 1981 'Botham Test' at Headingley. Let Barrie take up the story. "When Botham arrived at the crease England were five down and needing 122 more to avoid an innings defeat. Some hours later Ian was 149 not out and England had a lead of 129. An amazing 8-43 from Bob Willis saw the Australians all out for 111. Nelson had struck again." Meyer's fellow umpire that day, David Evans, was making his debut. Barry told me that as they came off Evans said, "Blimey BJ, I hope they are not all like that!" After listening to him relate the events of that amazing test I asked if he had managed to be in on the 500-1 bet, allegedly placed on behalf of Dennis Lillee and Rodney Marsh by the Aussie's coach driver. He laughed and said "Unfortunately not."

He was a very successful umpire and stood in 26 Tests. He regrets that this was in the days before neutral umpires came in and he did not stand in a Test outside England. His first Test appointment was for an England v New Zealand match at Old Trafford in July 1978. His last Test as an umpire was also at Old Trafford, for the Manchester Test against Australia in August 1993. In addition to his 26 Test matches he also umpired 23 One Day Internationals, and he stood in consecutive World Cup Finals in 1979 and 1983.

Only a chosen few can truly claim to have spent a life-time in sport. Barrie Meyer is certainly one of them. He signed for Bristol Rovers in 1949 and retired from umpiring in 1993 – an amazing 44 years. His son Adrian was a professional with Scarborough when they were in the Football League. He was twice in the squad against Argyle but failed to win a place.

One of Barrie's sons, Adrian, was a professional footballer with Scarborough and played 119 times and scored on nine occasions. Although he was in the squad for both League Cup games against Argyle in 1995 he did not make the bench for either game. He did, however, play in Scarborough's famous League Cup win over Chelsea.

After coaching and teaching umpiring in South Africa for many years, 11 years ago Meyer moved to Natal permanently. As my call to South Africa came to an end Barrie told me how his ability as a sportsman, with a good eye for a ball, surfaced extremely early. He told me that at three years of age his father threw a ball in his direction. "It fell a bit short and I half-volleyed and smashed the family's Swiss Clock."

SECRETARY AH (BERT) COLE
1891-1966

In AH (Bert) Cole, Plymouth Argyle's Secretary from 1947 to 1959, the club had one of the most experienced football administrator's in the land. He first came to the club as assistant to the great Secretary/ Manager Bob Jack. He was also a prime mover in the Supporters' Club, serving as its first propaganda secretary. After Jack Tresarden resigned his post in 1947 Plymouth Argyle elected to divide the Manager/ Secretary post. Jimmy Rae took over as manager while Bert Cole resigned his post with the Admiralty to become the company's first Secretary. He remained in that post until 1959.

Cole's 30 year association with the club embraced many crises, but it was the last one which had the most effect upon him personally. In a three day period in November 1958 he found himself first as full-time Secretary, then as a Vice President before being invited back as Honorary Club Secretary. His retirement at the end of October 1958 was delayed a few days so that he could read the notice convening the Annual General Meeting on Thursday 6 November 1958. After the meeting he was to become a Vice-President, but also would be on hand to offer advice if needed. As was seen in Chapter Five, the next few days were some of the most tumultuous in the club's history. Blindell, Cole's nemesis, was gone and he returned as Honorary Secretary. When he finally resigned the Honorary post, hours after Blindell's return was confirmed, he remarked that none of the pre-war directors was left on the Board and that David James was the sole survivor of the first post-war Board. He had a wide and varied responsibilities at Home Park, including organising a Youth international in 1955, several major Rugby representative matches and the organisation of some great FA Cup ties.

There were many parallels between Robert Jack and Bert Cole. Away from Plymouth Argyle both had a great love of Bowls and were important members of the Sir Francis Drake Lawn Bowling Club. Both were at one time first Captain and then President of the club, which shared Argyle's club colours of green and black. Each won county and international honours.

In 1964 Cole was chosen by the England Bowling team for a tour of Canada and the United States. He volunteered to be Secretary, Treasurer and Press Relations Officer on that tour, attracting great praise for his work. He was England's representative at the International Bowls Board meeting in Pasadena . In some remarkable papers lent to me by the current Sir Francis Drake President, Brian Edwards, I found an exchange of correspondence between Cole and Lyndon B Johnson, President of the United States. Not only that, during the tour the team played at Beverley Hills Lawn Bowling Club. Bert was informed that Walt Disney would be watching his rink. Cole was introduced to the great man and they struck up a friendship. Both died within days of each other in December 1966. Mrs Cole received a sympathy letter from a close friend of Disney, saying that Walt had often asked about her husband. What an amazing man!

Tommy Barrett, one of the Busby Babes who had to fly the nest and try his luck elsewhere. After he finished playing football he had a second career as a policeman in Manchester.
He is pictured on 27 September 2008 after receiving his silver salver, Argyle Legends tie and replica Argyle shirt.
Photo by the author

CHAPTER TWENTY

TOMMY BARRETT

Tommy Barrett must have been some player in his youth. After attracting interest from Manchester City, he joined Manchester United shortly after the club had won the 1951-52 League title. When he signed, in August 1952, the benchmark could not have been any higher. Amongst his contemporaries were Duncan Edwards, Eddie Colman and Jackie Blanchflower. Each was to become a household name, with Edwards, in particular, already looking like becoming the greatest player this nation had ever produced. Regrettably fate stepped in. Eddie Colman was killed at Munich and Duncan died of his injuries some days later. Blanchflower never played again. But in 1952 Tom found himself in a queue behind those three, with Freddie Goodwin also part of what became an unequal struggle.

Salford born Barrett was just past his 18th birthday when he signed for United. An only child, he was born on 16 March 1934 and he looks back on a happy and comfortable time as a child. His dad was a railwayman and his mother worked part-time as a packer in the local Kellogg's factory. In 1937, when Tom was three, the family moved into a new semi-detached house in Stretford, bucking the traditional trend by buying their property. War was not far away, and the family's new home was quite close to the huge Trafford Park Industrial area, which is still one of the biggest industrial sites in the north west. He clearly recalls going to a Christmas party at an aunt's house. They ended the party in an air raid shelter, emerging to find that her house had disappeared!

Before long, it was a place thought to be untenable for children and Tom, complete with gas mask, was evacuated to Congleton in Cheshire. His first port of call was Walfield School, now a site for cattle auctions. There he was met by a Mr Parks and taken to Sandy Lane Farm to join the rest of the family. At first he hated being away but eventually came to love his new life on a farm. Although it is almost 70 years ago, Tom has excellent recollection of his time there. "I particularly enjoyed harvest time, sitting on the side of the tractor as Ted, my surrogate dad, cut the corn. "As he cut in the straight lines it would disturb a lot of rabbits. Ted would shoot them and his wife Dorothy would cook them." Continuing, he told me, "By 1943 the Russians were getting on top of the Germans and I was allowed to return home".

It was about this time when he started to take an interest in football, and often got into trouble at school for kicking a ball around the playground. He joked, "The same happened when I moved up to the next school. About the only thing that changed was the name of the teacher inflicting the punishment". In 1947 Tom managed to qualify for Stretford Technical College. "It was great there; they had two football pitches so I stopped getting the cane". By the age of 11 or 12 he felt that, in football had the edge over most of his classmates. Despite the grief playing football brought him, to this day he remains grateful for the help and encouragement of Miss Jones at his primary school and Mr Luby, his sports teacher at Secondary School.

Leaving school at 15 he found work as an apprenticed electrical fitter. "I got £1/11/- (£1.55) a week – I think that lad Oliver Twist got more than me!" Playing for his department in an inter-departmental competition he was spotted by a man by the name of Harold Shaw. "Shaw brought a Manchester City scout along and they seemed impressed. "They gave me the thumbs up at half-time and said they would talk to me on Monday." But Monday was too late. Tom's dad went for his traditional Sunday lunch-time pint , thrilled and proud that his son had attracted the interest of a Maine Road scout. He was quick to tell his friends that "our Tom is going to be taken on by City". One of his dad's friends knew Walter Crickmer, then the Manchester United Secretary. Crickmer acted quickly and called around to see Tom, who was out. But he left a set of Central League forms for young Barrett to sign. The problem would be that immediately after his 1945 appointment, Matt Busby had completely re-vamped the Manchester United scouting network. By 1952 there was a virtual conveyor belt of outstanding, exciting and talented young players.

Tommy Taylor was purchased from Barnsley, Johnny Berry came in from Birmingham but most of the prodigious youngsters came from within. Roger Byrne was already in the side in 1952, the great Duncan Edwards had his first outing in 1953. Jackie Blanchflower, Mark Jones and Eddie Colman were all pressing for permanent places. David Pegg and Albert Scanlon vied for Rowley's left wing role. Meanwhile, a certain young man called Bobby Charlton was making significant claims to be a first choice at inside forward. Like all of those great names, once he joined United Barrett worked under coaches Jimmy Murphy and Bert Whalley, two of the mainstays of Matt Busby's hugely successful post-war renaissance at Old Trafford.

These men were the prime movers in turning the Busby Babes from raw talent to highly skilled footballers. They missed nothing, taking an interest in each of the five levels of sides that United fielded in those days. The coaching was of a high quality covering every aspect of the game. Murphy, in particular, was a hard taskmaster while Tom saw Whalley as both talented and benevolent. There was a traditional format, especially at the top level of the game. The youngest played for the Juniors team, then progressed through the Colts, on to the 'A' team and then to the Reserves. A lucky few made it to the First XI. At some of the bigger clubs, their staffs were large enough to field more than one side at the three lower levels. The competition was fierce, and from the 'A' team up, second place was less than acceptable.

It is to Tom's eternal credit that he made it as far as the second team, where he played regularly. It is a clear sign that he had outstanding ability—it was just that many around him were simply exceptional. Like many others at that time, conscription interrupted the flow of his career. Those with a special talent could maybe take it in their stride, but the mere

Tommy Barrett pictured just after arriving at Home Park in the summer of 1957.He had been competing for a place at Old Trafford with the great Duncan Edwards.
Courtesy Harry Penk/Plymouth Argyle

mortals often found it to be their undoing. Tom was called up in 1955 and served until 1957. He deployed to the Suez Canal Zone and also at RAF Khorkmakser in Aden. He acknowledges that United were right to release him when they did. "There were so many good players blocking my route, I would have been wasting my time if I had stayed. "But I think that having to go into the RAF affected my long term prospects at Old Trafford." At the time of his release from conscription he was based at RAF Locking near Western-super-Mare. Clutching his final railway warrant he made for Bristol Temple Meads station, to board the first train for Manchester. It was a rail journey that would have an immediate affect on his football career.

What followed was a football version of *Brief Encounter.* Once on the train he was surprised to see Plymouth Argyle manager Jack Rowley, who was travelling with his team to a fixture in the north and who introduced him to the director travelling with the team, Colonel Hunt, and the players too. The rest, as they say, is history. Rowley had not forgotten the strong young wing-half cum inside forward he had seen on the Old Trafford training ground. He knew that the young man could do a job for him, for Barrett was already one of a number of names on Jack Rowley's list of potential targets. In July 1957 Barrett, a great admirer of Jack Rowley, travelled to Plymouth to discuss terms. He did not take much persuading, though Jack in his customary way, made no promises about an immediate first team place. But at least now there was only one in the queue before him. Whoever it was (probably Rex Tilley), it would not present anything like the competition at Old Trafford.

Married players with children were normally allocated a club house to rent. Those married without children generally made their own arrangements, traditionally renting 'rooms' in a house. The single men followed a similar route, often moving in with a family and sharing the facilities. No smart flat on the Hoe for the 50s footballer! Barrett had two separate landladies during his spell in Plymouth. First he moved in with Graham Little's mother in Weston Mill, but because he delayed informing her he wanted to return the next season, he lost out on the room. Fortunately Neil Dougall's wife Monica had some friends in St Gabriels Avenue who were had a room to let. Tom recalls, "Mr and Mrs Downing were like a mother and father to me – and they had three beautiful daughters too! It

207

was close to the football ground and handy for the Hyde Park Social Club as well. I often played snooker there, and with Wilf Carter living close by we had many a game to pass the time".

Like many of those around Home Park in the late 50s, he found it to be a very happy group of players. "They were all good lads but I suppose my best friends were Geoff Barnsley, Bryce Fulton and Neil Dougall. That said, I cannot remember a cross word with any of the lads there at the time. I usually roomed with Neil on away trips". When quizzed on who was the best player in his time at Home Park, like many of his colleagues at the time he immediately nominates Wilf Carter. When asked whether or not he thinks Johnny Williams could have made it at the very top, he is positive that he could have, while qualifying his opinion by adding "but may be not at Manchester United at that time."

When I made my first telephone contact with Tom Barrett I did not immediately realise the significance of the date - it was the 50th anniversary of the Munich Air Disaster, 6 February 2008. Inevitably our conversation turned to the occasion. It was interesting to talk to someone who had been there at the time when the Busby Babes had started to carry all before them. He was the same age as many of them and knew them all personally. I asked Tom if he thought that they would have gone on to be the best club side the world had ever seen. His response was interesting. He told me, "Clearly they were a fantastic side but what the club could pay them in Europe was constrained by the maximum wage system. I believe there was every chance that a number of them would have followed the example of John Charles and gone to play abroad. Eddie Firmani too had gone to Italy from Charlton. Players talk and word spread about what these lads were on in Italy".

Whilst that is the first time I had heard anyone suggest some of the players may have moved abroad, it fits in with some information I came across during research for *Thanks For the Memory*. I read that disgruntled team captain Roger Byrne had frequently discussed bonus payments for European ties with Matt Busby. United players were conscious of some of the vast bonuses (up to £200) being offered to their opponents in the later stages of the competition. Byrne knew that Borussia Dortmund had been on £100 a man to beat United and then heard that Atletico Bilbao were on twice that amount. He told Busby that something should be done. Under FA rules a player could only earn a maximum of £10 for the first round, £20 for the second, £30 for the third and £40 for the semi-final. Had they made it to the European Cup Final they would have been restricted to £50 per man, and in all cases only those who played and the travelling 12th man could be paid. Busby was sympathetic, and although the club could do nothing about it, the manager told the Press "I believe the prestige being brought to English football by our success in the European Cup deserves more than praise".

With United's playing staff devastated by the crash there was talk of Rowley, Barrett and Bryce Fulton being offered back to Old Trafford to help the club out. If the offer was made, Tommy was never told. He does recall returning to Manchester for some of the funerals, travelling both ways with his manager. Tom made his debut for Argyle on 12 October 1957, in a 5-0 reverse at the County Ground, Northampton, which the football club shared with Northamptonshire County Cricket Club. He took over at inside left from Peter Kearns, who *Pilgrim* reported was the first to shake Barrett by the hand prior to his debut. He was left out for the next game and had to wait until a home FA Cup second round tie against Dorchester Town in early December. He played the next two league fixtures, scoring in a 2-2 home draw with Shrewsbury. Towards the end of the season he won a regular place in a side which was to form the basis of the team that would open the 1958-59 term at Boothferry Park. In that season he made a solid start and played in the opening seven fixtures before losing his place after a knee injury at Reading. He eventually needed a cartilage operation. He played only one more game that season, replacing Johnny Williams who was away representing the British Army against their French counterparts. Barrett put in an impressive performance in a hard fought 0-0 draw at Bradford City. Though nobody knew at the time, that was to be his last first team appearance for Argyle. In all he made 26 first team appearances and scored a solitary goal. For the reserves he played more than 50 times and hit four goals.

As well as being an extremely elegant wing half Barrett was a fine amateur cricketer too. He had a trial for Leicestershire but did not take the game up professionally. Harry Penk, no slouch himself with a cricket bat, still remembers Tom's powerful 93no against Plymouth Cricket Club's Midweek XI, a match played shortly before the promotion season.

In June 1962 Tom married his wife Marlene and they have a daughter and a son and five grandchildren. It was during their second Christmas together that they had their best present ever, their daughter Jane. Son Nicholas, who was born five years later, became a champion dinghy sailor. He now has a couple of boys who Tom thinks show a bit of promise at football. After a spell at Cheltenham Town, before they were in the League, he returned to Manchester and became a policeman. I can imagine he was a jolly good policeman, certainly more Dixon than Regan.

Tom and Marlene at the 50th anniversary dinner at the Astor Hotel
Photo by the author

PLYMOUTH ARGYLE

versus

ALL STARS XI

George Robertson Testimonial Match

Wednesday, April 22nd, 1964

Kick-off 7.30 p.m.   *Programme Price 6d.*

George Robertson served Plymouth Argyle for so long and so well that this turned out to be the first of two testimonials. In this match the Plymouth Argyle team included trainer George Taylor, Geoff Barnsley back on a visit to support his old friend and Wilf Carter at left back. It was Carter's last ever appearance at Home Park. Also playing was Peter McParland, the former Aston Villa and Northern Ireland outside left. Although still on the staff, McParland had long since lost his place to young Nicky Jennings. The All Star XI included the great wing pairing from the early 50s, Gordon Astall and Alex Govan, former left back Pat Jones plus at left half Malcolm McDonald. The referee was popular local man Charlie Nicholls, one of the city's best ever. He was supported by Johnny Newman (Red Flag) and Johnny Williams (Amber Flag).

Programme courtesy the Colin Parsons collection

CHAPTER TWENTY ONE

GEORGE ROBERTSON, BRYCE FULTON & REG WYATT

George Robertson was the very first Argyle player I ever heard about. Mr Quirke, the milkman who delivered to our house in Saltash Passage, was George's father-in-law and gave us regular reports of his daughter's husband's progress at Home Park. That must have been the first jab of green into my veins!

Robertson gave yeoman service to Plymouth Argyle. Prior to coming to Devon he had played for the same Scottish Junior club as manager Jimmy Rae, Gairdoch Juniors. He was originally something of a utility player before settling down as a very competent and reliable right back. George's consistency was a manager's dream. If in his day the players had been given stars for their performance, he would have rarely got all five but equally he would seldom warrant less than three.

He was still in the Royal Air Force completing his National Service when he was spotted by Argyle. He was given an outing for the reserves at Kenilworth Road. It was at the end of the 1948-49 season and he was part of a defence that had a real off day—Luton scored nine without reply. Based at RAF Lyneham, he returned to camp dismissing any thoughts about becoming a professional footballer in England. Once he had completed his time in the military he returned to Scotland, in time for the opening of the 1950-51 football season. He was looking no further than playing for Stenhousemuir, where he was born, when Argyle came in at the last minute and offered him terms. It was a decision neither of the parties would regret. After making his debut in the 1950-51 season his final first team game came at St James Park in a 1-1 draw on 21 December 1963. Peter MacParland was the Argyle scorer.

He won a place in the first team during his first season on the books. Another long journey east, this time to Colchester, saw Argyle go down to a 3-0 defeat on 17 March 1951. George deputised for the indisposed Chisolm. Less than a month later he again took Chisolm's place, this time in a 4-1 home win over Northampton Town. The team had been relegated the previous season and finished 4th in the Third Division (South). He had to be content with a place in the reserves for the entire 1951-2 season when Argyle won promotion. His opportunities were limited by Paddy Ratcliffe at right back, Pat Jones at left back and 'Jumbo' Chisolm each playing in all 46 League fixtures and the only FA Cup tie.

The 1952-53 season, enshrined in history after that 4th place finish in Division Two, was fantastic for the club and better for George himself. He managed 14 games. He was clearly seen as the automatic deputy for Chisolm and played on New Year's Day at Bury (2-3) and then in a home fixture against Leeds United (0-1) two days later. He now began to show his versatility. After missing two matches he returned at right half in place of Neil Dougall. He then missed another two before playing in 11 of the final

12 games, six at left half, two at right back and three more at centre half. He also replaced Dougall at right half for two FA Cup matches, including the disappointing 5th round home defeat at the hands of Gateshead. He managed 16 games in what was a strong first team, in some eyes the strongest side Argyle have ever had.

He started the 1953-54 season at right back. He missed only one of the 42 League games but the team struggled throughout the campaign, finishing 19th. After the opening 10 games he was switched to centre-half to deputise for Chisolm for two matches. In his other 29 outings that season he was picked to play only six of them in his favoured right back role. He also replaced Chisolm another five times and then finished the season playing 17 times in place of the injured right half Dougall and once at left half.

1954-55 was another struggle for the side, with the influential Chisolm gone. George played the opening 25 games in the centre, and after missing a few games through injury returned to his role as the utility man. He played another nine games in three different positions. Another of the future 1958-59 champions was now making his mark, with Peter Anderson playing only two less games than Robertson. George was out of the side when Jack Rowley arrived in February 1955 but finished the season as first choice right half. The team finished a place lower but survived. By 1955-56 Robertson was an automatic choice, mainly at right back though he had 12 of his 41 outings at right half. More of his future 1958-59 compatriots were breaking through now with Reg Wyatt (11), George Baker (9) and Johnny Williams (5) getting into the side. Interestingly none of them played in the positions they would make their own in the promotion side. 1956-57 was, at that time the team's worst on record. They finished 18th in Division Three (South) and for much of the season flirted with re-election. Robertson only missed a single game. He started the season at right half, moved to centre half for a game and then finished as the regular right back. In three seasons of perpetual struggle he never once let his head drop. His remarkable consistency saw him play another 45 games out of a possible 46 in the 57-58 campaign, as well as three FA Cup outings. All of them were at right back.

Of the seasons he was first choice, 1958-59 was by far his most successful. He played in 33 of the 46 games in that Championship season, missing a run of games having suffered a nasty gash in the home encounter with Colchester on 7 February 1959. Although it was hard on his deputy Bryce Fulton, he returned for the last five games of the season. It was fitting that a man who had known the down times at Home Park was on the field when the Third Division title was secured. Few men in that side deserved it more. It was his 255th League outing and it was 10 years, almost to the day, since had suffered that humiliation at the hands of Luton Town reserves.

The 1959-60 season was not so good in a couple of ways. First, along with Harry Penk, George Baker and Peter Kearns, George became a victim of a poor start to the season. In all he played just 13 games of that first term back in the Second Division. In addition to that he became embroiled in a controversy that would lead eventually to a libel action against Odhams Press, owners of the *Daily Herald*. Under a banner headline "Five Players In Argyle Bust-Up" journalist John Bromley wrote, "Five senior players are worried about their futures and are considering asking for a transfer". This was a time when professionals were not supposed to talk to the Press without the club's permission, a rule which former Secretary Bert Cole vehemently defended during his cross-examination in the High Court. The hearing did not get to the High Court for more than a year, with Jack Rowley being called as a witness for his former player and Bert Tann, the former Bristol Rovers gave expert evidence on how a player perceived to be troublesome would find it hard to get a new club. The case eventually went in his favour but there is no doubt his reputation suffered some damage.

Robertson played in 23 of 42 games in the following season but made a triumphant return in 61-62. The younger Terry Stacey, a former Carshalton and England amateur right back was signed at the start of the 59-60 campaign, but flattered to deceive. He had made only 19 starts in his first two seasons but Dougall went with him at the start of 1961-62 term. After a 3-0 home defeat at the hands of Luton Town Robertson was recalled and played in all but two of the remaining 39 games. (A local youngster by the name of Dave Roberts played in the matches he missed)

A change of manager in October 1961 re-vitalized the season. At one time it looked as if George Robertson would be around long enough to see his adopted home city in the top flight. Unfortunately five defeats in the last six games put paid to that. Robertson had outstayed most of the 1958-59 side. Of those who were mainstays in that promotion team only Johnny Williams, who was ever present, Wilf Carter and Peter Anderson featured regularly. In 62-63 he started the season at right back and played in the first 18 games. After a 6-1 hammering at Elland Road he lost his place to Saltash youngster Mike Reeves and played only four more times that term. The last of those four games was a 6-3 reverse at the Valley.

The 1963-64 season was to be his last. After 13 seasons he was entitled to look for a slightly easier life. Stuttard opened with Mike Reeves at right back, and then after two games gave Dave Roberts six starts. The poor opening had not helped either of these young men and Robertson was recalled. During a run of six games he helped Argyle to their first win—in the 12th fixture of the season! After a 3-0 reverse at Northampton he was left out again. Although he had not expected to play in the first team again, he did turn out on three more occasions, all of them at centre half. It was a neat symmetry. He finished the last of his 359 first team games for Argyle as a centre half, precisely as he had begun.

For such a quiet, unsung hero, George Robertson holds a couple of unique records. With his goal in the 3-2 home defeat to Liverpool on 28 April 1962 he must have become the last man to have scored a Second Division goal against Liverpool. And also he is the only man to have undertaken both of Argyle's post-war foreign tours. He went on the tour all 10 games. Playing in Chicago, St Louis, Denver, Los Angeles, Detroit,

The late Bryce Fulton who was immensely popular with his colleagues at Home Park. He joined Argyle in 1957 in the same deal which brought Tommy Barrett to the south west.

Courtesy Harry Penk and Plymouth Argyle

Philadelphia and New York certainly had a different ring to it than games in Lincoln, Blackburn, Bury and Oldham. If George Robertson was pleased at seeing off the challenge of the young Terry Stacey, then 1961-62 was a defining season for **Bryce Fulton**, who was ever present. Fulton did not fully prosper at Home Park until very late in Jack Rowley's reign. *Pilgrim*, in his *Football Herald* round up of 28 February 1959 saw things that Rowley may not have. He lavished praise upon Fulton, tipping him to become Robertson's replacement. This was during a run of 12 games Fulton had in the promotion side when George was injured. Paradoxically, Bryce fared a lot better after the manager who had signed him was sacked.

Bryce arrived as a part of the July 1957 deal with Manchester United which brought Tommy Barrett to Home Park. He played only nine times in 57-58, another 14 in the promotion campaign and three early in the 1959-60 season. After a 4-1 home defeat at the hands of Bristol City, on Boxing Day 1959, Rowley recalled Fulton at left back in place of Bellett. That signalled the end of Bellett's first team career at career at Home Park. In all Fulton played in 22 games that season, then 40 in 60-61 and then came that clean sweep the next term. In that ever present season he also played in the two glamorous home FA Cup ties against First Division sides. First West Ham arrived on 6 January 1962 and were hammered 3-0. That remains, in my view, the best 90 minutes of one touch, flowing football I have ever seen from an Argyle side. Three weeks later Tottenham Hotspur, League and Cup Double winners the previous season ended the dream with a 5-1 victory. Fulton had an excellent tussle with Welsh international Terry Medwin that day and, like all of his team mates that day, was beaten but far from disgraced.

The burly Scotsman was a very likeable man. All of his former colleagues spoke well of him. He and his wife were said to be a popular couple who lived life to the full. It would appear that Bryce Fulton often followed an ancestral passion for a dram or two of fine malt. My memory of Bryce Fulton is of a dark, heavy set man who was always laughing and joking with his colleagues. He always had time for the kids and a cheery word. Longevity is no longer a word associated with many professional footballers, and his seven seasons at Home Park never saw him do than try his hardest. No more so than in his last season, the 1963-64 campaign. Argyle started disastrously, having come from a comfortable 12th the previous year. They spent the entire season in the bottom four. Fulton did not start, with youngster Richard Davis being preferred to him. Then he came back in for two games before injury saw the shirt go back to Davis. He came back too early and lasted a single game. The increasingly desperate Ellis Stuttard decided against the inexperience of Davis and opted to put Wilf Carter in the number three shirt, a job he had done at West Bromwich many years before. After a disastrous run of nine defeats new manager Andy Beattie recalled Fulton. He played in 16 of the last 18 games as relegation was averted by 0.05 of a goal. And Fulton was something of a talisman that season. Despite Argyle's disastrous record overall, in the 22 matches he played in their record was W7, D11 and L4. In view of the fact that they lost 17 matches out of 42, for Fulton to only taste defeat four times was quite remarkable.

Reg Wyatt was another greatly admired figure at Home Park. Supporters liked his indefatigable approach and his colleagues could not pay him enough compliments.

Courtesy Plymouth Argyle

Before joining the exodus to Torquay in 1964, Bryce played 193 first games for Plymouth Argyle, which included 12 League Cup ties. He never managed to score a goal.

Interestingly, Fulton and **Reg Wyatt** were brought in for the second match of that 1963-64 season after the team had lost 5-0 at Middlesbrough on the opening day. And both were discarded after playing in the next two matches. Wyatt returned more permanently three or four games before Fulton was brought in. He played in 19 out of the last 20 games of the season and, like Fulton, seemed to bring an immediate improvement. He was only on the losing side three times during that spell. For a team that had shipped 20 goals in the first nine games, once Wyatt and Fulton returned they were difficult to score against. Doug Baird and Johnny Newman were the other members of that effective backline. Johnny Williams was another of the class of 58-59 who played regularly that season, turning out 39 times. Carter played 30 times and George Robertson nine, including his final game at Newcastle. The rest were gone.

The old "more comebacks than Frank Sinatra" cliché fits Reg Wyatt as well as anyone. He was written off so many times yet always had the guts and determination to come back. 1958-59, in terms of getting a medal and his overall level of performance, may look to have been his best season. However, it was remarkable how the team's fortunes turned around after his recall in 63-64.

Reg arrived at Home Park in 1950, a product of the same Plymouth Schoolboys side as Peter Anderson. They were close friends. Even their birthdays were close, with Peter's on 11 September 1932 and Reg's just a week later. Peter had already broken into the first team in 1951 but Reg had to wait five years for his first start. At first he was seen as an inside forward but made his debut at left back, on 14 January 1956 at Ewood Park. Pat Jones had suffered one of his rare injuries. Within a fortnight Jones was out again and Wyatt played in a 4-1 reverse at Lincoln. Jones was back for the next game, a 4-1 home defeat against Lincoln City. Jones hurt himself again and Reg returned for a visit to Filbert Street that again saw Argyle go down 4-1. Seven games later he made his home debut in a 1-1 draw with Notts County. The press reported that there was no prouder man that day than Reg Wyatt. As the team dropped out of the Second Division Rowley rang the changes towards the end. Wyatt played in six of the last seven games, four at inside right and one in each full back position. But it was a start. He now had 11 first team games to his name, plus his first goal for the club. Unfortunately it was the only goal against Bury in a 7-1 defeat at Gigg Lane!

He only made 19 appearances during the 1956-57 but in football terms it was a life changing season for him. He had made nine appearances at the very start of the season, mostly at right back but with one at inside right in the catastrophic 6-0 home defeat against Reading. Argyle had only three wins in their first 19 games and were real candidates for re-election.

It was a time when clubs looked towards floodlight friendly matches to boost income. The players, wages were fixed so all it cost the club was a maximum £2 bonus for each man, plus the expenses of the opposition. On 4 March 1957 Plymouth Argyle entertained an All Star Managers' XI. The match report read, "A crowd of 8,379 saw a gay and skilful game at Home Park with Argyle running out winners by 6-3." Jack Rowley and his brother Arthur played for the Managers, as did former keeper Bill Shortt who was by then at Wadebridge Town. But the great success of the night was Reg Wyatt at centre-half. *Pilgrim* could not have been more complimentary to Wyatt. "Argyle's 'big man' was Reg Wyatt and his intelligent use of the ball clearly justified Jack Rowley's decision to use him at centre half. His passing was ruthlessly direct and there were times when he looked a very useful centre half. If he improved his tackling it seems inevitable he will get into the League side in this position." Prophetic words indeed! The starring role saw him selected for the next two games and then for the last five. He really seemed to have found his niche. He was first choice from the commencement of the 1957-58 season. He missed only one game and the defence was the meanest in the League. They narrowly missed promotion, finishing third behind Brighton and Brentford. He played five or six more games with a degree of success. In the following season, 57-58, he missed only one match and the team managed to shut out the opposition on 19 occasions. Reg Wyatt was now undeniably the first choice centre half back.

At the beginning of the 1958-59 season he was again the number one. He was not the typical centre half of that era. They were usually huge, uncompromising men with faces straight off a wanted poster. He had skill and guile from his days as an inside forward.   *Pilgrim* was delighted, reporting how Wyatt had gone from simply a member of the playing staff to a star centre half worth £20,000 in the transfer market. (The record fee between two British clubs at that time stood at £45,000).

But it wasn't all sweetness and light. At about the time of the Coventry cup tie in 1958 Reg had issues over the payment of his Benefit. He was on the verge of asking for a transfer. He admitted afterwards "I acted rashly and Mr Pengelly and me have sorted it out. "I love this club and don't want to go anywhere." He began to 'hit the wall' after about 30 games and *Pilgrim* felt at one time that the edge had gone from Wyatt's game. He wrote "One of the directors has told me that Reg has played himself into the ground." And he agreed, offering the explanation that Reg had been playing on through niggling injuries. Furthermore, he was under the pressure of reading every week the rave reviews of reserves centre half Fincham. The big man from Leicester had been remarkably patient but wanted some of the first team's success. He acknowledged that Rowley had not promised him a berth in the chiefs, "but at the same time I did not come here to play in the Combination."

Although the whole team had a bit of an off night in the 4-2 home defeat to Accrington Stanley, Wyatt along with goalkeeper Barnsley seemed to take most of the blame. There are those who were there that felt Wyatt did not look himself throughout the match. Barnsley was left out for the next game while Wyatt gave way to Fincham through injury. The former Leicester man took his chance and Reg would not play again in the number five shirt that season. Once he was fit again Wyatt was annoyed at not getting straight back in the side. *Pilgrim* reported that he had written out a transfer request early in the week, but that the next day he had gone to see Jack Rowley and told him to tear it up.

He was recalled for the vital promotion clash with Brentford at Griffin Park, playing at left back in place of the injured Bellett. But he paid the price for a 3-0 defeat and lost his place for three more games. He again replaced the injured Bellett, for the 1-1 draw at Wrexham, but this time retained his place for the final five fixtures. It was fitting that this man, who had done so much to get Argyle to the top of the Division, was given

STORY OF A SUPPORTER
Colin Parsons (1)

Colin Parsons seems to have been born into supporting Plymouth Argyle. From 1921-1977 his grandfather missed just five games, all due to stoppage of leave in the Dockyard for different RN emergencies. When the new stand was built grandfather and Colin's father had seats C143 and C144 from the start. From 1957 Colin took C142 and still has it today.

Basingstoke based Colin has a truly fantastic archive of Argyle memorabilia, and *Thanks For The Memory* has benefited greatly from his collection. Here are just a few of his match day memories:-

Argyle 3 Swindon 2—*It was obvious from the outset of this game that Swindon knew all about Jimmy Gauld. It was one of many games in which he was fouled in the box for Wilf Carter to score the penalty. He scored the second and third goals himself. Swindon revelled in the heavy mud on that October day and got back to 2-2. Stand by for Gauld! He picked up the ball on the halfway line, performed one of his amazing dribbles and ran through the field into an empty net and Argyle ran out narrow winners, with many spectators having already left the ground.*

Argyle 3 QPR 2—*This Boxing Day game was another in which Jimmy Gauld excelled. Over 30.000 saw QPR take an early lead but Jimmy again ran the length of the field, this time to lay the ball off for Carter to score. I remember being incensed when Gauld had his shorts torn off as QPR tried anything to stop him. I think he relished having new shorts when everyone else was splattered in mud. Alex Govan had been recalled after a long period in the reserves and it was his cross which Gauld converted at the near post. 20 minutes later Gauld scored another of his sensational goals. He collected Govan's corner, beat four defenders along the by-line and scored his second. Argyle remained at the top of the league, ahead of Hull City.*

Argyle 2 Accrington Stanley 4—*It was not all sweetness and light during that 1958-59 season. Argyle lost seven games, one of which was at home in their first ever game against Accrington Stanley. I have built an extensive Argyle programme collection and now have a copy of all home programmes since the war. However, one of the most difficult to obtain is this wet Wednesday evening game. This is not only because of Accrington's prolonged absence from the Football League , which makes their programmes very collectable, but also because of the circumstances of the game. The rain was torrential, and with very little covered terracing, most programmes became a sodden pulp. Only 12,000 brave souls turned up, half the number who had seen Norwich (the first home defeat of the season) in the previous home match. The heavy pitch and slippery surface did not suit Argyle's style. Although Gauld scored yet again, joined on the scoresheet by Harry Penk, Stanley won the battle of the mud by two clear goals.*

STORY OF A SUPPORTER
Colin Parsons (2)

Argyle 8 Mansfield 3—*When the dust settles on my Argyle life, this is one game I shall always remember. So romantic is my recollection of it that I needed a newspaper report to stop blaming Geoff Barnsley for failing to handle Delaphena's crosses. He wasn't playing! After the inconceivable home defeat by Accrington Stanley, I doubted the certainty of promotion. It was Bob Wyllie's debut in goal, and Gordon Fincham came in for the first time, replacing the injured Reg Wyatt. Argyle were three up after twenty minutes and nerves about promotion became less frayed. Swinscoe scored the first of two own goals after two minutes and wingers Govan and Penk scored. However, four minutes after half-time Mansfield were level and Argyle were in tatters. The man who brought Mansfield back into the game was ex-Middlesbrough Jamaican winger Lindy Delaphena. He delivered a succession of delightful corners, all causing problems for Wyllie. He placed precision crosses on the head of Downie who scored twice and Ripley, to underline the fact that Mansfield had lost only one of their last ten games. Whatever might have been said about this Argyle side, they had a lot of resolution. Jimmy Gauld scored from a very narrow angle after cutting in along the left by-line and then Johnny Williams scored twice, either side of a Wilf Carter penalty, to make the score 7-3. The luckless Swinscoe finished as he had started—with an o.g.*

Argyle 1 Bradford City 1—*Argyle won promotion away at Accrington in the penultimate match of the season by drawing 1-1 – slightly fortunately since goalkeeper Bill McInnes sliced the ball to Penk who blasted it into the roof of the net. However, they had still not been confirmed as champions. They were level on 61 points with Hull City but had an inferior goal average. They had to better Hull's result at Wrexham with their own result at home to Bradford City. They were welcomed onto the field by the Bradford team who formed the traditional line of honour to greet them onto the pitch. The score was 1-1 at half-time and Jimmy Gauld received a back injury which caused him to miss the first quarter of an hour after half time. He resumed on the right wing. There were no further goals but Hull were surprisingly beaten 5-1 at the Racecourse ground. I remember the euphoria but also feeling a bit flat. We were the first champions of the new third division but were still open to boardroom disputes. We had the foundation of a good side but were short of the class which we would need to face Liverpool, Sunderland, Middlesbrough and Aston Villa. Only time would tell.*

Colin was a vociferous child. During the 4-3 win at Swindon Jimmy Gauld had a wonderful day and scored a hat-trick. Such was his excited shouting in the stand that two local supporters commented to my Dad that, "If we had a son like that we wouldn't take him to a football match". Quick as a flash his dad came back—"if he had to watch this rubbish every week he wouldn't want to come!!"

the opportunity to see the job through.

Fincham remained first choice at the start of the 1959-60 Second Division campaign. Wyatt was called in for a run of 16 games after a stunning and inept 5-0 home defeat at the hands of Derby County. Not only did he regain his place but took over as captain from the overlooked Len Casey. But after a 4-1 home defeat by Bristol City, Rowley recalled Fincham for Wyatt, as well as dropping both full backs. Reg returned for the final 12 games of that season, but at right back. 1960-61 was a better season for the team but Reg played only 29 games, again alternating between centre half and right back. The 61-62 season found Fincham and Robertson in outstanding form and Wyatt managed just three outings. The following term was little better and he saw action on only six occasions, three games at centre half and three at left back.

Then came that triumphant recall for the end of the 63-64 season, when many thought he was consistently back to his outstanding 1958-59 form. He played in the first game of Malcolm Allison's reign, a 2-0 defeat at Highfield Road, and never represented the club again. In some ways it was inevitable. In terms of flamboyance and lifestyle Wyatt was at the opposite end of the spectrum to Allison. In all he made 216 first team appearances for his home town team, scoring just twice. He clocked up more than 150 appearances for the reserves scoring 17 goals.

In the October of that season he decided to join his friends Peter Anderson and John 'Cardiff' Williams at Plainmoor. With Wilf Carter already at Exeter City only Johnny Williams now remained from the triumphant 1958-59 side. Reg played more than 70 games for Torquay and helped them to promotion in season 1965-66. He scored six goals, a prolific return compared to is time at Home Park.

Anyone who did not know what Reg Wyatt did for a living would never have guessed that he was a professional footballer. He displayed none of the trappings of football life and the only bright lights in his life were his wife and his daughter. He was immensely popular with his colleagues. Reg, Peter Anderson and John L Williams were particularly close. After Torquay he played part-time in the South Western League, as well as working for the Ministry of Public Building and Works as a heating engineer.

It was sad that these three lovely men had passed away before the 50th anniversary of the 1958-59 promotion celebrations were held. I know that all of the players who went out on to the pitch on 27 September 2008 mentioned their former colleagues. In their eyes they are gone but not forgotten. George, Bryce and Reg were three completely different men, but each shared a special kinship during their time together with the Andersons, Penks, Carters, Bakers, Barnsleys and Barretts of this world.

CHAPTER TWENTY TWO

GORDON FINCHAM, REG JENKINS & BOB WYLLIE

Throughout the 1958-59 success Jack Rowley tended to make changes to the team. In all he used 21 players, for those days quite a high number for a successful side. The change at left back was forced on him through Doughty's injury, but even then the turnover of players was greater than would be expected. But there was a strength in depth that the other teams in the promotion hunt did not have.

In Penk, Govan and Anderson Argyle had three wingers who would have each got in most other sides in the Division— perhaps only Southampton with the emerging Paine and Sydenham were better served on the flanks. At half back John L Williams showed at the end, when he returned to the side while his namesake was pushed further forward, that he could hold his own in the League's best side. Tommy Barrett was recalled for a single game at Bradford City when Johnny Williams was away, and starred in a 0-0 draw.

When Barrie Meyer was around, and fit, any two out of Carter, Gauld, Baker and him would have scored goals. When Meyer went earlier than expected it gave an opportunity to Reg Jenkins. But the side was losing confidence and he was a very young man then, though his ability was there for all to see. Unfortunately, when he needed some of the senior pros around him to be at their best, they were actually struggling themselves.

In defence when Reg Wyatt was injured, the introduction of Gordon Fincham did not weaken the side. Bryce Fulton replaced   the evergreen

Robertson for a dozen games and the transition was almost seamless. Goalkeeper Bob Wyllie came into the team vice Barnsley, at a time when they were beginning to struggle, but anyone who had watched the reserves regularly could see the man was a class act. It was unfortunate for him that he never got a chance when the team were steam-rolling all comers.

Gordon Fincham (left) was a big man. He arrived from Leicester City on the same day as JL Williams signed from Cardiff City. He had 50 appearances to his name for the Foxes and fitted both of Blindell's criteria—he had played in the First Division and he had completed his National Service. Indeed, during his military service he had played for the full British Army XI, including a visit to Home Park. When he joined the Army he served in the Catering Corps. Some of his fellow professionals used to rib him about it. Fincham was always keen to point out that he was not a chef. "If the truth be known I had a cushy number as waiter in the Sergeants' Mess" was his slant on his time at Aldershot. Like many of his professional football contemporaries he spent a lot more time on the football field than the parade ground. Whilst at Aldershot in addition to his games for the full Army XI he played regularly for both his unit and the battalion side. Such was the high standard of opponents, Fincham makes the point that it was no trouble maintaining fitness and skill levels. One team mate in the Army was Albert Quixall.

On the field he was a tough competitor, relishing the weekly battles with the centre forwards of the day. In a September 1958 interview with *Spectator* Gordon recalled the day he had come up against the great John Charles of Leeds United. "I was more than pleased with the result of our tussle. John told a leading soccer critic that he had thoroughly enjoyed our battle, and was looking forward to the next one. Unfortunately it never happened because I got injured. Then John got the move to Italy".

Whilst no one could question Fincham's pedigree, there must have been a nagging concern over his fitness. Gordon sustained a serious knee injury which saw him on the sidelines for 18 months. He underwent what we now call reconstructive surgery. It should not be forgotten that this was an era when the quality of medical science was light years away from today's standards. Prior to that he had already had a cartilage operation. He often wondered if he was ever going to complete a pre-season without injury. He reassured *Spectator* that his knee was completely all right. "I have a silly, nagging injury to my ankle at the moment. It is nothing at all to do with the knee. When I get rid of it I shall look forward to a crack at the first team". Although he had completed 50 games with the Leicester first team, he was still only 22 when he arrived at Home Park. What with injuries and National Service, this was a young man who had packed a lot into his years. Injury concerns apart, he looked a very useful acquisition.

John L Williams told me that they were both advised by Jack Rowley that he was going to give the previous season's side every opportunity to prove that last season was no fluke. Whilst John L got a chance much sooner than expected, Fincham had to wait until the 34th game of the season to make his first team debut. It was particularly frustrating for Fincham because he had been outstanding in the reserves for week after week. When he did break into the chiefs he made up for lost time and was a towering presence during the run-in. Unlike other newcomers Jenkins and Wyllie, he survived the 3-0 trouncing at Brentford and went on to complete the run in to promotion. He was as strong as the proverbial ox, seemingly a man with an extremely high pain threshold. During one of his early games in the first team, the 2-0 defeat at Tranmere, he looked to have been badly hurt. As George Taylor prepared to run on to treat the injury, Fincham angrily waved him away, got up and played on.

A native of Peterborough, where he and his wife Anne (a Plymouth girl) live today, he signed for Leicester City in 1952. He was spotted playing for his local works side but had played for the Huntingdonshire county side. In 1953, after one or two games covering for injured players he soon became a regular in the Foxes side.

Gordon Fincham stayed at Home Park for five seasons, making 136 League appearances and scoring four times. He played another 14 Cup games and had 52 outings for the reserves, where he found the net on five occasions. His last game for Argyle was in a 3-2 defeat at Scunthorpe on 23 February 1963. It was the end of the road for a half back line which most supporters from that era could recite—Williams, Fincham, Newman. They first game together on 16 January 1960 in a 2-2 home draw against Middlesbrough. They played together a remarkable 111 times, including all but three of the 42 matches in the very successful 1961-62 term. In Fincham's final season the trio were unchanged for the first 27 matches, until Fincham was injured at Scunthorpe. For most of that sequence Bryce Fulton had the left back spot to himself so the 3, 4, 5 and 6 slots were automatic picks for the best part of three years. With Robertson, Anderson, Carter, Kirby and McAnearney also playing very regularly at that time, there was a consistency of selection that has rarely been seen since.

When he left Argyle he moved slightly closer to his Peterborough roots, signing for Luton Town. After 64 games for them he then moved to Port Elizabeth, South Africa, spending time there as a player and a manager. He has been back in this country for more than 20 years.

Bob Wyllie pictured shortly after moving from Blackpool to London to try his luck with West Ham United. *Courtesy of Scott Drummond, Bob's nephew*

In 1979, when Bobby Saxton signed Forbes Phillipson-Masters from Southampton, the joke going around was that Saxton had told his Chairman that he was getting three different players for the fee. In the summer of 1958 Jack Rowley and Bert Cole could have tried the same story when they signed RGN Wyllie, West Ham's reserve goalkeeper. **'Bob' Wyllie**, a native of Dundee, was christened Robinson Gourlay Nichol Wyllie. Septimus Atterbury, who joined Argyle 40 years before Wyllie, still gets my vote for the grandest named player the club has ever had, but Wyllie surely runs him close. That really is some moniker!

Bob graduated into professional football by a traditional Scottish route. He was spotted playing in Junior Football for Monifieth Tayside and joined Dundee United in September 1949. The resident custodian was Alex Edmiston and for two years they vied for the number one jersey. Wyllie made his debut two months after signing, in a match against Morton. Edmiston was called up and had to go to Korea with the Black Watch. United were pleased that they had a ready made replacement. Bob grabbed his chance and went on to play 86 games for the Tannadice outfit. Lifelong Dundee United supporter Bill Grieg knew Bob well. He recalled two fantastic Scottish Cup derbies with Dundee. "It was in January 51 and the first game was at their place, ending 2-2. There were 38,000 there, a record for a derby. On the Wednesday they did us 1-0 at Tannadice with a goal from Billy Steel, a Scottish international for whom Dundee had paid Derby £17,500 a month or two before. Bob played in both games and did well". Bill also remembers Bob playing cricket for Elmwood CC. "I played against him; one of the last times I turned out. He was a fast bowler and for a laugh he bowled beamers at me".

In May 1953 Wyllie decided to move to England. He first went to Blackpool, where he understudied Scottish international George Farm, giving up a regular place in the United side and a good job outside football. At the time he simply said "I want to try my luck in England". The Tangerines were a fine team at that time and had just won the FA Cup, in the game which ever since has been dubbed the 'Matthews Final'. Although he played only 13 times for Blackpool he enjoyed himself there. His debut was against Manchester City and he found himself in the tunnel beside the great Bert Trautmann. Bob's nephew, Scott Drummond, told me that he remembered his Uncle Bob telling him about the day. "Bob said that when he first shook hands with Trautmann he noticed he was full of the cold. The man could hardly breathe yet went out there and was brilliant." Bob Wyllie must have had a good game too. Scott went on "My dad was telling Bob after how well he had played but my Uncle just kept on about how good Trautmann was. After the match England 'B' selectors who attended enquired about his availability for a forthcoming match. Needless to say, once fully informed, they did not pursue their interest".

Listening to Scott, it is clear that Bob was full of anecdotes about his time in football. He sounds a really good raconteur. Scott related one tale from not long after Bob had moved to Lancashire. "They were doing their pre-season work and my Auntie got home from a shopping trip to find she had left the key indoors. She hurried down to Bloomfield Road, understandably in a bit of a panic. On encountering the first person she saw she shouted in her broad accent 'Can ye go and get Boab? I've locked masel oot'. "That man she came across, and who calmed her down, was one Stanley Matthews!" Not surprisingly, Scott told me that his Auntie Nan took a long time to live that one down.

In May 1956 Bob was on the move again, this time to West Ham. He had not been able to dislodge George Farm at Blackpool and now he had to contend with another long serving custodian, in the form of Ernie Gregory. The serving West Ham goalkeeper was one of the best uncapped 'keepers of his generation and Wyllie would have to be at his very best to dislodge him. And so it proved, though Wyllie got off to a very good start. He took the eye in the public practice game (Colours v Blues) which

Hammers' star was newcomer Wyllie

STAR of the West Ham trial was the only newcomer on view— Ron Wyllie, ex-Blackpool goal-keeper.

Ernie Gregory will have to be in top form to keep his place in the senior side, for Wyllie really looks the part, with fine anticipation, safe hands and a firm throw. He also saved two with his feet!

Mike Grice moved well as

A cutting saved for 54 years by Jim Howie in

ended 2-2. As it was Ernie Gregory's reputation saw off the threat posed by the newcomer's ability. Bob played 13 times for the Upton Park club, before Jack Rowley invited him to come and assist with his tilt at getting Plymouth back into the second tier. It was to be another move which ended with disappointingly few first team appearances. I saw quite a lot of Bob Wyllie. With my season ticket getting me into the reserve fixtures for free, I often went to the Saturday home games. Although Geoff Barnsley was one of my favourites, it was easy to see, even as a child, that Bob Wyllie was a good goalkeeper. My memory is that he was a bigger man than Barnsley and a man with very large hands.

He did actually get a 'break' in England, but unfortunately it was of the wrong kind. During his time at Tannadice the club took the players to Wembley for an England against Scotland Home international. They were then to travel on to Swansea for a friendly. Whilst watching the international he saw the great Wilf Mannion carried off the field with a broken jaw. In his first interview with *Spectator*, Wyllie related the tale of the Mannion incident. "It is quite remarkable really. We watched that game at Wembley, travelled on to Swansea the next day and then I had my own jaw broken in that friendly on the Monday night. It was an awful injury and I couldn't eat for weeks".

Bob and family moved into Harry Brown's old club house on 15 July 1958. Rowley went as expected with Geoff Barnsley for the opening fixture, though again Wyllie had looked very competent in pre-season. Having joined at the same time as Gordon Fincham, like the Leicester man he would be kept waiting for his first team debut. It came, with Fincham's, in that remarkable fixture against Mansfield Town on 7 March 1959. Argyle won 8-3, and for that reason it really sticks in the mind. Argyle had been beaten at home to Accrington last time out, a surprising defeat. Such was the fall out from the Accrington defeat that the Board held an emergency meeting prior to the fixture against the Stags. The announcement afterwards was that the team was discussed but the final choice was down to the manager. Who knows? Did Harry Deans give Bob his debut?

The team were determined that they would put Mansfield to the sword. And for 42 minutes everything went to plan. Argyle had raced into a 3-0 lead after 20 minutes and looked as if they would run up double figures. The swagger and confidence of the early season home games was back. Bob Wyllie must have thought that being Argyle's number one was a doddle. But three minutes before half time it all began to unravel. Two goals in three minutes meant that the visitors sent Argyle in for their cup of tea with much to ponder. Two minutes after half time it was 3-3. I can still recall the bemused look on the new goalkeeper's face. He had barely touched the ball yet had conceded three in a match Argyle had looked capable of running away with. But Rowley stuck with the new custodian and on the following Saturday he gave what *Pilgrim* and *Spectator* both described as a masterful display at Notts County in a 2-1 win. The team then stayed north, with Geoff Barnsley in the travelling party, but Rowley persisted with the new man. Argyle went down 2-0 in an outstanding game, with Wyllie again getting the plaudits for his superb handling and distribution. Game number four enabled him to record his first blank in a 2-0 stroll against Chesterfield. The goalkeeper at the other end was a young fellow called Gordon Banks. As the Easter programme approached Wyllie still held the jersey. In front of 30,000 at Griffin Park, Argyle succumbed to a 3-0 defeat. Although the match reports do not attach any blame to Bob, it turned out to be the last appearance of a short career at Home Park. He left Plymouth in October 1959 for Mansfield. But there was time for one more event that is worth recording.

I was warned by his nephew Scott that the final story may well be apocryphal, though his dad swears it to be true. Scott's dad and mum made the long journey south to visit Bob and his wife during their time in Plymouth, taking with them a couple from Dundee that they are still friendly with today. It appears that they went out for a drink one evening to a Plymouth pub. As the evening wore on the ladies asked for a Bacardi and Coke, at that time an increasingly popular tipple in Scotland. The barman raised an eyebrow, having never heard of such a mix. By the end of the evening half the pub were on BCs! So, did Bob Wyllie's brother introduce Bacardi and Coke to Plymouth—he is adamant he did.

Once at Mansfield Bob Wyllie finally took up where he left off at Dundee United and became the first choice goalkeeper. Under manager Sam Weaver he made 37 League and Cup appearances in his first term there, missing only one game after his debut against Shrewsbury. Although they lost 6-3 he went on to enjoy a good spell at Field Mill. He had two years as first choice, before losing his place on 14 October 1961 to Colin Treharne.

At the beginning of the next season, 1962-63, Bob and his colleague Don Bradley moved into the non-League game with Alfreton Town. He started as first choice and enjoyed a quiet debut in a 4-0 Midland League outing against Stamford. That was the first of 74 League and Cup matches for the Derbyshire club, and at the end of that first season he got a runners-up medal against Ilkeston Town in the Derbyshire Senior Cup Final. His final appearance for Alfreton came in another Derbyshire Senior Cup fixture, a 3-2 reverse at Matlock on 21 March 1964. He was by now just a few weeks from his 35th birthday.

After a spell with Ilkeston he was back at Alfreton in 1971, ostensibly managing their reserve side. But the first team manager Alf England often asked Bob to assist with the first team. Not too long after the start of the 1972/73 season adverse criticism drove England out of the club and Bob decided to follow him. They had a spell together managing Belper Town. By this time his health was deteriorating and he died in 1982 at the relatively young age of 53. Here was yet another of the 1958-59 promotion group who never seems to have attracted a bad word from anyone. It was good that his Football League career finished on a relative high at

THE LOCAL JOURNALISTS

In 1958-59 football journalists wrote under a *nom de plume*. Locally, the *Western Evening Herald* football coverage was written by Ray Head, using the pen name *Pilgrim*. To the 1958-59 players he was known as the penguin, a reference to a long black coat he often wore. Graham Hambly told me that for many years Ray also covered Argyle for the *Western Morning News,* using the alias *Tamar*. He covered both jobs until Graham succeeded him in 1968. Ray Head died suddenly in 1982, still covering Argyle.

On the few occasions *Pilgrim* did not write the match reports or Argyle news, his replacement would write under the name *Twelfth Man*. As well as the weekly match analysis *Pilgrim* would write a summary column in the *Football Herald*, outlining all the news and events at Home Park during the preceding week. It was high quality writing and is now a researcher's dream.

The *Western Independent's Argyle* soccer writer used the pseudonym *Spectator*. At the start of the 1958-59 season Arthur Schofield was *Spectator,* but during 1959 Frank Sloan, son of a former Argyle player of the same name, was given the job. Despite extensive enquiries, no one can quote a precise handover date in 1959. The change was seamless in terms of the style of writing. Sloan became only the third person to carry the mantle. The first, Walter Taylor, was promoted to editor in 1947 and Schofield took over. On 29 July 1959 the three *Spectators* were in the same room together. They were all guests at the club's Promotion Celebration Dinner at Dingle's Dartmoor restaurant. Frank Sloan was disappointed that his time in the job—he handed over to Harley Lawer in 1964—was somewhat spoiled by Boardroom events dominating the news at Home Park. He later became Sports Editor at the *Herald.*

Pilgrim's weekly *Football Herald* summary was excellent; the coverage in the *Western Independent* was superb. On an inside page would be a detailed match report, while on the penultimate page would be a one to one interview with a player or team official. The back page consisted of an extremely detailed commentary of events at Home Park, covering the week since the previous publication. The back page was six columns of news covering every facet of life at Home Park. Nothing was missed. After a short summary of the previous day's game there were details about forthcoming events, news about trialists, transfer targets, the Supporters' Club, finance, Boardroom news (of which there was plenty in 1958-59) and he always solemnly reported the death of any former player or official.

Head, Schofield and then Sloan played an important role, for there was no broadcasting alternative. Plymouth had just one television channel, the BBC. They did not even cover local news on TV, until the Westward ITV channel started transmitting in 1961 or 1962. There were no local radio stations. Sound broadcasting was mainly restricted to three national stations, all run by the BBC. All that was available was the occasional local programme or bulletin, but within the national framework.

Mansfield, for he was definitely far too good a goalkeeper to have languished so long in reserve team football.

Apart from Neil Dougall, Bob Wyllie was the oldest player in the 1958-59 group. The youngest was a man who is one of the few Argyle players ever to have moved on and achieved legendary status at his new club. That man was **Reg Jenkins.** Born on 7 October 1938, Reg was the fifth member of the group whose dad had at one time mined coal for a living. Once in Millbrook his dad then took on a painting and decorating job while his mum scrubbed the floors of the Millbrook Baptist Church and the Freemasons Hall in the village. He had a brother John who was 19 years older and had played for Truro City.

We have seen in previous chapters that some of this group of players did not come into the professional game by the traditional Schoolboy or County honours. None found football more by chance than Millbrook born Reg. At under 11 he was clearly an outstanding young player. His goals shot little Millbrook Infants and Primary to the All Cornwall Cup. Watched by four coach loads of supporters they were, at that time (circa 1948), the smallest community to achieve that feat. As we sat in his beautiful bungalow in a quiet corner of Millbrook, he points out the school building where he first tasted soccer success. Despite that triumph he was considered too small at Secondary school and was nearly lost to the game from the age of 12. He was limited to the odd kickabout in the village square. Reg recalls that the games only broke up "when we all went home to listen to Dick Barton on the radio."

After four of five years with no organised football, Millbrook were short on the last night of the season. Reg explained that one Friday Mr Ryder, a well known football man in Millbrook, asked him and a friend if they could play for the village side tomorrow. What would become the Jenkins phenomenon was off and running. After just three months playing regularly with Millbrook he was involved in a game with Argyle Reserves. He scored four in a 5-0 win. He joined Truro City and became the talk of the South Western League circuit. By this time he was an apprentice shipwright in the Dockyard, something he was determined he would complete.

At one time Portsmouth showed an interest in the player and invited him to play a trial match at the Valley. Portsmouth went down 5-1 to the Charlton side but Reg showed his knack for scoring. Portsmouth's idea was that they would contact the authorities to switch Reg's apprenticeship to the Hampshire yard. He was not impressed, especially as he would have remained an amateur. He eventually signed forms for Argyle when he was 19, with the club making an exception to their new no part-time rule. On 14 August 1958 he had transferred in from Truro City while Geoff Peach made the reciprocal journey. He had already had outings for the reserves the previous season but made a big impact in the 1958 public practice game. *Pilgrim* could not believe the improvement from the previous season and predicted that Jenkins would be a menace to defences.

In a second public trial, which attracted 5,543, Reg netted both goals for the Possibles in a 6-2 defeat. On the 31 January 1959 Reg became a full-timer at Home Park. In 1957-58 he had hit a creditable 12 goals in 26

20 year old Reg Jenkins challenges future England goalkeeper Gordon Banks, playing here for his home town team Chesterfield. Wilf Carter waits to see if the ball will drop his way.
Courtesy the Sunday Independent

Frame by frame! Gordon Banks has just failed to hold a rasping shot on the turn from Wilf Carter. The left hand picture shows Banks trying to recover the situation while the right hand one shows that Reg Jenkins has prodded the ball in for his first League goal. *The left hand picture is from the Colin Parsons collection, the other from the Sunday Independent*

outings in what was a poor reserve side. By the time he signed full-time forms, and got his £10 signing on fee, he had notched seven in 13 reserve games. In terms of wages, the club was about to balance the books as Meyer was pushing to move back closer to Bristol. Reg was seen as the ideal replacement.

He made his League debut at Swindon on 28 February 1958. He was given George Baker's number nine shirt and helped his colleagues to a 4-3 win. Jimmy Gauld was on top of his game that day and scored a wonderful hat trick. But in truth the side had been struggling since Boxing Day, scraping results here and there. Jenkins came into the team on the back of a first home defeat of the season, when the side were beaten 1-0 by Norwich. He retained his place after the win at Swindon but then got caught up in the Accrington home defeat. He then lost his place for three games before returning for the 2-0 success over Chesterfield and that important first goal. It was another unconvincing display by the team. Jenkins, a young man making his way in the game, needed support that some were unable to offer. He played his fourth and final game of the season in the 3-0 defeat at Brentford on Good Friday.

It was a familiar story the following season. He was brought into the side as they struggled to come to terms with Second Division football. By the time he was given his first start, at the expense of inside left Peter Kearns in a 6-2 defeat at Middlesbrough, Rowley had already used eight forwards in five games. He then missed a game before getting the centre forward berth for a 5-0 defeat at home to Derby County. He was given another three outings, scoring in a 4-1 defeat at Anfield. That was the tenth game of the season and Jack Rowley had already used 20 players. Later he got another seven games, scoring in a 5-3 success at home to Bristol Rovers. He played in first of two Christmas games against the other Bristol club, but a 4-1 home defeat saw him sidelined again. Rowley then went into the transfer market, signing George Kirby and Jimmy McAnearney from Sheffield Wednesday and Johnny Newman from Leicester City.

Rowley was dismissed in March 1960 but the Dougall-Taylor partnership did not turn to Reg again. Indeed, Reg was quite emphatic when he told me that he found George Taylor hard to handle at times. He sees Neil Dougall as the most helpful person on the staff during his spell at Home Park. "Neil really encouraged me and I was very grateful for that. On the other hand there was one senior pro who really wound me up with his 'them and us' attitude to the reserves." One gets the distinct impression that there isn't a lot of forgive and forget about Reg Jenkins. He is the most placid and pleasant of men, but it doesn't seem too good an idea to get on the wrong side of him.

Like many of the players he remarked on Jack Rowley's will to win attitude, and how he would keep the weekly practice matches going until he scored. It was surprising to hear that players like the young Reg did not seem to get one to ones with the manager. If anyone could have improved a young striker's game it was Jack. Reg laughed when he told me about a Thursday tradition at Home Park. "As we returned from training we would look to the area where the manager's car was parked. If it was gone or disappearing out the gate, that was a sure sign that the team sheet was on the dressing room wall—and there were changes for the next match."

He first went to Exeter and then Torquay, where in both cases he gave notice of his ability to get goals on a regular basis. In the 1960-61 campaign he hit six goals in 20 games for Exeter before spending from September 1961 to July 1964 at Torquay. There he upped his average to more than one every four outings. In Cups and League he played 95 times for Torquay and scored 25 goals. Apart from the football side of his life, during his spell on the Devon Riviera he met his wife Norma. They have now been married for 48 years and have a son and a daughter, both born in Torquay. Although he loved his time at Torquay, he was disappointed to find that the day after he committed to the Gulls Bristol Rover's Bert Tann came in for him. "They were a Second Division side and it would have been a really good move".

But no one, not even Reg Jenkins himself, was prepared for what happened after his next move. When Rochdale offered Torquay United £3,000 for Reg Jenkins' signature he and Norma had one small query. "Where is Rochdale?" After consulting a map they located it in the north west of England, not too far from what was then a new M6 motorway. "Norma saw it as an adventure really, something we both felt we had to do. "I met up with Tony Collins their manager, in a hotel in Bristol. He told me that I would get 10% of the fee anyway, but that if I signed they would give me another £300 on top". So the deal was done and I signed there and then. It took the couple more than 12 hours to reach Lancashire. From day one they found the locals as friendly as any group of people they had ever encountered. He settled quickly off the field and once playing he more than justified the club's investment. He opened with two on his debut and by the season's end he had accumulated 25 goals in all competitions. By the summer of 1965 if someone said that Reg Jenkins had been seen walking across the local canal, Rochdale supporters would have believed it. In all he turned out for Rochdale 305 times in League games and scored 119 goals. In various cup ties he added another 22 goals.

10 May 1969 was a great day in Rochdale's history; they went up to the Third Division, their one and only promotion success. And they did it the hard way too. For the early part of the season they were in the lower reaches of the league. They then went on a tremendous run which saw them into the third and final promotion spot. More than 9,000 showed up to cheer them to the victory they needed. The last game was against a Southend side who themselves could be promoted, but they had to beat Rochdale. A draw would be enough for the home side but the crowd deserved a win. Reg Jenkins had a part in Steve Melledew's opener after a quarter of an hour but they needed a second to make them feel more secure. It came from the spot, just after the hour, when Reg himself netted the penalty kick. With 10 minutes left Reg's second saw Spotland change to Dreamland, when he blasted home a cross from the right. Manager Len Richley was delighted and the players were pleased for Chairman Fred Ratcliffe. He had kept the club going when lesser men would have quit long before. Ratcliffe's broad smile was quite understandable.

Reg scored 13 in that memorable season, but that has to be put into context. He seemed out of favour with manager Bob Stokoe and rarely played in the period they were languishing near the bottom. He returned as soon as Stokoe took an appointment at Carlisle and Richley came into the club. After promotion he grabbed another 20 in the Third Division. The team finished a very creditable ninth, still their highest ever placing.

It wasn't all roses for his time at Spotland. In his first season his 25 goals had helped guide them to sixth, their highest placing for nearly 20 years. But then they struggled with a run of 21st, 21st and 19th. Then surprisingly it all came together and they were promoted. Despite an almost unbroken run of good fortune, his time in Lancashire did not end the way he would have wanted. He had played eight seasons at Spotland but towards the end was beset by a number of niggling injuries. As he rightly points out the treatment available in those days is nothing like now. But what hasn't changed is that the star player is always rushed back too quickly, especially one as talismanic as Reg Jenkins was for Rochdale.

At the end of what became his last season Walter Joyce had taken over as manager. It became clear that someone had told Joyce that Reg's injuries were not as debilitating as the player was making out. The final straw was Fred Ratcliffe, the Chairman who Reg admired so much, asking Reg to undergo a three month trial at the start of the following season, before being offered a full contract. He saw it as an affront and decided it was time to go.

There was a time he could have gone from Rochdale before. Stanley Matthews and Ernie Taylor, former team-mates at Blackpool, were both at Port Vale. They were prepared to invest £10,000 in Reg but Rochdale were not persuaded. "I would have got a £1,000 as my share of the fee, a fair amount of money back then. As it was I stayed at Rochdale, waiting two hours for Fred Ratcliffe to clear the wage cheques every week." But clearly, when you listen to his memories of his time at Spotland, just maybe it was worth that £1,000 to stay.

When we met during April 2008 I asked him about the summer of 1966. Connecting his first League goal against Chesterfield with the World Cup Final at Wembley, I was looking to examine the different directions the two player's lives took after that day at Home Park seven years before. For Reg he was either staying at his mother's house, "with the two kids sleeping either side of our bed or I may have been working on a chicken farm in Rochdale. Our wages went down in the summer so we had to other work to make ends meet." The whole world knows what Banks was doing that summer. That is the stark contrast between footballers who simply make a living out of the game and those who get the big breaks.

After Rochdale he was given the opportunity to work as assistant to the Oldham manager but the money wasn't any better than a lorry driving job he had been offered in Cornwall. He shrewdly put £25 down on a plot of land in Millbrook and the bungalow he still lives in was started as soon ashe returned.

Nearly 40 years after he left to return to Cronwall, Reg Jenkins is still a legend in Rochdale. At the Millennium he was voted 'Dale's best ever player in a poll by fans. He told me when we met in Millbrook that he could be at some function or other in Rochdale every week of his life. "I love Millbrook but if I could have brought a few of the Rochdale people back down home that would make it perfect".

Once he returned to Millbrook he took an active part in making the local football club more successful than it had ever been, leading them from the lower reaches of the Plymouth Combination League to an established position in the South Western League. He had to pay 50p to become reinstated as an amateur before he could take the player-manager's job. A hip injury forced him to retire. At 55 he took up golf and now plays off 11. They are a real golfing family with his son playing off 2 and his daughter a 5 handicap. Reg is now retired and when we met he looked tanned, content and relaxed.

In the weeks after I spoke to Reg Rochdale continued to have a very successful season, having picked up after the appointment of former Blackburn and Plymouth Argyle man Keith Hill. Rather like 1969 they surged up the table and made it to a play-off final against Stockport on 27 May 2008. I watched the TV coverage with interest, knowing that Reg Jenkins would be there and that Sky would *have* to interview him. Sure enough, just before kick off he wished his former club all the best, with his grin showing how genuinely he felt for the club. Millbrook got a mention too! His attractive shyness shone through during that television appearance. It made me think that not only did the Rochdale fans idolise him for his scoring exploits, those who got to know him realised what a smashing fellow their hero was. That was clear from every article I read about him during the research for *Thanks For The Memory.*

A SUPPORTER'S STORY
Roger Elliott

The 1958/59 season was memorable to me for a number of reasons. Each season we watched in rain or sunshine from the terraces as on the pitch the Argyle players orchestrated the huge, feverish, swaying crowd with the exciting highs and lows of their team play. We were ecstatic as Johnny Williams slotted home 40 yard pile-driver goals, as Jimmy Gauld scored after sprinting with the ball almost glued to his feet, and as Wilf Carter coolly yet clinically converted penalties. Then there was the lanky centre half, Reg Wyatt, who would chase and slide from behind to hook the ball off an opponents toes safely into touch. I could mention all the squad but I'll focus on the ultimate utility player and tackler, Neil Dougall.

In a previous season I remember vividly a fifty-fifty ball in front of the new stand on the half way line. Neil Dougall and an opponent catapulted themselves at the ball only for them to bounce off each other, fall backwards, scramble up again and challenge like lions for the ball once more. They were true professionals, masters of the skill of tackling, hard but clean. In those days you could use the shoulder when on the ball and it reduced the chances of broken legs. On the other hand, if you held, tugged or pushed, then the whistle would go immediately.

By coincidence, in the early 58/59 season Neil Dougall then coached me to tackle in the very same area in front of the new stand. I had arrived (hiding an ankle injury) from West Hoe United, recommended by Maurice, their manager, for trials with the Under 18 Juniors. After evening practice matches on outside fields, where I came off worse going for 50/50 balls against the fair but hard tackling Dido Grey, I found myself one evening with another junior on the Home Park hallowed turf, being coached by Neil Dougall. At first I knocked my knee but the coach told me to use my shoulder and I found I could win many 50/50 tackles.

Neil was also aware that I had an ankle problem, so beside arranging electrical treatment with the physio, he took me to the bathroom area for hot and cold treatment. The area was twice the size of our family of five's two bedroom flat. I thought it was a palace! There were at least twelve spotless turquoise baths. I was able to sit and lift my leg from a hot bath to a cold.

My chance came to play in Argyle colours. The Junior's captain, Truscott, was away on one of his many representative games, so I took his place at right half. We played on the pitch opposite the boating pond. At the end the Junior's manager told me that I wouldn't get a regular game but that he wanted me to cover every time Truscott was away. I thanked him but said that I had a date at the Prince Rock Hospital to have my ankle manipulated under general anaesthetic. In fact, I played again for several decades, avoiding bad injuries.

Yes, I remember the 58/59 Argyle promotion team. In particular, I remember the player coach, Neil Dougall.

CHAPTER TWENTY THREE

NEIL DOUGALL

A constant thread through *Thanks For The Memory* has been how pleasant and approachable almost everyone in the 1958-59 side was. Neil Dougall was the elder statesman of the side, some eight years older than the next oldest player Bob Wyllie. Maybe it was he set the example because he was a most considerate and courteous man.

Neil (christened Cornelius) Dougall was born at Falkirk on 7 November 1921. If ever a man was born to be a professional footballer it was Neil Dougall. His father Billy first played for Falkirk before moving on to Bury and then Burnley. Dougall senior was also chosen for the Scottish League XI, at a time when Scottish football was much stronger and competitive than it is now. His Uncle James played professionally for Preston, Cardiff and Halifax and won a solitary cap for Scotland. Neil's brother was a fair player too, though he stayed in the amateur ranks with a top club of the day, Pegasus FC. Due to injury Bill Dougall was forced to retire early, but Burnley took him on to their management staff. It is acknowledged that it was he who laid the foundations for the Burnley 1960 League Championship success. Indeed, Neil's father was manager for most of the previous season, but was forced to hand over to Harry Potts through ill health.

Neil's pedigree saw him sign for Burnley in 1940, but the War prevented him appearing for their first team in an official League fixture. Dougall attracted the attention of a number of clubs during the war when his fine displays for the RAF drew many plaudits. When Harry Storer took over at Birmingham City in June 1945, one of his first acts was to persuade the St Andrews Board to spend nearly £3,000 on Neil Dougall. The partnership was immediately successful and they won the Southern League Championship as well as getting to the FA Cup semi-final. 1945-46 was the last of the war-time League competitions but the 1946 FA Cup was for real.

From the start of the 1946-47 season, until he retired from playing during the 1958-59 campaign, he was always involved in either a promotion, relegation or re-election tussle. 12 consecutive seasons of either joy or struggle. It was a fitting end to his playing career that he played sufficient games to earn a Third Division Championship medal for the 1958-59 success, a season he had not intended to play competitively. In all he played 274 League games for Plymouth Argyle, scoring 24 times. He also had 15 FA Cup outings and added another two goals to his tally. He arrived at Home Park late in season 1948-49 and played only three times. He found it difficult to settle and injuries also affected his form. But from the start of the 1949-50 season he began to show why Jimmy Rae saw fit to spend a record £13,000 to secure his signature. After an indifferent start he

into Division Three (South). In his first 'mini-season' the team only finished one place above the trap-door. Their fate was sealed this time mainly due to 18 games where they failed to register a goal. Signed as an inside forward he only wore his customary number eight shirt for six of his 30 appearances. He played once at centre forward and in the last 24 games he appeared at right half. Two seasons completed and already a near miss and a relegation.

In terms of appearances, the 1950-51 campaign in the third tier was his most productive in his entire career at Home Park. He missed only four of the 46 fixtures and weighed in with six goals. His first goal for Argyle came at Dean Court, Bournemouth, when his friend and flatmate Alex Govan got the other. His first goal at home was in a 5-1 win over Aldershot, with the elegant Maurice Tadman getting the other four. Argyle stayed in the promotion hunt for most of that season.

The team were well fancied the next season to follow their fourth place finish with promotion. They duly delivered, with Dougall alternating between the right half and inside right berths, just as he had done the season before. Injuries restricted him to 26 appearances and three goals. Whereas the team was almost expected to have won promotion in the previous campaign, most realists could see the team struggling in the Second Division.

Reality was different, of course, and the team finished fourth in a powerful League. Dougall missed just one game, playing the entire season at right half. Pat Jones played every game, goalkeeper Shortt missed only two and Astall and Tadman just three each. Dougall took his total Argyle goal tally to 13. Thus far the team had never lost when he scored. Promotion was often tantalisingly close, but then one would expect nothing else with Neil Dougall around! 1953-54 saw excitement of the wrong kind, with the team never too far from the wrong end of the table. Injury restricted Neil to 27 appearances and he did not find the net in any of them. 1954-55 was even less successful, with the team looking likely to be relegated until Jack Rowley arrived. Again injury interrupted his season and he played only 17 games and scored once. That goal, in a 3-2 reverse at Doncaster, spoiled his record of the team never losing when he scored.

In his first six seasons in Plymouth he had so far had one promotion to his name, one near miss and four struggling seasons at the bottom end. 1955-56 did nothing to break the sequence. In a dismal relegation season, where he made 29 appearances with two goals, he was again injured almost as often as he was fit. He would have hoped that his eighth season on the books at Home Park would bring some much needed success. Back in the Third South, it was a Division where Argyle had never struggled. They had finished 11th in the first ever season of the competition (1920-21) but, thereafter, had never finished lower than the fourth place achieved in 1950-51.

1956-57 kept his record for seasons with interest, but once again it was of the wrong kind. It was a season to forget, with Dougall playing 26 times in the League. His nine goals was his best single season return and on two occasions he 'bagged a brace.' As well as his normal inside forward

Neil with George Taylor. They once shared the manager's job. *Courtesy Margaret Callan*

position, he played 12 games on the right wing. Eventually the team pulled away from the re-election zone, but finished a lowly 18th.

The war years apart, this was considered the club's nadir. Neil was now approaching his 36th birthday and was having trouble staying fit. Increasingly too, Jack Rowley saw Dougall as the answer to the languid displays by the reserve team. In addition to his first team games he turned out for the reserves on more than 60 occasions, probably more than a third of those games as reserve team trainer.

The summer of 1957 saw an influx of players who promised to improve the club's fortunes. Wilf Carter took the eight shirt that Dougall had worn with such distinction, while Johnny Williams was making the right half spot his own. Neil did not expect to play very often for the first team, and that is how it turned out. He did get 13 games but in six different positions. He played six games at left back (one of six people tried there that season while Pat Jones was injured). Those outings would develop a significance for the following term.

Neil was delighted with the role Jack Rowley had given him with the reserves. With the summer signings of Fincham, JL Williams, Bob Wyllie and Meyer, there would be some substance to his charges. For too many years the reserves had under achieved through a policy of employing average part-timers and promising amateurs. There was clear and recent proof that a strong reserve side can increase the first team's chances of success. From 1950-51 to the end of 1952-53 the second string had finished 4th, 2nd and then 3rd place. This mirrored the first team's 4th and 1st in Division Three (South) and then that famous 4th place finish in the Second.

But almost as soon as Neil arrived home from the opening match of the 1958-59 Football Combination season, he was having to tell wife Monica that he would have to travel north to play for the first team. The first team had gained a hard draw at Hull on the opening day, but at the expense of a serious injury to debutant left back Eric Doughty. Typically he answered the call and so began an unexpected run of 23 League and Cup appearances. It would lead to him playing until just past his 37th birthday.

He was ready for the call to arms, and missed only one of the 23 games prior to Bellett signing. That is a remarkable tribute to the way Neil Dougall looked after his body. Of the matches he played after his recall, just the game at Colchester ended in defeat. The game he missed during his surprise run in the team was the 5-1 debacle at the Dell on 29 November 1958. He pulled on a first team shirt for the final time on 13 December 1958, aged 37 years and 36 days. One can only assume that Jack Rowley had turned to Dougall because Bryce Fulton had missed part of pre-season due to a wages dispute. John L Williams was the travelling 12th man, but he had made it clear to the manager before they left that he was injured. Although Fulton was supposed to he the future and Dougall the past, during the season before Dougall had often been preferred to Fulton at left back. Whatever the merits of the decision, in terms of results Rowley was proved right by going for the man he saw as the most reliable. Bellett and then Wyatt filled the shirt for the remainder of the season but the defence was never as sound again.

Following George Reed's untimely passing, and once Bellett was signed, Neil Dougall was confirmed in the Assistant Trainer's job. His good friend and colleague Pat Jones, by now playing at St Austell, was also interviewed but it would have been something of a shock if Dougall had not been chosen. He continued the rest of that season overseeing the reserve side and continued into the 1959-60 season. The Boardroom conflict created uncertainty at Home Park, though many people thought that Blindell's return at the start to that season would put Jack Rowley's job at risk. The manager survived until March 1960. While they looked for a successor it was decided that Trainer George Taylor and Neil would be given joint charge of the first team, with a third former player Tony McShane coming in to assist with the reserves. It worked well for the remainder of that season and the team gradually pulled away from the threat of relegation.

The partnership continued at the start of 1960-61 and the side got off to a better start than the previous campaign. By the middle of September they got into their stride, recording consecutive 5-1 wins at home to Portsmouth and away to Huddersfield. The season was something of a goal fest. There was a 5-2 away win at Eastville, a 4-0 trouncing at Anfield and, on 17 December 1960, a 9-0 drubbing at Stoke, quickly followed by the two famous 6-4 games with Charlton Athletic. The Wednesday before the Stoke collapse, the team had forced a creditable 3-3 draw at Villa Park in the 4th round of the League Cup.

Although there was a mid-table respectability about things, the Board decided to appoint Vic Buckingham. When he left, almost as soon as he had arrived, Neil Dougall was given sole responsibility for the first team. It was an appointment that pleased the supporters and the players, plus there was no ill feeling from George Taylor. The campaign got off to a poor start. Huddersfield avenged the previous season's 5-1 home defeat by Argyle—with a 5-1 win at Leeds Road. It was clear from those who knew him that Neil Dougall was not himself. After an amicable meeting with the Board, it was announced that Neil would become Chief Coach and Chief Scout. In a statement after the meeting he said "I don't think I was made to be a leader of men. My father warned me about it enough times. Things haven't been going too well and I've not been sleeping at nights". He admitted that he had been taking things out on his family and he saw that he must quit. Dignified as ever, he finished by saying "This is a much more natural appointment for me". *Pilgrim* added that he had known for some time that Mrs (Monica) Dougall was worried about her husband and the pressure he was under. For many years Neil and Monica had a flower shop in Hyde Park. Later he worked at the Mayflower Centre, retiring in 1986. He always looked smart and had time for everyone. On match days he would stroll through the concourse to the players' entrance. He passed no one without acknowledging them.

Neil Dougall played for Scotland on three occasions, two of his caps coming in April 1946. At Hampden Park nearly 140,000 saw a strong England team beaten 1-0 in a Victory International. Then at Maine Road he played in an unofficial friendly against England. It finished 2-2 and was in aid of the Bolton Disaster Fund. On 9 March 1946 33 people had been killed at Burnden Park during a Bolton v Stoke cup tie. His first (and only) official cap came in October 1946, in a 3-1 Home International Championship defeat against Wales at Wrexham. Unusually, every member of the Scotland team was winning their first cap. How good could Neil Dougall have been if the War had not taken seven years of his career away?

On 5 October 1959 he was granted a Testimonial and the club where it all started for him, Burnley, flew their full side to Home Park. The visitors won 6-1, with Pointer 3, Pilkington, Harris and White getting their goals. Neil was not fit to play but his long time pal Alex Govan got a consolation for the home side. 12,996 turned out to pay tribute.

Sadly, Neil is now in the grip of Alzheimer's disease. Alex Govan, who goes to see him says "Its very sad, he still looks a million dollars but he doesn't always know me now. We were really good mates".

PLYMOUTH ARGYLE SUPPORTERS' CLUB — FINANCIAL STATEMENT, 1958-59

GENERAL ACCOUNT

INCOME

	1957/58 £ s. d.	£ s. d.
By Balance from 1957/58 Account	670 3 1	1273 15 5
Bank Interest	1 6 0	1 6 6
Subscriptions and Donations	90 6 3	152 14 1
Sale of Club badges and Brooches	27 15 0	34 7 3
Sale "Argyle" Ball Pens and Refills	23 9 2	138 18 0
Revenue from Competitions	2 17 6	1 3 6
Revenue from Excursions	346 3 1	428 3 0
Revenue from Handbooks, Fixture Cards and Team Photographs	33 1 9	34 12 0
	90 18 10	102 1 10
Revenue from Cushion Hire Service	127 2 0	118 16 6
Revenue from Catering Service	570 10 8	412 1 4
Revenue from Programme Sales	1406 5 3	1637 10 2
"Green and Black" Club—Donations for specified purposes	10467 4 6	16629 6 5
Collection and Donations—Bert Cole Testimonial		
Donations—Late George Reed Fund		38 0 0
Collection—George Taylor Benefit Fund		50 0 0
Other Items	69 5 3	11 0 0
	13926 8 4	**21063 16 0**

EXPENDITURE

	1957/58 £ s. d.	£ s. d.
To Hire of Halls for Meetings	14 8 0	12 2 0
Annual Meeting Expenses	3 9 0	2 16 3
Printing and Stationery	74 0 8	67 7 3
Postages, Telegrams and Telephones, including rentals	47 6 4	58 12 2
Maintenance and cleaning Club property at Home Park	14 3 9	108 9 0
Purchase Club Badges and Brooches	25 0 0	85 10 0
Purchase "Argyle" Ball Pens and Refills		144 16 6
Purchase for Home Park		5 18 1
*Purchase of Footballs	324 3 5	270 19 3
*Purchase Forms and Chairs for Home Park	22 2 6	88 0 0
*Fitting out new Club Headquarters		448 16 10
*Presentation of Blazers to players and officials		243 10 0
*Promotion Celebrations	1 0 0	306 18 11
*Ground Improvements—Direct payments		804 3 0
Small Lotteries Act Registration Fee, 1959		1 12 6
Members' Insurance Premium	11 12 6	
Plymouth Argyle Football Club—Transfer revenue from Programme Sales	1406 5 3	1637 10 2
Mr. Bert Cole—Presentation		59 4 0
Mrs. George Reed—Late George Reed Fund		75 0 0
Mr. George Taylor—Benefit Presentation		11 16 8
Ball Boys—Equipment replacements		3 0 0
Floral Tributes		3 15 0
Cup Tie Expenses	19 7	5 0
Gifts to Officers during illness		
Cheque Book		
Honorariums 1957/58:		
Hon. Gen. Secretary and Treasurer	40 0 0	50 0 0
Hon. Asst. Gen. Secretary and Treas.	15 0 0	25 0 0
Donations:		
St. John Ambulance Brigade	5 5 0	5 5 0
Toc H Wireless for Hospitals Fund	5 5 0	5 5 0
Plymouth Council of Social Service	2 2 0	2 2 0
Royal Dockyard Orphanage	2 2 0	2 2 0
Plymouth & District Blind Aid Society	2 2 0	2 2 0
Hospital Patients' Disabled Fellowship Club		2 2 0
Hospital Patients Voluntary Welfare Fund		2 2 0
Lord Mayor's Christmas Appeal Fund	2 2 0	2 2 0
*Plymouth Argyle Football Club	9500 0 0	14467 7 0
Gratuity to Groundsman for services rendered		5 0
Other Items	1132 1 11	
Balance to 1959/60 Account	1273 15 5	2031 18 5
	13926 8 4	**21063 16 0**

NOTE—*Denotes items met from "Green and Black" Club donations.

F. T. PRING, Chairman.
RON A. LUCAS, Hon. General Secretary and Treasurer.

We have examined the financial statements and accounts of the above Club, have received all explanations required, and in our opinion they are properly drawn up.

HENRY A. SHEPPARD
JOHN D. BERRIMAN
E. L. SMYTH
Hon. Auditors
23rd July, 1959

The Plymouth Argyle Supporters' Club, run by Ron Lucas, was a tremendous asset to the parent club. For all his perceived faults, Ron Blindell greatly admired the organisation and did as much as anyone to bring the two organisations much closer together. That Supporters' Club Chairman Fred Pring agreed to become one of Blindell's nominees, when he wanted to oust Harry Deans, was a clear indicator of where the Supporters' Club loyalties lay. This fascinating balance sheet, from *the Colin Parsons' Collection*, shows the myriad of tasks they undertook.

CHAPTER TWENTY FOUR

FINANCES & THE SUPPORTERS' CLUB

We have seen in earlier chapters that many of the post-war years had been something of a financial struggle for Plymouth Argyle. But leading up to and during the 1958-59 season the figures were much better. Ron Blindell's business acumen, bringing with it better attention to costs, was a major factor. The repeal of Entertainment Tax was a huge bonus. Success on the field during the 1957-58 and 1958-59 seasons drew the fans back in their thousands. The average attendance at Home Park during this promotion season was 22,526. That was 1,800 more than the next best in the Third Division, Norwich City, and it bettered the average numbers who went to First Division games at Preston, Blackpool and FA Cup Finalists Luton Town. Only five clubs in the Second Division attracted higher average crowds.

During the1958-59 season the total attendance at Football League matches was 33,571,238 – and that was 10 million down on 1948-49! The highest average home attendances were at Old Trafford at 53,258. Liverpool, despite finishing fourth in the Second Division, averaged 36,749. Plymouth with 22,296 had the highest 3rd Division average.

Because the manager picks the team and the players score the goals and win the points, it has always been the way of things that it is their names which are remembered when people talk of greatness and success.

This small chrome lapel badge achieved iconic status as the Supporters' Club went from strength to strength. Across the white background was a green cross, with the chrome lettering picked out on black.

When the definitive history of Plymouth Argyle is written Sammy Black and Jack Leslie, Wilf Carter and Jimmy Gauld, Gordon Astall and Alex Govan, Tommy Tynan, Maurice Tadman, Paul Mariner and Billy Rafferty and the great Jack Chisolm are all sure to feature. Managers Robert Jack, Dave Smith and Paul Sturrock are others whose names will be engraved on the placard of distinction, and deservedly so.

Yet over the years there are others, ordinary men without the necessary skill to take the field or coach the team. Men who are often the very bedrock upon which a club is built. Their names are unlikely to be writ large in any chronicle of times gone by, yet some will have made monumental contributions. These are men without whom Plymouth Argyle may have floundered, even during successful eras.

In 1958-59 there were three such men, Supporters' Club Chairman Fred Pring, their Honorary Secretary and Treasurer Ron Lucas and WE Jutson. The Supporters' Club was reconstituted

RON A. LUCAS—Hon. Gen. Sec. and Treas., Plymouth Argyle Supporters' Club. A graduate of local amateur football, having been the secretary of the successful Gas Company team of the 1930's. Appointed Hon. Treas. in 1945, and to his present position on reconstitution of club in 1958. Is joint Hon. Promoter of the Green & Black Pool which has done so much for Plymouth Argyle.

in 1958 and immediately became a phenomenal success. The club's motto was *To Help, Not Hinder* and with their Green and Black Club, run by Jutson, they certainly lived up to their motto, or what would now be better known as a Mission Statement. By the end of the 1958-59 season 60,000 people were competing in the pontoon goal competition they ran. The Supporters' Club notes in the 1959-60 Handbook, produced and funded by that organisation, paid a generous and deserved tribute to Mr Lucas. It described his exceptional organising ability, expressing the view "It can only lead to one thing—success".

The Supporters' Club did more than just raise money. They ran the catering for the first time that season, produced and sold the programme, looked after the match announcer's role, organised away travel and sold things like pennants, biros (and refills) - and those prized lapel badges. They also looked after and kitted out the ball boys, all of

The Plymouth Argyle Supporters' Club, prior to the start of the 1958-59 season. They were all volunteers and made an immense contribution to the finances of the parent club.
Back Row (l to r): R Whitfield, J Salsbury, K Buckler, Mrs P Buckler, Mrs F Jarvis, A Pearse, R Hatton and W Keith
Front Row (l to r): E Geach, G Hawkins, Ron Lucas, Fred Pring, J Wills, S Cox, P Cox and J Muir
Both photographs courtesy Plymouth Argyle

whom before being chosen had to report to Mr Lucas's Desborough Road home to ensure they were all precisely the same height. They planned and financed ground improvements, where possible finding voluntary labour to take on smaller jobs. The itemised balance sheet on page 240 shows the wide spectrum of influence they exerted.

During summer of 1959 *Spectator* reviewed the season's finances, having pored over both the parent club's balance sheet and the contribution of the Supporters' Club. The figures may look trifling by today's standard, but should be judged against the £20 maximum wage for a player and the 33p it cost for a centre stand seat. As a rough rule of thumb, the Retail Price Index (RPI) indicates that what cost £1 in 1958 would now be £17. It doesn't work for everything, especially when it comes to footballers' wages and the price of admission to the ground.

He reported that the football club's financial year closed on 9 May 1959 and that there was a record profit of £14,900. He highlighted the massive influence of the Plymouth Argyle Supporters' Club, explaining that it was entirely responsible for the promotion season delivering that (then) record profit. Deduct their contribution of £22,630 (four times greater than any previous injection of funds) and it will be seen that the promotion season would have shown a loss of around £8,000. With the total costs for the season set at £87,821 *Spectator* posed the question "Is there now any doubt that soccer has become 'big business'?" If only he had lived to see it now! The figures also showed how fortunate the current Board were that Entertainment Tax was no longer levied. It would have been around £15,000 on that season's turnover. At £20,767 net transfer fees were the second highest in the club's history, mainly due to the signings of Meyer, Bellett and Casey. Players' wages, benefits, signing on bonuses, management and officers' salaries amounted to £32,033, an increase of £2,000 on the previous season. Other principal items of expenditure included travel costs of £8,232, up over £3,000, and Football Association and League charges of £3,604, marginally higher than the previous season's £3,512.

The club got no allowances from the Football League to compensate them for their travel and accommodation bills, which were surely the highest in any Division. Take the promotion season as an example. In the north Hull, Tranmere, Bradford City, Mansfield, Halifax, Doncaster and Chesterfield could all travel to each other on the day. Similarly, amongst the southern element the same applied to Southampton, QPR, Brentford, Bournemouth, Swindon and Reading. Norwich City and Newport were perhaps the odd ones out, as like Argyle they had no real local derby. Colchester and Southend had several long journeys but at least they had each other to play twice a season. Wrexham could get to Birkenhead and back in a day when up against Tranmere Rovers. Only Bournemouth was sufficiently close to Plymouth for a return journey in a single day. It would have been tough going though. One thing the former players all agreed on was that no one could accuse the club of skimping on hotels. To a man they all told me that accommodation was always satisfactory. Some were disappointed to see a clampdown on rail journeys. Their nights out in London, paid for by the club, were an attractive perk which most of them were sorry to see reduced when increased road travel was deemed more economic. Peter Anderson mourned the loss of the Saturday nights in London, where they passed time waiting for the sleeper at a nice sandwich bar by Paddington station.

Over the season Argyle's average home attendance of over 22,000 brought in £69,828 at the turnstiles and another £11,142 in season tickets. This was an era when prices were set by the Football League. The standard admission to the ground was 2/- (10p) for an adult and 1/- (5p) for under 16s. At Home Park the best stand seats were 6/6d (33p) while the wing stand was 5/- (25p). Wolves had been a lone voice at the 1958 Football League AGM, calling for a reduction. One key difference to today's arrangements were the payments to the opposition from the home gate. Once match expenses were deducted—things like policing, match official fees and turnstile operators (which totalled £4,204 for the season) - the travelling club were entitled to 20% of the balance.

To meet their travel costs Plymouth needed to play in front of 15,000. Apart from Argyle only Norwich averaged above that figure, though Hull with 14,325, Brentford (13,922) and Southampton (13,718) came close. Only on a few occasions did they cover their travel and accommodation costs from their share of the gate. That exciting 4-3 win at the County Ground saw Swindon hand over £247, £100 more than Argyle's outlay. From Reading they took away £228 against £125 spent. After the early season, back to back games at Bury and Stockport, they received £383 against outgoings of £255. On only a few occasions did they give their opponents less at Home Park than they had received in the reverse fixture. On Good Friday the mammoth 29,000 at Griffin Park, for the promotion clash with Brentford, provided Argyle with a return of £490. When the Bees came to Home Park on Easter Monday Brentford's share was £38 less at £452. Generally it was Argyle who lost out. The Christmas fixture at home to Queens Park Rangers was a classic case. The Londoners received £536 as their share of the 30,000 plus Home Park crowd, while the next day Argyle came away from Loftus Road with only £278. Some clubs must have loved their visits to the League's farthest outpost. Bury took away £467, Swindon £435, Tranmere £371, Mansfield £305 and Chesterfield £370. Stockport and Accrington were the unlucky ones, their fixtures both coinciding with prolonged heavy rain. Both recouped less than £200 against their travelling, though in both cases that was more than either had to hand over when Argyle visited Edgeley Park and Peel Park.

The club had quite a lucrative FA Cup run, even though they perished at the third round stage. They cleared £4,000 from the four ties. The gate money for the first two rounds was divided evenly amongst the two sides, again after match expenses were deducted. The first hurdle proved a difficult one, and after a 2-2 draw at Home Park they had to journey to Gillingham for a replay. The 21,759 paying supporters at the home game provide each club with £1,392 and Argyle with a 4-1 success. With the Priestfield game being played on a Wednesday afternoon, the crowd was less than 11,000. Argyle took £634 before expenses. Their second round visit to Highfield Road, Coventry, was watched by an impressive 27,295 and each team earned £1,874, with Argyle then having to deduct travelling and accommodation expenses. Then came the Cardiff City home third round tie, which attracted a bumper gate of 36,247. The gross receipts were £4,176 which had to be divided three ways. After match expenses were deducted each club got a third and the other portion was paid to the Football Association. Each share was worth £1,392.

Including the management salaries, wages accounted for less than 40% of the Home Park turnover that season. Nationally there were those who thought the players deserved a larger share of the income. It was in 1958 that the old Association of Football Players' and Trainers' Union (the AFPTU) changed its name to the Professional Footballers' Union, (the PFA). Jimmy Hill, then of Fulham, had just taken over as Chairman from the former Portsmouth player Jimmy Guthrie. The name change was Hill's attempt to rid the Union of its blue collar image. In 1955 Guthrie had given a famous speech to the Trades Union Congress (TUC), "I stand here as a representative of the last bonded men in Britain ... we seek your assistance to unfetter the chains and set us free".

Hill took the mantle and by 1961 the maximum wage was no more. To repeal the Retain & Transfer agreement would take another two years. It is often misunderstood that the players had two battles to fight. The fight to prevent the Football League imposing a maximum wage structure, including lower wages in the summer, was separate to the famous 'George Eastham case' which overthrew the Retain and Transfer rules. The latter meant that until 1963, any player in England had to put in a transfer request if they wanted to move. If the club were not prepared to sanction a transfer he would be tied to the club, provided his wages were kept to the level of his previous summer contract. It meant that clubs could control the players, in addition to having a predictable costing mechanism for each season.

It may have been a contributory factor as to why we saw many more 'one club men' in earlier eras of the game. Preston's Tom Finney and Billy Wright of Wolves are two who come to mind. The great Jimmy Dickinson at Portsmouth played an unbelievable 764 League games for his club. But as we saw in the case of our own Johnny Williams, there was no real incentive for a player to move if his current club were paying the maximum, and he was happy there. In 1958-59 season a First Division star could earn no more than a maximum of £20 per week. In addition they were entitled to strictly regulated bonus payments. In all League and FA sanctioned friendlies the bonus was £4 for a win and £2 for a draw. Friendly matches also attracted an extra payment of £2 minimum and £3 maximum to each player, plus an extra £2 if that particular match was televised. When on tour outside England or Wales, the players receive an extra £2 per day out of pocket expenses.

In FA Cup ties the extra win payment was Round 1 £4, Round 2 £4, Round 3 £5, Round 4 £6, Round 5 £8, Round 6 £10, Semi-final £20 and Final £25. In the case of drawn matches only a half bonus was paid. Under Blindell's regime, Argyle were one of the few lower League clubs to pay first team players the full maximum. But that was only to those in the chiefs and the officially nominated 12th man. Everyone else, at every club, would be reduced to their contracted summer wage. In the summer the mandatory out of season maximum was set at £17, but was always proportionate to whatever first team wage a club paid. For reserve team matches the win and draw bonuses were half what they were for first team games.

There was no commercial sponsorship, shirt advertising or prize money. There was something called Talent Money, shared amongst the players of successful Clubs as follows:-

First & Second Division Clubs: No.1 Club £1,100, No.2 Club £880, No. 3Club £660, No.4 Club £440 and No.5 Club £220.

Third Division Clubs: No.1 Club £550, No.2 Club £440, No. 3 Club £330, No. 4 Club £220.

Fourth Division Clubs: No.1 Club £330, No.2 Club £220, No.3 Club £110, No.4 Club £55.

FA Cup: Winners of the Cup, £1,100; Runners-up £880; each defeated Semi-finalist, £660; each defeated Club in Round 6, £440; each defeated Club in Round 5, £220.

This meant that our men who won the Third Division shared £550 prize money between them. To establish a player's share the sum of £550 was divided by 506 (46 games multiplied by 11 players per match). That came to the equivalent of £1.08 in today's money. Each player's payment would be determined by multiplying the number of appearances he made by £1.08. Big money!

The source of annoyance amongst the Manchester United players, which Tom Barrett spoke of in an earlier chapter, can quickly be understood when looking at the European Cup bonuses determined by the FA: Round 1, £10 on each appearance; Round 2, £20 on each appearance; Round 3, £30 on each appearance; Semi-final, £40 on each appearance; Final, £50 on each appearance. Compared to the cash and prestige generated, these figures were pitiful.

In addition to all these entitlements, clubs were able to, and in most cases did, pay removal expenses when players were transferred, plus an additional sum of up to £300 if the player was transferred at the request of his Club. There was also a Benefit system. As a reward for loyal service, the club would pay the player a sum up to a maximum of £150 a year for the first 5 years and £200 a year for succeeding years of service with the same club. Many clubs were reluctant to pay decent Benefits, sheltering behind the words 'up to a maximum of'. Finally, the Football League Provident Fund put aside a sum equal to 8% of all these earnings each year which was paid to a player, free of Income Tax, on the 1st January following his 35th birthday, or following his retirement from League football, whichever was the earlier.

It was clear that the Football Association and the Football League were concerned that removal of the maximum wage would see costs spiral out of control. The idea of this system was to limit player mobility and wages, thus preventing all the top players simply finishing up at the richest clubs. Perhaps history has proved the FA and Football League's fears were not unfounded. So anxious were they that, by order of the FA and the Football League, on 7 March 1959 every programme across the land carried a mandatory open letter from the Presidents of the FA and Football League. Apart from listing all the terms and conditions for players it made a big play about players being able to stay in the game in "Managerial, Secretarial, Training and Coaching appointments." Of the 1958-59 Argyle promotion side only Neil Dougall stayed in game at first team level, and that appointment lasted no longer than a few years. Not one of the others managed to make a long-term living out of the game.

The management teams and support staff of that era were nowhere near as big as they are now. There would be a manager, a chief trainer and an assistant trainer, the latter often looking after the reserves. The old Secretary/Manager role was almost extinct, so increasingly the Club Secretary would come from an administration background, as against a football one. Without the education programmes that young players have today, many professional footballers retiring in the late 50s faced only manual work. There were not the vast media openings of today. On any current Saturday now television, radio and newspaper coverage is predominately by former players. At the time of this Argyle promotion the unlucky ones who did not go into coaching or administration, got taken on as a groundsman or assistant groundsman, but on a poor wage.

It was interesting to talk to the players about the abolition of the maximum wage agreement. Those I discussed it with had a very high opinion of Jimmy Hill, appreciating what he was trying to achieve for them. But that group of players at Home Park were an enlightened bunch. George Baker remembers meetings with the PFA representatives. Whilst glad to hear about Johnny Haynes becoming the first £100 a week footballer George recalls that most of the players realised that clubs in the lower reaches of the League would not be able to afford huge wages of that nature. "What we were looking for was a higher maximum really." he told me. "£30 a week instead of £20 was probably the height of our ambitions back then. Look at what it is now!"

The PFA will claim that they have done an excellent job for the players. For the better ones, recipients of the riches that Sky brings to the game, it has been a good deal. But compared to the average wage of today, it is doubtful that a great number of Third and Division players are *that* much better off. George Baker was keen to make the point that there were perks, especially when the side was going well. "You rarely paid for much if you went out for the night. The cinemas would not take money from you; it was rare if you had to buy your own drink in a pub. Businesses were glad to be associated with success."

But there is another side to the PFA. One of the senior players from the 1958-59 side recently required an operation on in-growing toe nails. He has free membership now and a representative, the former Manchester United captain Martin Buchan. He looks after a group of former players. The private medical fee for nearly £1,000 was paid for by the Union. It is good to know that these heroes of 1958-59 have not been forgotten by the current generation of players.

PLYMOUTH ARGYLE SUPPORTERS' CLUB

ROAD EXCURSIONS, 1958/59 Members only

In pursuance of the requirements of the Road Traffic Act, we are precluded from advertising our 1958-59 Season's Coach Excursions, and we therefore give below, for your information, details of our proposed programme:

Date		Excursion	Fare (including stated meal)	
			s.	d.
1958				
Sept.	20th	Colchester—returning to London for evening (Breakfast)	34	0
Oct.	4th	Norwich (Breakfast)	35	6
Nov.	1st.	Chesterfield (Breakfast)	33	6
Nov.	29th.	*Southampton (Luncheon)	23	0
Dec.	27th.	Queens Park Rangers (Breakfast)	30	0
1959				
Jan.	31st.	Reading (Breakfast)	25	0
Feb.	14th.	*Bournemouth (Luncheon)	21	0
Feb.	28th.	*Swindon (Breakfast & Luncheon)	32	6
Mar.	27/28th.	Brentford and Newport (Breakfast and evening meal on Friday. Bed & Breakfast)	72	0

* Denotes day excursions

Additional excursions will be arranged for any away Cup Match if within reasonable travelling distance.

All bookings must be made at least TEN days prior to date of excursion—In the case of the Brentford/Newport tour at Easter 1959, all bookings must be made by 31st December 1958.

Bookings may be made or further details obtained at Club Headquarters and Huts at Home Park, or direct to:—
Mr. R. A. Lucas,
Hon. General Secretary and Treasurer,
134 Desborough Road,
St. Judes, Plymouth.
Telephone: Plymouth 65280.

May we remind members that a Thrift Club is operated for excursions—Full particulars gladly given on request.

Please retain for future reference

The Supporters' Club ran all supporters' travel. The note about the Road Traffic Act is interesting. This was a one-shot leaflet and if you did not see it or retain it, the detail would have to be passed by word of mouth. The Supporters' Club as we knew it in 1959 was closed in 1967, and reformed as the Supporters' Association. The bad feeling between them and the parent club was due to interference in away travel arrangements.
Note that only three of the fixtures were day trips. On the roads of the day they would have been arduous journeys.
From the Colin Parsons' collection.

Summary Of A Promotion Season

Statistics from   1958-59

PLYMOUTH ARGYLE

Third Division Champions 1958-59

One of the most iconic pictures of an Argyle side. It was taken on 25 August 1958, shortly before the away game at Rochdale.
Back Row (l to r): JL Williams, Robertson, Downs, JS Williams, Manager Jack Rowley, Barnsley, Wyatt, Barrett, Dougall, Chairman Ron Blindell, Doughty and Trainer George Taylor
Front Row (l to r): Anderson, Gauld, Carter, Baker and Penk

League Appearances and Goals

Carter	45	22	Dougall	20	1
Gauld	45	21	Govan	20	6
Williams JS	45	7	Bellett	18	0
Barnsley	41	0	Fulton	14	0
Wyatt	39	1	Fincham	13	0
Penk	37	9	Barrett	8	0
Robertson	33	0	Meyer	8	5
Baker	32	6	Wyllie	5	0
Anderson	30	7	Jenkins	4	1
Casey	24	0	Doughty	1	0
Williams JL	24	0	Own Goals		3

In the late 50s professional football was much more prescriptive than it is now. The Football Association and the Football League exerted great control over every facet of the game. If the manager made positional changes before the game, the player would have to change into the shirt that corresponded to his new position.

A good example of this was seen towards the end of the promotion season. Manager Rowley decided to switch Johnny Williams to inside forward and bring in the other John Williams at wing half. It would have made no difference to the performance if Johnny Williams had retained his usual 4 shirt. John Cardiff could have taken the 8 or 10 shirt but lined up at half back.

Another example is wingers Peter Anderson and Harry Penk. They frequently swapped wings during a game. However, if Rowley told Anderson to start on the right he would wear 7, but if he was told to take up the left wing role from kick-off he would wear the 11. Only in the home match against Halifax Town did Argyle players 'break the rules.' Anderson lined up in the 10 shirt but played at outside right while Baker wore the 7 but played in the centre forward position. Some of that was to do with the fact that Wilf Carter suffered a barren spell in the 8 and 10 shirts so switched to the number 9 shirt for the final 13 games.

Goalkeeper jersey colours were also tightly controlled. The only colour allowed for keepers in Football League games was green. Across the whole country, only the Argyle keeper and the opposing one could wear another colour, which had to be red or blue. Yellow was exclusively reserved for international matches. On several occasions opposition goalkeepers had to take the field at Home Park wearing the Argyle keeper's spare jersey, their kitman having automatically packed a green one.

Shirt	Position	Appearances
1	Goalkeeper	Barnsley 41 Wyllie 5
2	Right Full Back	Robertson 33 Fulton 13
3	Left Full Back	Doughty 1 Dougall 20 Wyatt 6 Bellett 18 Fulton 1
4	Right Wing Half Back	JS Williams 36 Barrett 1 JL Williams 9
5	Centre Half Back	Wyatt 33 Fincham 13
6	Left Wing Half Back	JL Williams 15 Casey 24 Barrett 7
7	Right Wing Forward	Anderson 24 Penk 16 Baker 6
8	Right Inside Forward	Gauld 22 Carter 22 JS Williams 2
9	Centre Forward	Baker 24 Meyer 7 Carter 13 Jenkins 2
10	Left Inside Forward	Carter 10 Meyer 1 Jenkins 2 Gauld 23 Baker 2 JS Williams 7 Anderson 1
11	Left Wing Forward	Penk 21 Anderson 5 Govan 20

HOME RESULTS AND ATTENDANCES

Football League Division Three
1958-59
(Argyle scores first)

Opposition	Result	Scorers	Attendance
Tranmere Rovers	4-0	Carter 2, Baker, Gauld	22,518
Rochdale	2-0	Carter, JS Williams	26,961
Reading	2-2	Carter, Penk	25,966
Bury	3-0	Meyer 2, Gauld	27,589
Doncaster Rovers	4-0	Carter 2, JS Williams, Govan	24,827
Bournemouth & BA	3-1	Dougall, Meyer, Wyatt	24,822
Southend United	3-1	Costello og, JS Williams, Gauld	25,349
Swindon Town	3-2	Carter pen, Gauld 2	26,051
Notts County	3-0	Baker, Gauld, Penk	25,910
Newport County	3-2	Baker, Gauld 2	23,482
Wrexham	2-2	Penk, Gauld	21,056
Hull City	1-1	Carter	20,305
Queens Park Rangers	3-2	Carter, Gauld 2	30, 036
Stockport County	2-1	Govan, Baker	10,099
Colchester United	1-1	JS Williams	22,686
Norwich City	0-1		24,532
Accrington Stanley	2-4	Gauld, Penk	12,022
Mansfield Town	8-3	Govan, Penk, JS Williams 2, Gauld, Carter pen, Swinscoe 2 og	17,597
Chesterfield	2-0	Jenkins, Carter	17,334
Brentford	1-1	Govan	27,073
Halifax Town	1-1	Carter	19,571
Southampton	1-0	Carter	23,775
Bradford City	1-1	Carter	26,717

Over 525,000 people clicked through the turnstiles at Home Park at an average of 22,926 per match. Attendances dropped below 22,000 on only seven occasions. A crowd of 30,036 watched the Boxing Day defeat of Queens Park Rangers.

In addition another 58,006 turned out for the FA Cup home ties against Gillingham (21,759) and Cardiff City (36,247).

AWAY RESULTS AND ATTENDANCES

Football League Division Three
1958-59
(Argyle scores first)

Opposition	Result	Scorers	Attendance	Home Av
Hull City	1-1	Gauld	14,318	14,375
Rochdale	2-0	Carter, Penk	8,442	4,810
Stockport County	2-2	Penk, Gauld	11,300	9,255
Bury	1-1	Anderson	12,188	9,441
Colchester United	0-2		10,038	7,756
Doncaster Rovers	6-4	Anderson 3, Meyer 2, Penk	5,300	6,664
Norwich City	1-1	Carter	22,200	21,101
Mansfield Town	4-1	Carter 3, Anderson	12,488	8,463
Chesterfield	2-1	Baker, Carter	10,976	9,028
Southampton	1-5	Carter	21,830	13,718
Bradford City	0-0		11,908	11,090
Queens Park Rangers	2-1	Gauld	15,656	9,155
Southend United	0-0		12,410	11,226
Reading	2-0	Govan, Baker	13,595	12,660
Bournemouth & BA	1-1	Govan	15,107	10,680
Swindon Town	4-3	Gauld 3, Anderson	13,090	11,359
Notts County	2-1	Gauld 2	7,369	9,529
Tranmere Rovers	0-2		15,811	11,815
Brentford	0-3		29,000	13,922
Newport County	1-0	Carter pen	8,108	6,611
Wrexham	1-1	JS Williams	8,817	10,338
Halifax Town	1-0	Anderson	8,523	6,685
Accrington Stanley	1-1	Penk	4,000	6,030

With few Argyle supporters travelling to away games the team were clearly an attraction for opposition fans. In 23 away fixtures, they drew more than the home team's average (in the extreme right hand column) on all but five occasions. At Brentford on Good Friday the attendance was more than double the home side's average home crowd. An average of 12,722 spectators watched each away game Plymouth Argyle played.

Summary Of A Season

Season 1958-59

Distances travelled to away fixtures

Opponents	Miles Travelled	Detail
23 8.58 Hull City 25.8.58 Rochdale	677	4 nights away First visit to Rochdale
06.09.58 Stockport County 08.09.58 Bury	594	4 nights away
20.09.58 Colchester United	622	2 nights away First defeat of the season
02.10.58 Doncaster Rovers 04.10.58 Norwich City	798	4 nights away
18.10.58 Mansfield Town	540	
01.11.58 Chesterfield	552	
19.11.58 Gillingham **FA Cup**	506	Travelled by train
29.11.58 Southampton	308	
06.12.58 Coventry City **FA Cup**	434	
13.12.58 Bradford City	650	Travelled by train
27.12.58 Queens Park Rangers	470	Travelled by train
04.01.59 Tranmere Rovers	596	Match postponed on arrival - travelled by train
24.01.59 Southend United	588	
31.01.09 Reading	398	
14.02.59 Bournemouth & BA	258	Shortest journey
28.02.59 Swindon Town	322	
14.03.59 Notts County 16.03.59 Tranmere Rovers	659	After a night in Nottingham the players were taken to Southport to prepare for the Tranmere game. 4 nights away.
27.03.59 Brentford 28.12.59 Newport County	599	Travelled by train with two nights away
11.04.59 Wrexham	516	First visit to Wrexham
20.04.59 Halifax Town 25.04.59 Accrington Stanley	783	First ever visits to Halifax and Accrington. 7 nights away. Team stayed in Southport 19 to 24.04.59 and then at Wolverhampton on the night after the Accrington fixture
Total miles travelled	**10870**	

254

THIRD DIVISION CHAMPIONS

A post season photograph of the 1958-59 Third Division winners.
Back Row (l to r): JL Williams, Robertson, Carter, Anderson, Baker and Bellett

Centre Row (l to r): Trainer George Taylor, Wyatt, Fulton, Gauld, Barnsley, Secretary AH Cole, Fincham and Assistant Trainer Neil Dougall

Front Row (l to r): JS Williams, Govan, Director Bill Pengelly, Chairman Harry Deans, Director Cliff Crookes, Manager Jack Rowley, Casey and Penk

Note that the socks are completely different than those they started the season with at Hull City

Courtesy of Plymouth Argyle FC and the Argyle Legends

Supporters who watched the 1958-59 promotion campaign may wonder why there little mention of Len Casey and Wally Bellett. They preferred not to participate in *Thanks For The Memory* and I have honoured their wish.

Main Books of Reference
Plymouth Argyle A Complete Record 1903-89: Brian Knight
All About Argyle: WS Tonkin
Snakes and Ladders: Andy Riddle
Argyle Classics: Harley Lawer
Plymouth Argyle Handbooks 1958-59 and 1959-60

Web Sites
Greens on Screen, PASOTI, PASALB
Argyle Review
Swindon Town
Newcastle Brown

Organisations
Plymouth Central Library Services
Plymouth Evening Herald
Portsmouth Evening News
Andy Riddle, Tom Finnie and Paul Hart at Argyle Legends
John Collings and Graham Hambly at *Sunday Independent* Newspaper
Chris Errington & Owen Ryles at the *Plymouth Evening Herald*
Gordon Sparks & Stuart Geddes at BBC Radio Devon
Rick Cowdery and Peter Hall at Plymouth Argyle

Colin Parsons	Nigel Springthorpe	Colin Bolton
Margaret Callan	Susan Watson	Nicola Walker
Joyce Woolridge	Cleeve Carter	Barry Pearce
Mike Curno	Trev Scallan	Roger Elliott
Pete Sanders	John Lloyd	Colin Cameron
Paul Brown	Dick Mattick	Ian MacDonald
Bill Grieg	James Howie	Scott Drummond
Sam Bailey	Gerald Taylor	Jed Griffiths
Caroline Smith	Pete Sanders	John Simmons
Alan Rundle	Jeremy Wills	
Steve Dean	Danny Thomas	